M000234276

PopDaddy

Michelle,

I hope you love
PopDaddy. It was
great to meet you!

PopDaddy
Copyright © 2016 Jeffrey Roach

All rights reserved. No part of this may be reproduced in any form or by any means without the prior consent of the Publisher, excepting brief quotes used in reviews.

The stories in this book reflect the author's recollection of events. Some dates, names, locations, and identifying characteristics have been changed to protect the privacy of those depicted. Dialogue has been re-created from memory.

POPDADDY
PRESS

ISBN: 099727400X
ISBN-13: 978-0-9972740-0-4

DEDICATION

This book is dedicated to my family, by birth or otherwise. It has taken a lot longer than I thought to get this out of my head and onto the page. I appreciate the years of patience and support you have shown me.

More than anything, this one is for Ken and Jackson. Thank you for allowing me to tell our story. I love you guys.

ACKNOWLEDGMENTS

Thank you to everyone who has played a role in helping our family to become a reality, and in helping me to tell our story. I especially want to thank my early readers: Ken, Fara, Betty, Marti, Sydney, Mariah, Mary and Corby. PopDaddy would be a mess without your eagle eyes and helpful insights.

When early readers asked me if everything in the book really happened, I told them yes. But not necessarily in the order in which it is told and with much better dialog. I have shuffled things around a bit to shorten the timeframe and improve the overall narrative.

PROLOGUE

Decatur, March, 2007

"Daddy, I'm bleeding."

I push back the blankets and sleep, swinging my legs out of the bed before I bother to open my eyes. When I finally pry them open I can see that it's very late, or very early I suppose.

My feet complain when they hit the hardwood floors. According to reliable sources on the Internet, the muscles in your feet contract at night and you need to stretch them out in the morning before you try to walk. To me it's just the latest battle in the never-ending war against old age.

I fumble around in the dark for my robe. I could have sworn I laid it across the bench at the end of the bed. I'm really not much of a robe guy, but I would certainly want to have one at my disposal if the house caught on fire. I would hate to be standing around on the lawn in my underwear.

Wait, did he say bleeding? A couple of scary images pop into my head as I continue sweeping my hands across the bench.

"Where's my stupid robe?" I mutter in the darkness. I can't find it and so I stand here for a moment, confused about what comes next. The two Tylenol PMs I took before going to bed are certainly not helping.

Standing here in just my underwear I realize that it is freezing in the house. The weather has turned warmer this week and I turned the heat off before going to bed, so that it won't be so hot tomorrow. I didn't take into account how cold it would get in the middle of the night.

Goosebumps appear on my arm, which is a clear indication that at least my body seems to be functioning, even if my brain feels like it's running a few minutes behind. I stand there, lost in thought. *What am I doing? Should I turn the heat back on? And where the hell is my robe?*

"Daddy?"

Jackson's voice snaps me out of my daze and gets me moving. The cat darts out from under the bed and races past me. She seems convinced that something important is happening. *Bleeding?*

"I'm coming sweetheart," I whisper, as I hobble down the hallway that connects our room to our son's. I'm not sure why I'm whispering. There's no chance that my husband Ken is going to wake up. Ken is a sleeper. Just give him a few quiet minutes in the bed (or on the couch, or anywhere remotely flat) and he is out. Seriously, when his head hits the pillow he falls asleep and sleeps soundly, through anything. I lay awake and resist the temptation to get up and check to make sure the front door is locked. Or plan what I'm going to fix for breakfast. Or worry if I'm going to need a walker when Jackson graduates from high school. Still, the middle of the night is a time for whispering, so I whisper.

I round the corner and poke my head into Jackson's room, my eyes adjusting to the sudden brightness. Between his Nemo lamp and his Mickey Mouse clock there's enough light to read by, or in this case to reveal him sitting up in his bed with both his hands extended. He is staring at them, as if they belong to someone else. They are covered in blood.

"What happened, big guy?" I ask as I step into his room. My voice sounds way too cheerful for the middle of the night. But I've learned that Jackson's level of stress in these situations is directly related to my level of stress. That's why the first words out of any parent's mouth when their child is hurt are, "You're okay." Your child could have just been nearly sideswiped by a city bus, and you'll immediately begin chanting you're okay, you're okay. Maybe we are just practicing positive thinking and willing our child to be all right. You have to be okay. You must be okay. Please be okay.

"My nose is bleeding, Daddy."

"Yes, I can see that."

Despite the blood, I'm relieved. Jackson has been prone to nosebleeds since he was a baby. It's likely hereditary, but we will never know for sure. One of the most frustrating things about adoption is the complete lack of history. A little person just appears in your life one day without any stories of his or her own. Not that any baby comes with an owner's manual, but there is no shared heredity between adopted children and their new parents. There is no comforting yourself that whatever your child is going through you have lived through as well. On the other hand, who wouldn't like to begin life with a clean slate; no preconceived notions?

Nosebleeds offer up so much blood so quickly that in the beginning I was convinced that each epistaxis (yes, I looked it up) was the first step on the road to some *Dark*

Victory. Ken says it's because I've watched too many old movies, or at least too many old Bette Davis movies. He's probably right. In my mind, behind every headache lies a potential malignant brain tumor.

I blame my hypochondria on an old, well-worn medical dictionary my mom always seemed to keep within reach, and referred to religiously. By ten, I'd memorized the entire thing cover to cover and diagnosed myself with any number of terminal illnesses. My adolescence was marked by weeks of planning my fond farewell to family and friends from my sickbed. I'd look in their eyes, smile serenely and implore them to be brave, that mine was just a passing sorrow. Maybe there's an upside to this lack of shared heredity. Maybe Jackson will be spared some of my dramatic tendencies. Although Ken seems to have picked up a few in our sixteen years together, so Jackson is not in the clear yet.

Lost in thought, I momentarily forget what has me out of bed at this hour; little drops of crimson abruptly snap me back to the present.

"You're okay handsome," I say, "but let's get you cleaned up." I lean over and lift Jackson out of his bed, careful to avoid knocking our heads on the rainbow canopy that stretches in a graceful arc from the footboard to the headboard. The canopy is an ill-thought-out purchase from IKEA that Jackson will not part with, despite the fact that the brightly-colored silk fabric hovers dangerously close to his face as he sleeps. The very idea makes me anxious.

We make the short trip to his bathroom so that I can get a better look at his nose. I grab a handful of tissues. "Press these to your nose, sweetheart."

He dutifully takes the tissues and presses them against

his nose. We've been through this before. Over the next few minutes we go through half a box of tissues while I keep up a steady conversation with him, trying to keep his mind on something other than the nosebleed. We spend several long moments discussing the merits of playing as Mario or Luigi in his latest game for his DS. I slyly try to insert Peach into the equation but he shuts that down immediately.

Eventually, we've patched things up well enough to get him out of his pajamas. I carry him back to his room, sit him on the edge of the bed and pull open his closet to find him a clean pair to sleep in.

"Daddy, why are you in your panties?"

I glance down at my white briefs. Hanes. Not even Calvins. Oh how the mighty have fallen.

"They're not panties, silly."

"Granny calls them panties."

He's right. If you are under a certain age my mom refers to your underwear as panties. I can actually hear her voice in the back of my head telling my nephews to put their panties on and stop running around naked.

"That's because your granny is crazy," I say. "We boys call them underwear."

"Why are you in your unders?" I smile at how he has shortened underwear to unders without even thinking about it.

"Because it was hot when we went to bed and sleeping next to your papa is like sleeping next to a furnace."

"I'm cold."

"Me too. So, enough with the questions, Chatty Cathy, we have to get you back in bed. You've got school tomorrow."

"Okay."

"You don't want to be tired and grouchy tomorrow do you?" He doesn't answer me and I can tell that he's already starting to wind down again. Now I'm the one who can't seem to shut up.

"Do you guys still take a nap at school?"

"We're not babies, Daddy," he says.

"Sorry. I didn't know you Pre-K kids were so grown up. Come on, let's get you into these pj's and back in bed."

"I'm tired, PopDaddy."

My heart does a little flip at the nickname. It's been a while since I've heard it. From the very beginning I've always been Daddy and Ken has always been Papa. But when Jackson was a toddler he would often mix up our names, or fumble around between Papa and Daddy until he got the one he wanted. At some point he just combined them and started using PopDaddy.

I toss the pj's back in the dresser and scoop him up.

"How about you sleep with me and Papa for the rest of the night?" I whisper to him. He's fading fast and doesn't bother to answer. He is practically asleep by the time I get him to our room.

I nudge Ken and he wakes up long enough to take Jackson and a wad of tissues.

"Keep those handy in case his nose starts to bleed again," I mutter. He grunts an acknowledgement. As I'm walking out of the room, I glance back and see Jackson propped up on two or three pillows, with Ken's arm draped across him. The tissues seem to have already disappeared. So much for keeping the tissues at the ready. For one crazy moment I regret putting white pillowcases on the pillows this morning.

Back in Jackson's room I finally flip on the overhead light. His pillows are covered in little drops of blood. I know from experience that blood is like gossip, it doesn't take much to do permanent damage. I pull the pillowcases and sheets off and see that a good bit has soaked through to the mattress, going from crimson to rust as it moved through the layers of cotton. I am reminded that the downside of having a kid who never wets the bed is that you don't bother with a mattress cover.

I gather up the bedding and head to the laundry room. A few minutes later, the sheets are loaded in our efficient-looking, front-loading washer. The soothing sounds of water pushing the sheets first clockwise and then back will soon be replaced by the high pitched screams of rotation as the washer labors to wring every last drop of water out of its cargo. *"Quiet Operation"* a little metal placard on the side of the machine boasts. I'm convinced that would only apply in a tornado. I want to be asleep before that kicks in, so I pick up the pace.

I pull the mattress off the bed so that one end is on the floor and the other is propped up on the box springs and scrub at the stains until they begin to disappear. When the last red rings are no longer visible, I flip on the ceiling fan, turn off the light, drop my cleaning rags into the laundry basket and head back to bed.

It's 4:10.

2001

CHAPTER ONE

Dallas, January, 2001

"Honey, I'm pregnant."

Marti and I were seated at the little round table where the five of us typically met for lunch. I had begged the corporate office for the table under the pretense that we needed it for meeting with clients and prospects. The truth is we just wanted it as a makeshift lunch table. There was no way we would ever let one of our fancy law firm clients within one hundred yards of our building.

About a year ago, our company had moved us out of our prestigious Turtle Creek location and leased space for us north of Dallas, just off Central Expressway. While the location was convenient enough to where most of us lived, and the actual space was roomy and newly renovated, our co-tenants included Alcoholics Anonymous (a non-smoking branch!), the Social Security Office and a test prep center. If they had any clue about what we actually did our company would have realized that it was highly unlikely that we'd invite our conservative clients to come by and mingle with our neighbors.

Not that we had anything against the drunks, the seniors and the skateboarders—in fact, just the opposite. With the bar set so low, we knew we'd be less likely to stand out when we started singing show tunes during lunch, something we did fairly regularly. *Gypsy* was one of our favorites: *Why did I do it? What did it get me?* These were questions we asked ourselves nearly every day.

The little table was plopped in the middle of our office space, since we didn't have anything as practical as a conference room. There were two exterior offices for Ken and me, and three cubes for Marti, Kim and Julie. In a moment of inspired lunacy, we had combined Kim and Marti's two cubes into one big space that we had affectionately dubbed the double-wide.

Julie was across the room in a private cube. Without ever discussing it, we all knew that communal living and Julie would make for strange and hostile bedfellows. It turned out to be a good thing that Marti and Kim got along because, after we combined them, we realized we couldn't figure out how to separate the two cubes again. Most of the good stuff either happened in the double-wide or at the lunch table and the five of us seemed to naturally gravitate toward those two hubs.

"Honey, did you hear me? I said I'm pregnant."

Marti clutched both my hands tightly with her own as she delivered her big news. I had initially thought that this hand-holding business was for dramatic effect. I now realized that it was a much more practical choice to keep me from slapping her face.

"What?" I gasped in my best *Mildred Pierce* impersonation, totally giving in to the drama of the moment. Sometimes I can't help myself. "You're going to have a baby?" I am a firm believer in the notion that, if you think about it long enough, there's always a line from a movie for just about any situation.

With the confession out of the way, she took a deep breath and smiled. "Yep, I got me a little something cooking up in the oven."

"But you can't be pregnant," I stammered. "You just started working here a few months ago."

Here was a training and support company that specialized in working with law firms on adopting new technology. That sounds a lot fancier than what we actually did. The reality was a lot more boring. When a law firm upgraded to the latest version of Microsoft Office, our job was to go on site and teach everyone how to use the new software, as well as support them at their desk in the first few weeks after the change. In the end, we were highly paid babysitters. We had staked our entire financial future on the idea that most people are hopelessly mouse impaired and terrified of change. So far, it had been a safe bet.

Although our office was based in Dallas, our trainers like Marti typically traveled all over the country on any given project. It was this last piece of information that troubled me. Some useless knowledge stored in the back of my brain insisted that pregnant women couldn't travel. Well, at least not gracefully.

"Yeah, sorry about that, but this," she said, indicating her stomach with a showy little swirl of her finger, "is officially no longer fat. It's now a baby." With that she threw her head back and let loose with one of her trademark laughs, which was something between a laugh and a bark and totally infectious. I couldn't help but laugh with her. From the moment we met, Marti and I had been firm and fast friends.

Like most of my friends, we had met on the job. In a typical project you might work through as many as one thousand people over the course of several weeks. As a result, you got pretty good at recognizing a kindred spirit. Within a few hours of meeting we knew everything there was to know about each other. It turned out that her father had played the classic *I'm living a lie!* card at dinner one night and announced that he was gay. Marti had not only accepted and loved her dad for who he was, but had spent the next twenty years helping her mother recover from the shock. It was still a work in progress.

"This is a disaster," I finally choked out. "Get the menus. We are going to need a lot of food to get through this." Just as I felt like there was always a line from a movie for every occasion I also believed that the right amount of food could make any situation seem less dire.

"Jeffrey!" Kim scolded me as she got up from the double-wide and teetered over to the lunch table on her fabulous hooker shoes. Kim was the only person I knew who strapped on heels to go to a job where no one would ever see her feet.

"Congratulations," she cooed, leaning down precariously to give Marti a hug.

She swatted in my general direction. "It's 10 o'clock in the morning. It's too early to start planning lunch. Besides, I think this is going to require drinks, and we can't get those delivered," she added with a grin. "Now, congratulate Marti on her good news."

"Yes, congratulations," I mumbled, "of course, congratulations. I'm thrilled for you—wait, was this on purpose? Is it Greg's?"

"Yes and yes. As hard as it is for you to imagine, I am still having sex with my husband."

"Gulp. Putting aside that little nugget for the time

being, let's focus on the big issue here. I have worked like a dog for months to get you hired so that we can hang out together all day in the double-wide. Laws were broken. I shredded contracts."

"A," she said, "I was the one operating the shredder, and B, we promised never to speak of that again."

"The point is that Michael is going to flip his wig when he finds out." Michael was my boss and I had lobbied him long and hard to get Marti hired. I'm one of those people who is only happy when those I love suffer as much as I do. From the moment we met, Marti and I started scheming a plan that would get her out of her job and into one of the cubes outside my office. Between us and our goal were a couple of non-compete clauses, some client goodwill and hours of begging and pleading with Michael. Ultimately, it had all come together and we had successfully stolen her away from one of our clients, while somehow not pissing them off. It was some of my best work and I was proud of it.

"Kim. Those menus are not going to get themselves! Chop, chop, lady."

"Honey, I will get the menus. Kim should sit down before she falls down. Just understand that after I get these menus for you I'm going to start playing the baby card, which means I will not get off of my ass for the next few months." Before Marti could retrieve the menus, the door to the office flew open and Julie and Ken fumbled through with coffee from Starbucks.

"Marti's knocked up," I yelled across the room. "She's claiming that it's Greg's, but my money is on our postman."

This earned me another swat from Kim. "Jeffrey! You're terrible! You know the shitter only has eyes for

Julie." Ken and Julie joined us at the table and it was hugs all around. I was secretly delighted with the visual of Marti and our postman, also known as the shitter, striking up a torrid office affair. Delighted, and slightly repulsed.

Our postman had earned his nickname from the peculiar habit he had of visiting the men's room every day just before delivering our mail. After a twenty-minute respite from his route, he'd arrive in our office, refreshed and ready to hand-deliver the mail. Literally, he insisted upon handing the mail to Julie every single day. Every now and then she'd challenge him by refusing to acknowledge that he was hovering outside of her cube. But he'd just wait her out. Eventually she'd have to turn around and take the mail from his outstretched hand.

"Two things," Julie said, choosing to ignore Kim. "First, I'm surprised you are still having sex with your husband. And second, holy shit is Michael going to be pissed."

"Finally the voice of reason!" I wasn't surprised that Julie was the one to just cut through all the niceties and get down to business.

Julie is a fiery redhead whose temper is only matched by her generosity and unwavering loyalty. She's another refugee from a law firm, but her story was a little different. When Julie left her firm, we didn't bother to go through the whole song and dance with the client. In theory, she quit one day and I hired her the next. But the reality is her former employer was too afraid of her to make a fuss.

Without a doubt, Julie was the sheriff in our office. When the maintenance people didn't empty our trash cans, it was Julie who took care of it. When the students from the test prep center started to get too rowdy, it was Julie who marched straight to the source and shut it down.

One particularly memorable day, three guys decided it would be really funny to go into the men's room, which shared a wall with the double-wide, get into the three stalls and pretend to take the shits of their career.

In a rare moment, we were actually quietly working away when we heard the exaggerated moans and grunts of someone struggling with a particularly large and disagreeable food baby. After this went on for ten minutes or so, Julie stood up, announced that she'd had enough, walked right out of our office and headed straight toward the men's room.

No! we thought. *She wouldn't dare!*

But she did. She threw open the door, silencing the boys immediately, and said, "Our place of business is right next door, and I would ask the three of you to conduct yourselves like the young gentlemen I know you to be." She returned to her cube, and that was the last we heard of the boys and their noisy food babies.

"Julie's right," Marti said. "My timing kind of stinks and we are going to need a really good plan. Let's review our situation."

I took a sip of my skinny vanilla latte and decided to get the ball rolling. "Okay, so I stole Marti away from one of our best clients."

"And this was after you stole Julie and me away from clients as well," Kim added.

Damn! I forgot that I snatched Kim as well.

"Yes, I'm nothing if not consistent. And you're not being helpful. Drink your latte and shut it. Where was I? Oh yeah, I persuaded Marti to give up her boring but stable job and then convinced Michael that she was so amazing, so incredibly talented, that it was worth the risk of alienating a client. Further, I talked about how flexible she was, and how she enjoyed travel. And now, a month later—"

"It's been longer than a month!" Marti corrected me.

"Right, a few months later, she is barefoot and pregnant."

Marti gave me a mock horrified look. "Honey, I'm wearing shoes. Oh, but it gets better. I checked into our benefits and our maternity leave package—I'm being kind when I say it sucks."

The five of us fell into a companionable silence. I could almost hear the wheels turning in each of our heads.

"Well, what do you think, Jeffrey? I don't see how we don't come out of this one without a black eye." Again, there was Julie not afraid to just put it out there.

"Jules darling, have a little faith," I said with a sly grin.

Suddenly, all eyes were on me, the master manipulator. I could tell that they were waiting to be dazzled by my sheer ability to reshape reality around what works best for me.

"Here's how I see it. If she stays here, Marti isn't going to be particularly useful to us. No offense, lady, but a pregnant woman can't be away from home for weeks at a time." I paused, letting that sink in. "And the clothing options are, well, limited, if I'm being kind."

"Agreed," Marti said at last.

"Then there's the problem of maternity leave. I'd hate to see you miss an opportunity to lay around on your ass for a few months."

"Uh, hello? I'd prefer you use the correct terminology: living the pregnancy dream."

"Indeed, the pregnancy dream almost makes pushing a

bowling ball out of your hoohaw worth it."

"Almost."

"Well, then there's only one solution. You've got to zip it on the pregnancy talk. As far as the world is concerned you're just carb loading. And we have got to find you another job, preferably back at a law firm. You're obviously qualified, the benefits are good and you won't have to travel. Plus we can spin a story that you decided the vendor side just wasn't for you."

"I'm completely prepared to lie," Marti said.

"Good, because you are going to have to make this sound convincing. Most importantly, we have to be quick about it. We have to do this while we can still pass that"— I motioned to her stomach—"off as fat. In short, we are dumping your ass."

Marti looked at me with undisguised awe. "God you're good. I'll get the menus."

"Wait!" Ken finally said. I realized that he had barely said a word since he and Julie arrived. "I'm so happy for you, Marti." With that he threw his arms around her and gave her a big hug.

"Careful, bun in the oven."

"Oh right! Sorry," Ken said, quickly letting her go.

"Honey, I'm kidding. Get over here and hug me like you mean it."

***

After a long day in which very little work was actually done, but Marti's entire future was carefully plotted, Ken and I were on our way home. It was only a ten-minute drive from the office to where we lived on Clearhurst Drive.

Our house was located in one of those brand new, manufactured communities that I typically can't stand called The Traditions at White Rock. Yes, it was a bit much, but its saving grace was that it was nestled in an older, middle-class neighborhood northeast of downtown Dallas called Lake Highlands. We could walk to the end of our street, cross the road, and be out of *The Stepford Wives* and right in the heart of old Lake Highlands, a name which proves that the fine folks of Dallas are capable of irony.

The lake part was reasonable, due to the close proximity of White Rock Lake, which was within biking distance, and one of the most beautiful parts of Dallas. Highlands, however, was a bit of a stretch as Dallas is essentially a prairie. It's true that we were within walking distance of Flag Pole Hill, which is often cited as the tallest point in all of Dallas. But tallest is relative; at a few hundred feet, it's more of a swell than a hill. The elevation of Lake Highlands is 571 feet, compared to downtown Dallas at 430 feet.

We ended up there because we were desperate for a new house. That's new as in new construction, because new construction definitely had its advantage. We wanted to experience the thrill of being able to blow our hair dry and run the dishwasher at the same time. After years of living with suspect wiring in New York this seemed deliciously luxurious. When we first moved in I stood in the kitchen next to the dishwasher blowing my hair dry just to revel in the excess.

Patsy, our aging and high-strung Dalmatian, would be waiting for us at the back door and, as usual, I had spent the drive home trying to figure out a way to get Ken to walk her. I was lost in my thoughts on how to pull this off. What concessions would I need to make? It's not that I minded walking the dog. Okay, I did actually. But it was cold for Dallas and after being stuck in the house all day

Patsy was never in a hurry for the walk to end, so she would hold her water and push the walk further and further toward Flag Pole Hill.

"So Marti's news is pretty amazing, huh," Ken said, as we turned into The Traditions. I pulled over next to the mailbox, which was inconveniently located at the end of the block.

"I could kill her."

Ken popped out to get the mail, leaving the door open and inviting in the cold air. I didn't even bother to tell him to close the door. He would only remind me that it didn't make sense to close the door for the three seconds it took to get the mail. I just put my face right in front of the heating vent and tried not to count the actual seconds that were ticking away.

He slipped back into the car with a stack of mail, most of which would end up in the trash. He finally closed the door and I pointed the Jeep toward home.

"What?" he said, picking up the conversation from where we left off. "Don't you think she'll be an incredible mom?"

"If by incredible mom you mean one that has true mastery over the F word, I'd have to agree."

"You are so mean." Now it was Ken who was swatting at me. Why did people feel like I needed to be swatted today?

"I'm just kidding! I think she will be great. Who wouldn't want Marti for a mom? She's hilarious and she knows the shop girls at Neiman's by their first names."

"Is everything a joke to you?" Ken didn't look or sound like he was joking at all. In fact, he looked downright peeved. "I can't believe you aren't amazed by the idea that she has a little, delicate life growing inside her that she'll one day hold in her arms. I'm jealous."

I pulled into the garage and shut off the engine, but neither one of us made a move to get out of the car. I looked over at Ken and saw that his eyelashes were wet with un-cried tears. He was definitely upset about something. Rather than try to guess what was going on with him, I decided to just take the direct approach and ask him.

"What's wrong, sweetie?" I attempted to slide over the console to put my arm around his shoulder. The movies had taught me that this was the right thing to do, but the center gear shift made the move incredibly awkward. So I ended up half hugging, half clinging to Ken.

"Of course I'm happy for her. You know I love kids. Why are you so upset with me?"

"I'm not," he said. I cocked my eyebrow at him. "Truthfully? I have no idea. I mean, ever since I heard Marti's big news I have felt so excited for her but at the same time I've felt—" Here he paused, searching for the right word.

"Jealous?" I offered.

"Yes. No. Not really. More like emotional." Ken scrubbed his hands across his face, as if he was trying to clear away the confusion. "What I really feel is this overwhelming *sadness*."

"But I thought you were happy for Marti."

"Not sadness for Marti, sadness for me. For us."

"Now you've really lost me. Why would we be sad that Marti is going to have a baby? If you are worried that it's going to change our friendship with her and Greg, I wouldn't."

22

"It's not that. It's just that I'm sad that it's not us. That we will never get to share that kind of surprise with our friends."

"Ah," I said as the light finally blinked on for me. "Well, that's ridiculous. We could have a baby if we wanted one." I realized how silly that sounded as soon as the words were out of my mouth.

"Well, I mean we can't *have* a baby. There's no way I'm putting on all that extra weight." I tried to grin at Ken, but he wasn't having it. "But we can, you know, adopt a baby. Rent a baby? Steal one?"

"There you go with the jokes again. This is important to me. I grew up thinking I would end up living the All American Dream." That much was true. Ken had even been engaged to a woman at one point. I felt the first flutter of panic when he said that. He must have seen it in my eyes, because he quickly added, "I love you and I love my life with you, but the white picket fence dream never goes away."

"Listen to me, Mr. White Picket Fence, just because we're two men doesn't mean we aren't qualified to raise a child. You understand?" Unlike Ken, I didn't grow up expecting to get married and raise a family. I grew up consumed with getting the hell out of my small town, but the look on his face had me scrambling to make it all better.

"Yes," he said, and sighed, "but it's my dream, not yours."

This time I did the swatting. "That's just silly. Your dreams are my dreams. They're our dreams. So if it matters to you, it matters to me."

"Really?" Ken said.

"Of course."

"So you'd be okay if I looked into adoption?"

"Wait. What just happened here?" How had I gone from trying to comfort Ken to becoming a father? I felt like I went into a car dealership to buy a Toyota and ended up with a Lexus.

"Uh huh," Ken replied. "That's what I thought. Your dreams, my dreams, our dreams. It was a moving speech, Mr. English Major, but it's all talk."

"Really, Mr. English Major? Who are you? Me? I didn't say no, and it wasn't just words. I meant what I said."

"Which is what exactly?"

"Mr. Manford," I said in my sexiest voice, "let's go inside and make a baby. And let's be quick about it because this gear shift is trying to make a baby with me right now." This was my standard way of distracting Ken, one part humor and one part sex. Usually it worked, but not this time.

"So I can look into adoption?" Ken asked again, determined to get a definitive answer from me.

I sighed and slid back into my seat before the gear shift could do any permanent damage. "Ken, if you really want to look into our options then do it. If you think that's adoption, then look into adoption. You could probably call James and Joe in New York for some advice." James and Joe had adopted a little girl from China a few years ago and were the only gay couple we knew with a child.

"That's right. I had forgotten about them. Maybe I will call them tonight. But I have to know that you are serious about this. You know me, I will make it happen."

"I never doubt your ability to make things happen," I said. "And yes, I'm serious. If you think that's what we should do. Besides, you would be an amazing father and I would do my best not to damage him. At least not too much."

"Him?" Ken asked, trying hard to hide his smile.

Had I said him? I suppose I had assumed if we were looking at adopting a baby it would be a boy. Again, I tried to distract Ken with humor. "Oh yes! Unlike you, I can't deal with lady parts. We'd have to adopt a boy."

"Don't try to joke your way out of it now," Ken said. "I'm on it."

Obviously my skills were subpar that day, since I didn't seem to be able to get anything past Ken. "I'm not joking."

"This is your last chance," Ken warned me. "If you say it one more time, I'm going to think you mean it."

I leaned into him until our lips were just a few inches apart and this time there was no humor in my voice. "Mr. Manford, will you have a baby with me?"

Ken threw his arms around me and held me so tight I started to see stars. After a few heartbeats I pulled away and gave him my most loving look.

"There's only one condition," I whispered.

"Anything. Just name it."

"You have to walk the dog."

"Naturally," Ken said, rolling his eyes and getting out of the Jeep.

"Forever," I added.

Ken rolled his eyes again. "You have to admit," he said as we headed inside, "that Mr. English Major was pretty good."

"Yeah. It was pretty good," I said. "Not stellar, but good Mr. I'm-going-to-be-walking-the-dog-for-the-rest-of-her-life."

Ten minutes later, Patsy was dragging me through the

winter chill, in search of the perfect spot to do her business, while Ken sat in front of his computer in heated comfort feverishly researching adoption. *God you are such a sap,* I thought to myself.

One part of me was terrified at the conversation we had in the Jeep, but there was another part of me that actually felt excited by it. That's why I had decided to walk the dog, despite extracting a life-long promise of dog walking from Ken. I needed a few minutes to figure out how I really felt about this. So while Ken was at home creating a whole new future for us, I was alone with my thoughts and an aging Dalmatian who couldn't relax until she shit in the middle of someone else's yard.

After reaching the end of our street, I decided to cross White Rock Trail and extend Patsy's walk beyond what we typically did after work. She looked up at me to see if I was serious and then almost broke into a slow trot as I led her across the street. Apparently, I was surprising everyone that day.

And no one was more surprised than me. I honestly didn't know what to think about how agreeable I had been to the idea of adopting a baby. But my sense of this unexpected turn of events was that this was the right thing at the right time. Although I wasn't sure what this would mean for us, my instincts told me that Marti's news was going to have as big an impact on Ken and me as it did her and Greg.

CHAPTER TWO

Dallas, June, 2001

As it turned out, the road to adoption was long, complex and paved with paper. There were endless forms to be filled out, background checks, and filing fees. As prospective parents we were fingerprinted, second-guessed by friends and family, scrutinized by social workers, and crushed by delays. Since Marti's big reveal, Ken had been moving the two of us methodically through all of the steps required to adopt a child, but it was sometimes difficult to connect those steps with the end result.

We had definitely made progress in the last few months. We had settled on an international adoption from Guatemala and were working with an agency called Casa Antigua. Still, something that was supposed to be fundamentally tactile, having a baby, had started to feel devoid of any human interaction. There was no morning sickness, no baby bump, no Lamaze classes, no swollen feet and no tiny little kicks to remind us of the prize at the bottom of this particular Cracker Jack box.

No doubt pregnant women would happily strike some of the more unpleasant items off of that list but, still, they do serve a purpose in helping to mark the time, of helping to create a real sense of forward motion, of progress.

I knew that Ken had accomplished dozens of important tasks but most of the time it felt like what we were doing was totally random and clinical. Unlike a traditional pregnancy, there was no blueprint for adoption, no dictated order in which things had to be done. There was just "the list", which we tackled from all angles, slowly but surely removing the obstacles between us and our future child.

By the time the home study was scheduled I was starting to feel a little desperate for some human interaction, something where I felt like I had some control over the situation. Up until that point everything seemed to be black and white facts on a report or form, something to be filled out in triplicate, filed and mailed off to some agency somewhere. Better yet, something to be hand couriered to its destination, since we had already lost days due to lost documents.

In other words, I had started to feel a desperate need to imprint some of my personality on the process. As it turned out, a little bit of me goes a long way.

"What time is she supposed to be here?" She was Diane, who was coming by the house to conduct our home study, which would become the centerpiece in our adoption package. In a sea of paper, the home study is that little bit of flair, something that helps to remind everyone that there are real, live people behind all the facts and figures.

Diane was one half of the dynamic duo of Diane and Susan, a lesbian couple in Dallas who had worked tirelessly to help guide future gay and lesbian parents through the complexities of adopting a child in Texas. They had both worked for child protective services for many years, trying to help the cause from the inside. Once they retired they set up a private consulting practice to continue their efforts. They were personally connected to the success of so many families in Dallas that you couldn't attend a gay and lesbian family affair without bumping into people whose lives they had touched. We had heard about them through a Guatemala family group that Ken had joined and had gotten to know them at the different meetings we had attended.

Ken looked up from the magazine he was reading. "For the four thousandth time, she is supposed to be here around noon."

"So like now?"

"Yep. Any minute now."

"But she could be a little later, right? Like closer to 12:30?"

"Yes."

"Okay. I'm just trying to figure out what to do about lunch."

Ken sighed and dropped his magazine on the coffee table. "Lunch? You do realize that she's not coming to just hang out with us. She's coming on official business."

"Official, huh? Is there like a uniform and everything? Perhaps a cute little hat?" Nerves always brought out the smartass in me. "I wonder if I should serve wine, or does that send the wrong message? Does that just scream day drinkers? Speaking of which, if I do serve wine, and I'm not saying I will, do not drink a drop. Not a single drop. Maybe I should just make some tea."

"Why are you going to make tea? You don't even like tea."

"I can't help it. You know I think tea tastes like pee."

"That right there," Ken said. "That is probably

something you want to keep to yourself during the interview, because it opens up way too many follow-up questions."

"You're right. We need to keep our answers short and sweet. Just like those interrogation scenes in a movie; the more you talk the more trouble you get into."

"Yeah, except it's not really the same thing. Diane isn't trying to finger us for a crime."

"Please don't say finger us while she's here."

Ken burst out laughing.

"Seriously, do not even say finger or I will wet my pants. And that will definitely send the wrong message."

By this point Ken was having trouble catching his breath from laughing at me.

"Shut up."

"Maybe you should serve *finger* sandwiches," Ken said with a snort.

"I hate you." Just then the doorbell trilled. "God I hope she didn't hear that."

Ken jumped up off the couch to answer the door but I cut him off at the path. "I'll get the door. You head to the kitchen and await further instruction." Ken rolled his eyes but headed toward the kitchen as I pulled open the front door.

"Diane! How are you?"

"Hey Jeffrey, it's great to see you. What a beautiful day."

"Isn't it," I said. "We took a long walk earlier. It's just gorgeous." We hadn't taken a long walk earlier, but it occurred to me that we probably should have, so I spontaneously added that to our morning narrative.

"Come in. Ken's in the kitchen scoping out our options for lunch. Are you hungry?"

"No, I'm good," she said stepping into the foyer. "Your house is beautiful. I didn't know you guys lived so close to us."

"Thank you, and, yes, we are really close." I closed the door behind Diane. "So where do you want to do this?"

"How about the dining room table? Then we'll have plenty of room to spread out."

"Perfect. Come on in and sit down." I led Diane through the living room toward the dining room. Our downstairs was essentially one big open space, so we could see Ken in the kitchen as we made our way to the dining room table.

"Hey Ken, Diane's here, so you may have to wait on lunch."

"Oh no, feel free to eat. I don't mind," Diane said.

Ken glared at me from behind the counter, well aware that I was the one who had positioned him in the kitchen so he could be prepared to whip up a snack or a drink for Diane. "That's okay; I'm not very hungry. Diane, can I get you something to drink?"

"Just water is fine for me, thank you."

"Coming right up." Ken managed to sound pleasant but I could tell he was preparing his list of *I told you so's* for the minute Diane finished up and left.

"Jeffrey, can I get you something? Maybe a margarita to settle your nerves."

"Ha! Very funny. Just some water please." I looked over at Diane. "He's totally kidding; I don't drink cocktails this early in the day."

Diane laughed. "Oh, I do whenever I can! But you won't need anything to settle your nerves. There's no reason at all for you to be nervous. I know you guys and

31

I've seen you around all of the kids at the events and I can tell you are going to make great parents."

Ken brought the two glasses of water into the dining room and pulled out the chair next to mine. He set one of the glasses in front of me and handed the other one across the table to Diane.

"Dallas' finest," he said, indicating the water.

"Thanks Ken." Diane took a big drink of water and smiled. Tap water? I was going to shoot Ken when this was over.

"Okay boys. Are you ready to get started?"

I nodded and Ken added a cheerful, "Absolutely."

"Let's start with something simple: Why Guatemala?"

I had prepared for this question. In fact, I had written out a well thought out answer on index cards earlier in the week and committed it to memory. I planned on talking about how we didn't care about the color of his skin, or his ethnic background. I planned on talking about how inspired we had been by the children we had met from Guatemala. There were elements of diversity and community and identity that I had managed to wrap into the kind of answer that would likely reduce Diane to tears.

Unfortunately, the only thing I could think of when Diane asked the question was my sister's reaction when we told our families that we had settled on adopting a baby from Central America. She had quipped that we were so lucky that we were going to have a kid who could play outside in the yard without going up in flames. Three of her children were fair-skinned and freckled and she never left the house without an ample supply of fifty level sunblock.

I always thought she was exaggerating until I accidently

cooked two of her kids in my Jeep one summer day by insisting on driving with the top down. We were out a fortune in Aloe Vera and they still have nightmares about open air vehicles to this day. Lesson learned.

"With this hot Texas sun we couldn't bear the thought of trying to keep up with all those layers of sunblock, so we knew we had to have a brown-skinned baby." Oh. My. God. Had I just said that?

I glanced over at Ken and his eyes had gone as wide as saucers. Diane managed a polite chuckle as if to say she appreciated my quirky sense of humor. Ken stepped in and answered the question in a very normal, non-rehearsed way. He also discreetly moved the glass of water he had gotten for me in front of him and took a quick drink.

"That's great," Diane said. "You can't help but fall in love with those kids when you start to hang around them. Okay, why don't you two tell me a little bit about how you grew up? How were your relationships with your parents? Were they strict? How did they handle discipline?"

I would love to tell you how I answered those questions and all of the following questions, but it was about this time that I experienced a brownout. In case you haven't experienced it yourself, in a brownout you do not completely lose consciousness like a blackout. Instead, your conscious just sort of dims and you enter a fugue state where you can't be responsible for anything that comes out of your mouth.

The only thing I can remember was telling myself over and over again to shut up. *Please shut the hell up.* Thankfully, Ken was there to smooth out the rough edges. He delivered one honest, well-considered answer after another and I could tell that Diane was impressed. In fact, I think she might have misted up at one point, but I can't be sure due to the brownout. I was a total train wreck. After what felt like hours, Diane announced that she had everything she needed and we all got up and made our way to the front door.

"Thanks for squeezing us in this morning, Diane. We are on a pretty tight timeframe and we really appreciate you giving up your Saturday."

"My pleasure, Ken. I should have the report ready for you in a week or so. I'll do what I can to speed it up. Susan is very good at keeping me on task."

"Perfect. We are anxious to get it to our case worker at Casa Antigua."

"You're working with Cathy aren't you?"

"We are."

"I thought so. She said you guys are chewing through the paperwork like a machine. If you like, I can copy her on the email."

"That would be great," Ken said.

No, I thought, that would be a disaster. I wanted a chance to read it before we sent it to Cathy so that I could do some damage control. I was just about to say so to Diane when Ken caught my eye and gave me a look that said, *I think you've said enough.* I shut my mouth and pasted what I hoped was a pleasant smile on my face.

"Alright then, guys. I'm out of your hair. Enjoy the rest of your weekend."

"Thanks again," I managed to mumble.

Ken closed the door behind Diane and turned to me. "What happened to keeping our answers short and sweet?"

"I don't know what happened. It was like the worst case of verbal diarrhea ever. I just couldn't stop talking." I staggered over to the sofa and collapsed. "We are never going to get a baby now."

"Don't be so dramatic. It wasn't that bad."

"Really?" I pushed up to a sitting position and gave Ken a hopeful glance that said, *please lie to me.*

He hesitated, so I collapsed back on the couch with a groan. "Really. It wasn't that bad. It was just kind of random. Why did you tell that story about the fringe vest in second grade?"

One fateful day, in the second grade, I had worn a fabulous suede vest with fringe to school. It was adorable and I wasn't the only one who thought so. A pack of girls had chased me all over the playground and had ended up ripping away most of the fringe. I came home in tears, feeling like a beautiful butterfly whose wings had been torn off. There was no connection to be made between that experience and adopting a baby. None.

"I don't know. It just came out."

"And why mention that they wanted you to skip the third grade?"

"Again, I have no idea. I just panicked and when I do my default reaction is to launch into the *Jeffrey* show. That's how I made it through high school. Keep them laughing and they won't notice that you are a big ol' queen."

"I'm pretty sure Diane was amused by most of it, but there were a couple of times I was tempted to put my hand over your mouth."

"Why didn't you? As my guy it is your responsibility to stop me from making a fool of myself." I fell back on the couch with another sigh. "I am such an idiot."

"Oh relax. It's not that big a deal. But now might be a great time to go get those frozen margaritas. Do you want to see if Marti and Greg want to meet us at Mi Cocina? Plus we can see little Mason."

Marti's delivery of Mason had served as a real boost for us. Any time we saw the little guy he seemed to recharge our baby batteries.

"You go. I'll just lay here and wallow in my own filth. In fact, you may just want to move forward with the whole adoption thing on your own. Clearly, I'm useless."

"Well, now that you brought it up, there is something I do want to talk to you about, but you have to promise not to freak out."

"Ooookay. I promise not to freak out." I had a feeling I was about to totally freak out. When someone says don't freak out it's a sure sign that it's about to happen.

"Alright." Ken took a calming breath. "So you know that on paper I'm officially the adopting parent."

"Yes."

"But in reality you are going to be just as much a part of his life as I am." Ken looked at me for approval and I gave him a stiff, little nod.

"I'm doing this all wrong. What I'm saying is that it doesn't matter what it says on paper. We are both going to be his dads."

I relaxed a little and he continued. "Right, so anyway, Diane is actually going to write two different home studies. One of them will include both of us, but the one we are submitting to Guatemala will only include me and my family."

"Why is she doing two then?"

"We may need the other one when we do the second parent adoption. And even if we don't, I want some official record that we are in this together." Ken paused and seemed to struggle with what to say next.

"I'm sorry, I shouldn't have kept this from you, but I didn't want you to worry about it, and—"

Before he could finish, I jumped up and threw my arms around his neck and burst into tears.

"I know," he whispered, trying to soothe me. "I hate cutting you out of the picture, but Cathy says it is the only way."

I pulled away and gave him a huge smile. "I'm not crying because I'm upset. These are tears of joy. I'm so glad that I didn't manage to mess this up."

"Really?"

"Really. I was afraid that Cathy would read that report and call the whole thing off and that would break my heart. Because not only do I want this for you, I really want this for me too now. It's just that all of those questions about actually raising a baby really freaked me out. But it is something I want to do with you and I was so afraid I had ruined everything."

"You didn't ruin anything and those questions have me freaked out too. I really don't know how I feel about discipline and preserving our future son's cultural identity. I honestly haven't thought about all of that, but I'm sure we can figure it out together."

"I'm so relieved. I thought it was just me."

"No. I'm as scared as you are."

I gave him another big hug. "Whew, I'm exhausted. I think margaritas sound like exactly what we need right now."

"Great, should I call Marti?"

"Sure, but first we have to take a walk."

"You mean walk the dog? She's been in the back yard

for the last hour. I'm pretty sure she has had a chance to do her business."

"No, we," I said, indicating the two of us, "should take a long walk."

"Okay, but why?"

"I told Diane that we had taken a nice long walk this morning and I feel like I need to do everything I can to course correct my karma. So we are taking that relaxing walk, even if it kills us."

"I'm not even going to ask why you lied to Diane."

"Thank you. I appreciate that. Now get the leash and let's get this over with so that we can enjoy some daytime cocktails."

Ken opened the door to let Patsy in from being exiled in the back yard and snagged her leash from the garage.

"Oh, and not a word about my little performance to Marti and Greg. I need your promise that we will never speak of this again."

"Yeah, that's not going to happen. Besides, even if I did promise not to tell them you would spill the beans within five minutes of sitting down."

I pushed him out the door with a sigh. I knew he was right, but I was hoping he would let me tell the story because I knew that I would tell it better than him.

"Alright," I said with a sigh as we stepped into a wall of heat. "Let's get to stepping, those drinks aren't going to drink themselves."

CHAPTER THREE

Dallas, October, 2001

"Does it sound shallow if I say we should choose the cutest one?"

Ken and I were hunkered over his computer screen, squinting at grainy pictures of three baby boys who had recently arrived at Casa Antigua, the agency in Guatemala we were using for our adoption. We had been waiting for this email for weeks, waiting for a baby boy to find his way to us on the back of misfortune. We were counting on Guatemala's devout Catholic population and disregard for birth control to make our wait a short one.

To be fair, part of the reason we chose Guatemala in the first place was directly related to that Catholic devotion. In most cases, birth mothers in Guatemala were not drug addicts or prostitutes. In most cases. Like so many other aspects of adoption, you have no control over the circumstances your future child is born into. As an adoptive parent, you do the best you can to stack the odds in your favor, make your choices, and try not to second-guess yourself.

And there had been so many choices to make. One of the things that Ken and I were never concerned about was the color of our future son's skin. White, brown, black or any shade in-between—it all sounded great to us.

"It does sound a little shallow," Ken said with a grin, "but you do tend to go for the cute ones. Just look at me." He wiggled his brows up and down a few times to emphasize his point.

I glanced over at him. As usual, he was selling himself short. At six feet tall, with black, wavy hair and true-blue eyes he is well beyond cute. Ask anyone who has ever seen him and they will tell you that Ken is well named. Fortunately for me, he wasn't remotely interested in setting up house with Barbie or Skipper.

"Besides, we are the ones who have to look at him every day for the next eighteen years. So, I say we go for cute."

I rolled my eyes and tried to focus on the pictures.

"What? You know you married me for my looks." Ken had obviously figured out how much this decision was stressing me out and was doing what he could to try to lighten the mood.

I leaned in and gave him a quick peck on the lips. "You are an idiot, but you're my idiot."

"Thank you—I think. Listen, don't let this make you crazy. Remember, this is the payoff. All of the hard work and endless waiting has been about this moment. Try to enjoy it."

He was right. This moment had been a long time coming. Like so many other people, we had no idea what we were getting ourselves into when we decided to wade into the parent pool. As gay men, we didn't have the luxury of testing the waters, of easing into the experience. We knew that there were people all over the world who had never met us, but did not want us to be parents, people who worked tirelessly to thwart us and our future family at every turn.

So we had jumped in feet first and quickly become experts on the pros and cons of adopting a baby from places as far flung as Eastern Europe and Brazil. Along the way we had also made our peace with the thousands of little moral questions and all the horrible stories of exploitation around international adoption. Some of the stories we had read were so terrible that we had nearly changed our minds about moving forward with an adoption and looked into fostering a child.

Fortunately, we had heard about Guatemala from a parenting group in Texas. They had invited us to one of their social events and, after spending time in the company of so many kids who had been adopted from there, we were hooked.

Guatemala had become the country of choice not only for prospective parents from the Dallas area but from all over the world. As was typically the case with adoption, this had attracted the notice of people determined to make a profit off of other people's unhappy circumstances. Stories were starting to appear in the media of people kidnapping children in Guatemala to sell them to rich, white families in America.

As a result, adoptions in Guatemala had come under increased scrutiny. It wasn't hard to imagine that the country would eventually shut down international adoptions completely. It had happened before in countries like China. It was really heartbreaking to think that agencies like Casa Antigua were trying to help children, many of whom were abandoned, and that their good work would likely come to an end very soon.

We knew that we needed to move quickly before things

went south in Guatemala. In other words, we had arrived at that place Holly Hunter so perfectly captured in *Raising Arizona* when she told Nicholas Cage "Don't you come back here without a baby!" At this point the end had to justify the means, because the means had been exhausting.

We had been in full-on baby mode for the last six months, as prepared to become parents as anyone who isn't a parent can ever be. The nursery was perfect, the home study was approved, and the checks had been cashed. We thought we had every contingency planned for, but never expected to be facing this *Sophie's Choice* moment.

"Why three? Why do there have to be three? We've waited for months without a single baby, and now there are three. Did someone turn on the baby faucet in Guatemala?"

"Maybe there was some magic in the air nine months ago," Ken said with a little twinkle in his eye. He circled his arms around my waist and tried to pull me in tight.

"Mitts off, Mr. Manford; there's no magic in the air here in Dallas." I shrugged him off and went back to obsessively staring at the computer screen.

He reluctantly let me go with a laugh. "Ya know, if it's really that hard to pick one, we could just take all three."

I cocked my left eyebrow and narrowed my eyes, a look that I have perfected to the point of trademark.

"Um, no."

I knew he was only half kidding and would take all three without a second thought if our finances did not dictate otherwise. But finances play a significant role in any private adoption. Even open adoptions were getting increasingly more expensive, and we had chosen a private international adoption, which financially sits near the top of the parenting food chain.

We could tell you from experience that adoption is not for the weak-hearted, nor is it easy. One of the first hurdles you have to overcome as gay men when you decide that you want to become parents is how you want to go about growing your family. The options include fostering, open adoption, private adoption, private international adoption and surrogacy. Each of these comes loaded with any number of complications, including a cost. As tacky as it sounds, cost is a huge consideration. You can get so caught up in the cost that you start to imagine a little price tag dangling from the toe of your new bundle of joy.

In some respects, it was like shopping. "Look at this one, darling, she's so precious," a wife might say to her husband.

"Well, isn't she cute? Kinda looks like my sister," he says, discreetly checking the price tag. "Oh, my. She's cute but she's not that cute. Keep looking, dear."

Most of our choices were behind us, for better or for worse. Except perhaps the most important choice, and now the clock was ticking down and I knew I needed to choose soon. Adoption is a high wire act that requires swift, confident movement. Leap! Plunge! Don't look down! Only I had a history of looking both down and back. Ken had more than shouldered the bulk of our choices up until this point, carefully researching all of our options to illuminate the path we should take. This choice was one he insisted we make together. But how can you make a connection to a child you've never met through nothing but a grainy picture snapped in a dimly-lit room under the worst of conditions?

I stared intently at the photos, willing one of them to

speak to me. I thought about placing my hands on the screen to see if I could get some kind of vibe. Fortunately, I resisted the urge. God knows that story would have made the rounds for years to come.

Instead, I mentally challenged the three boys: Okay, one of you will soon be saddled with the surname Manford-Roach. But which one? With that last name, and two gay dads deep in the heart of Texas, you'll need to be tough. Did one of these impossibly tiny things have an air of toughness about him? Unlike in real life, these babies were holding their tongues and keeping their counsel.

"This is too hard," I complained. "What if one of these boys is a future serial killer? Or worse yet, what if one of them is a little butterball? I can't relive my fat childhood. I barely made it through the first time."

I poked Ken in the ribs. "Look at that one on the left. Does he look a little fleshy to you? Hey, I know, why don't we print up all the pictures and just throw darts at them? Although that seems like we are getting our parenting off on the wrong foot, doesn't it? Can you imagine telling him his story? We threw darts at your picture—"

"Try to focus," Ken reminded me. "Besides, I've already picked."

"What!"

"Yeah. It's so obvious to me. Just keep looking and you'll figure it out."

"No pressure, huh? Well, if it's so obvious then you probably don't need my input." I made like I was about to move away from the computer, but Ken quickly put his hands on my shoulders and pushed me firmly back into the chair.

"Nice try. Serial killers and butterballs? I worry about

your mind sometimes. And, besides, I think you were awfully sexy in your husky years." Once more he tried to pull me in close and nuzzle my neck.

"Hey! I said mitts off. I'm trying to focus. And I worry about my mind all the time. I've told you for years I'm not right in the head and I'm fragile. Oh, and for the record, never use the word *husky* in context with me again. Remember a sentence that contains the word husky should not contain any reference to me. Got it?" Despite all the marketing efforts that went into it, everyone knows that husky is just a nicer way to say fat. Damn you, Sears, you've scarred me for life.

"I can't believe that I shared my painful childhood with you and you have warped it into something sexy."

Ken had lived with me long enough to know that I was stalling. For someone who has always been told they are so quick witted, I don't like to make quick decisions. This was a scenario we had not planned for and it seemed surreal to be shopping on the Internet for our child. Of course, even if there was just one baby we would still be looking at his picture and deciding whether or not to move forward with him. Now that it was happening it just seemed so unexpected and strange.

I mean, there I was looking at pictures of three impossibly tiny, impossibly cute baby boys and being asked to pick one that was going to be a part of my life for the rest of my life. Worse still, I knew I had to pick him right now. No doubt there was another family somewhere in the world who would get a similar email, but with one less choice. I hated making them wait one minute more than they had to.

"You think too much. Just act for a change."

He was right, I do think too much. I'm one of those people who is convinced they could outthink a lie detector. When it was time for our home study, I was determined to outthink our case worker. I synchronized mine and Ken's answers before she got there, staged the house and selected clothes that said "caring, but not cloying." Unfortunately, within minutes of starting the interview, I went completely off script, because my other major character flaw is that I talk too much.

"How about little Carlos?" I asked tentatively. "Carlos Enrique. How does Jackson Miguel Manford-Roach grab you? Are you up for a name change, little guy? Can you handle the Michael Jackson jokes? Will Michael Jackson even be in the collective conscious by the time you get to school?"

"Maybe we shouldn't change his name," I said, turning to Ken. "Are we setting ourselves up for some sort of Oprah moment? My gay dads took away my identity."

"See, sweetie, I knew you'd figure it out. It has to be little Carlos." Ken pulled me out of his chair and sat down in my place. He clicked the Reply button in the email. His fingers flew across the keys, confirming our choice with our case worker.

"Wait! Wait!" I protested to no avail. "Maybe we should get a second opinion. I think Ellen's home." Ellen was the single woman who lived next door to us and the only person in Dallas who possibly knew less about children than I did.

"Let me just go knock on her door. Or maybe we should send the pictures to our families and get some kind of consensus. At least we would be able to spread the blame around if things don't work out the way we want."

"There. All done," Ken said and pushed away from the computer. "Do we have any tuna? I'm starving. If I boil some eggs will you make tuna salad? Why is your tuna so much better than mine?"

And just like that, we were the proud parents of a healthy baby boy. I was still standing over the computer, staring at the original email.

This is it, I thought to myself, *the moment that sets our future on a particular path. And Ken is making a sandwich.* I slumped into his vacated chair, because all of a sudden I needed to sit down.

Of course, the roots of this decision went far deeper than clicking Reply to an email. The roots began with our good friend Marti. So if we turned out to be lousy parents, I was fully prepared to blame her.

"It's the dill," I said listlessly. "The dill is my secret ingredient."

I got up and made my way to the kitchen, thinking about dill and Marti, and the moment a few months ago when our lives took a sudden and unexpected turn toward a life less ordinary.

"I'll get you for this one day, Ms. Marti."

"What's that, honey?" Ken was in the pantry. I could see he was already pulling out ingredients, some of which didn't make any sense. Was that cumin? That man.

"I said get out the dill, and I'll make you some tuna."

I shuffled toward the pantry and started pulling together the ingredients for Ken's sandwich. I had avoided putting on any additional baby weight during our pregnancy but I had a feeling that stress eating was going to be an important part of my future.

CHAPTER FOUR

Dallas, November, 2001

In early November, Ken started worrying about my legal status as Jackson's parent. Actually, that's not true, he had been worried about it all along, but now that we had a baby to go with a name it was first and foremost in his mind.

After a couple days of endless Internet searches proved not to be particularly helpful, I finally convinced him to get in touch with a lawyer. He sent a message to the Yahoo group that the families who had adopted from Guatemala used to communicate and he was immediately flooded with responses. One name in particular kept coming up over and over from the gay parents on the board—Sylvia Browning. According to everyone who had used her, she was not only friendly to the cause, so to speak, she was actually part of the cause. Yep, Sylvia was a big ol' lesbian.

I had always had a healthy fear of lesbians but when it came to the baby game, they were pretty awesome. Lesbians had jumped on the baby wagon years ahead of most gay men and they were more than willing to extend a hand and help pull us on board.

One of the quirky things about gay people is that, whenever possible, we surround ourselves with other gay people. We eat at gay-owned restaurants, shop in gay-owned stores, and get our hair cut by gay stylists. Ken and I had even gone so far as to use a gay plumber when we had an issue with our dishwasher. This gay favoritism may seem a little weird, it's not like gay plumbers are automatically better than straight plumbers. Although in my experience they do give better butt crack. The reality is that when you've been made fun of and treated badly your entire life, you certainly don't want to pay for the experience. Maybe one day this wouldn't be a consideration, but for most of us it was a very real concern. So, Sylvia got my vote without any qualms.

Ken called her and scheduled an appointment for us to see her right away. He never was one to waste time. In the car on the way to the appointment, he slid his hand across the seat and gave my thigh a little squeeze and cleared his throat. After years of living together I knew I was in for one of his little *be nice* speeches.

"So I was thinking," he began, "that we should just listen today and let Sylvia do most of the talking." Oops, my bad. Apparently, this was the *be quiet* speech.

"That makes sense. I mean, I know you have a lot of questions, but I'm not sure we know enough to even ask them." I was pretty proud of how I had played that. With just a couple of sentences I had managed to insinuate that it was Ken who would be interrupting Sylvia instead of me.

"Okay. So we agree that we won't do all the talking?" Ouch. It seemed he was determined to keep me in the equation.

"Absolutely."

"Great."

"Great."

"Thanks honey."

I bit my tongue. I was trying to play it cool and not acknowledge what he *wasn't* saying. "You are such an ass," I muttered. So much for playing it cool.

"What did I say?" Ken was all wide-eyed and innocent but I wasn't buying it. I glanced over at him and raised an eyebrow. "Never you mind, mister. Just try to keep your yap shut."

After a few minutes of silence, Ken started laughing. "Just shut up!" I said with a grin. This just made him laugh even harder. "Seriously, just try to get us there alive." Ken kept grinning at me and he was still trying to keep from laughing ten minutes later when we pulled into the parking lot.

Sylvia's office was located in the heart of Cedar Springs, which was the unofficial gayborhood of Dallas. The office building was only a couple of stories tall and had a really cool seventies vibe going with lots of wood, windows and trees. Dallas may be a prairie, but it's a prairie that has been landscaped within an inch of its life.

"Ready?" Ken asked as we stepped out of the car.

"Ready as I'll ever be. Motormouth."

Ken chuckled, placed his hand on the small of my back and guided me into the building. Once we managed to locate the correct suite we were greeted by an adorable receptionist in a too-tight-for-the-office t-shirt with a rainbow flag on it. Sylvia clearly knew her audience.

He looked us over and seemed to like what he saw. "You must be Ken and Jeffrey," he said with a big smile that featured two Kewpie Doll dimples. I stepped forward and introduced myself and Ken.

"Ya'll have a seat right over there," he said, pointing to

a brightly upholstered love seat, "and I will let her know you are here."

"Thank you," we both said.

"Make yourselves comfortable. I will be right back."

Once he was out of sight, I turned to Ken and whispered, "Thinking of trading me in on a newer model?"

"Not a chance, baby. I'm afraid you are stuck with me for the foreseeable future."

"That's a relief, but I think rosy cheeks is going to be awfully disappointed."

"Please, he only had eyes for you." One of the things I loved most about Ken was how oblivious he was to the effect his good looks had on total strangers. Not only was he completely unaware, he always thought the lusty looks that were being thrown his way were directed at me. I was thinking about whether I should let him know that I might as well have been invisible when dimples, whose real name turned out to be something ridiculous like Leif, returned.

"Okay ya'll, she's ready for you." He motioned for Ken and me to follow him as he headed back in the direction he had come from. I wasn't paying attention and nearly collided into his backside when he stopped abruptly at a small kitchen that was tucked into an alcove and asked if either of us would like coffee or a glass of water. We both declined and he led us into Sylvia's office.

After years of watching L.A. Law and Ally McBeal, Sylvia was a little bit of a let down. I don't know what I was expecting, but she definitely wasn't it. There was no power suit or asymmetrical haircut with highlights. In fact, Sylvia was borderline frumpy and dressed a bit like a ranch hand.

After such a cute office and an adorable receptionist, I was expecting more. She must have noticed my surprised look because she shrugged her shoulders and said, "Leif is the beauty and I'm the brains." Then she smiled and the smile lit up her entire face. The smile took her from out-of-work ranch hand struggling with addiction to gainfully employed ranch hand with a heart of gold.

"Have a seat, boys, and let's talk."

Two hours later, Sylvia was still talking. I wondered if we were paying for this by the word. Despite my promise to Ken, I didn't keep my mouth shut, or at least I tried not to. But every time I would interrupt, Sylvia would shut me down and talk even harder. If I hadn't been so annoyed I would have been impressed.

The worst part was that, after all those endless sentences, I didn't know any more than I did when we walked in. I glanced over at Ken, who seemed not only to be paying attention, but also to understand every word she was saying. I was starting to think that I was the Leif in our relationship.

"So while there's not much we can do to establish Jeffrey as Jackson's second father, there's plenty we can do to protect his rights and access to him. When we are finally allowed to marry, this will be a moot point."

"When?" I said. "Don't you mean if?" The idea of two guys getting married seemed pretty far-fetched to me in general and especially far-fetched in Texas.

"It will happen," she said with complete conviction. "Maybe not this year, or even in the next ten years. But eventually I believe marriage between two men or two women will be recognized as the law of the land."

"Wow," I said. I'd never really thought about Ken and I being able to get married like *normal* folks do. But the way she said it caused my heart to beat a little faster. What would it be like to actually marry the man I had been living with for over ten years?

"Now the church," she continued with a little chuckle, "well, that's a whole other enchilada."

"You can keep the church," I said. "Just make it legal and we'll be the first two down the aisle."

"Hell yes. I like your spirit. I thought I lost you there for a minute, but it seems you are back." I gave her a sheepish smile and decided to make an effort to try to pay closer attention to the rest of the meeting.

"In any case, those are my recommendations. Does that make sense to both of you?" she asked. It looked like paying attention for the rest of the meeting was going to be a snap.

"Yes," Ken said without a moment's hesitation.

"Uh," I stumbled, "so Ken's *not* going to be my dad—right?" At one point I thought I heard Sylvia say something about Ken adopting *me*.

Her left eye twitched ever so slightly. "He is not. Let's go over this one more time. Flip your pages back to the beginning."

"Honestly, Sylvia, I probably won't pay attention the second time through either. If Ken is happy then I'm happy. I trust him."

She closed her book. "That's really sweet. Stupid, but really sweet." She looked at the two of us over the rim of her glasses. "Are you sure?"

"Completely." I reached over and picked up Ken's hand. "Do you understand what we are doing, honey?"

"I do. In a nutshell we are doing what we need to do to make sure your rights are protected when it comes to Jackson, but also that the two of us are as bound together as legally possible."

"Sounds like a plan." I turned back to Sylvia. "I'm good."

She took off her glasses and smiled at the two of us. "Ain't love grand?"

We both laughed and I started to get up from my chair.

"Hang on there, hoss. We still have one last thing to talk about. And I would love to have your undivided attention for this one."

Hoss? Seriously. "Okay. What is it?"

"Let's say you and Ken die in a terrible car crash. Your bodies are burned beyond recognition. What happens to Jackson?" Sylvia picked up her glasses and put them back on. "Do I have your undivided attention now?"

"You do," I said meekly. I had never thought about what would happen to Jackson if something happened to Ken and me.

"So with all the work we've done so far, if something happens to Ken, Jackson stays with you." She nodded at me. "In the eyes of the law, it doesn't matter if something happens to you, since Ken is his legal parent."

"But you know that you are just as much his parent as I am," Ken quickly added.

"Of course he is, and *when* we can legally marry it won't be an issue. But for now, we've got Jeffrey covered in case something happens to you. Legally, as long as you are around, Jeffrey just doesn't have a whole lot of options. So be nice to him, kiddo."

"Noted," I said. Someone else might have been put off by her ballbuster approach, but I found it refreshing and honest. Plus I was already working out my impersonation of her. In my version of her she was going to smoke.

"So back to the car crash scenario. What happens to Jackson? By default, he would go to Ken's family."

I looked over at Ken to see what he thought about this, because my inner voice immediately screamed, *I want him with my family.*

"I think I would want him with Jeffrey's family." Holy shit. My inner voice was powerful strong. "You think or you know?" Sylvia pressed.

"I know."

"Okay, so who specifically from Jeffrey's family."

"His sister."

"What's her full name?"

"Wait!" I couldn't let Ken just sign Jackson over to Fara without talking about it first. Even if it was what I truly wanted. "Are you sure about this, Ken?"

"I am. Here's what I'm thinking. Jackson is always going to have a connection to my family, since I'm his adoptive parent. If we name your sister as his guardian, if something happens to both of us then he also has a permanent bond to your family." I looked over at Sylvia for confirmation. She wiggled her hand back and forth as if to say, "Sort of." I raised my eyebrows at her, asking her to step in and say something.

"Look, family can be really shitty. A lot shittier than strangers, but what Ken is saying does go a long way toward making his intentions, and yours, very clear to your families. I'm not saying it's iron clad, but naming your family does create a legal bond between them and Jackson. Could they cut off Ken's family if they wanted to?"

"They wouldn't," we both said. Sylvia raised both of her hands, palms out as if to stop us from saying anything else.

"Like I said, family can be really shitty, but if they tried to cut Ken's family out they would have some legal recourse."

I looked over at Ken and he gave me a little nod. "Let's go with my sister as the legal guardian if the two of us go down in an epic air disaster on our way back from celebrating our *wedding* anniversary."

Sylvia sat back in her chair and eyed me for a long moment. "I like you. Are you looking for a job? I'll put Leif out on the street in a second if you are interested."

"I heard that!" Leif shouted from the reception area.

"Thanks for the offer, but I could never out-dimple Leif."

Sylvia picked up her glasses and put them back on. "Okay, let's get this all written up so the two of you can get out of here. Your days of footloose and fancy free are numbered so you may want to tip over to JR's and have a drink after this." JR's, the gay bar named after the patriarch of the Ewing family, was practically an institution in Dallas.

"Screw JR's," I said. "We are going to Mia's for margaritas and a boatload of Mexican food."

"Are you sure I can't keep you?"

"Sorry, I'm taken."

Sylvia gave an exaggerated sigh and then set about finalizing our paperwork. When we walked out of her office thirty minutes later, Ken and I had stitched our lives together as carefully and completely as we legally could. Well, at least until we could finally walk down the aisle together, assuming I was still ambulatory when that day finally arrived.

"Mia's?" Ken asked as we settled into the car.

"Mia's for sure. Do you want me to call Marti and Greg and see if they can meet us?"

"Sure. What about Kim and Ed?"

"The more the merrier as far as I'm concerned."

Ken eased out of the parking lot and I started making calls. I was so happy to have all of that legal stuff figured out but I was even more excited to reveal my Sylvia impersonation to our friends.

CHAPTER FIVE

Dallas, December, 2001

"Hey, we got another picture!" Ken was sitting at his computer downstairs messing around on the Internet. I was sprawled out on the comfortable but ugly sectional upstairs in the media room playing my brand new XBOX that Ken had bought me for Christmas, but had ended up giving to me just after Thanksgiving. Based on my experience, Jackson was going to be one lucky kid.

"Hang on, I just need to save my game."

"Better hurry up, I'm about to open it."

"Don't open it. I'm trying to get to a save point." *Halo* was supposed to be a great game, but I was having trouble finding the rhythm of it.

"Seriously, our child is playing second fiddle to your video game."

"I haven't made that much progress anyway. I'll just redo it." I shut down the XBOX and raced down the stairs. If I expected any kind of sympathy from Ken over the lost progress in my game, it wasn't forthcoming. Ken thought video games were boring and a waste of time, time that could be spent doing something with or for him, or, double bonus, doing something *with* him that was *for* him. Like shopping for a new pair of shoes. Personally, I'd rather face the zombies in *Resident Evil* than the zombies at the mall. Dallasites had a healthy appetite for plastic surgery.

I came up behind Ken and looked over his shoulder. "Okay, let's take a look."

Ken double-clicked the attachment in the email message and Jackson popped up on his computer screen.

I actually gasped. I couldn't help myself. "Oh my gosh it's his Santa picture! And he's wearing the outfit we sent him. He is so adorable."

Ken looked up at me. "He is. I think he is likely just about the most adorable kid ever."

"At least in the top five."

"At least."

"Can you send it to Fara? She is going to die. Look at all that black hair."

"Yes." He clicked the Forward button and typed in my sister's email address. "I'm so glad we didn't let them cut his hair."

The caretakers at Casa Antigua had written Cathy to ask about getting Jackson's hair trimmed. Even though he was only two months old he had a full head of hair. We had begged them not to cut it so that we could be there for his first haircut. They weren't happy about it, but they agreed to wait. The people taking care of the children who were waiting for their adoptions to be finalized took a lot of pride in caring for our baby. In every picture we saw Jackson was clean, well-dressed and seemed to be happy.

And we saw pictures of him on a fairly regular basis. We knew a lot of people who were adopting through the same agency as we were and every time one of them made a trip to Guatemala to pick up or visit their child they did their best to take pictures of all the babies who were still waiting to go home. In fact, we had even received a couple of pictures that weren't even Jackson. But this one was most definitely him in the outfit we had sent him for Christmas, smiling as he sat on Santa's lap. I was stunned at how quickly he was changing. Stunned and anxious. *I should be there for all of this*, I thought to myself.

"I am experiencing a cuteness overload." The phone rang and I reached over Ken's shoulder to grab it. "Hello!"

"We just got the picture," Fara said.

"How cute is he? I just told Ken that I was experiencing a cuteness overload."

"That hair!"

"I know. It's possible he has more hair than I do."

"He looks like Dad!" Our dad had a lifetime supply of *Just for Men* hair color and used it to maintain his black hair.

"Ha!" I put my hand over the receiver. "Fara says he looks like Dad with all of that wispy, black hair flying around everywhere."

"Put her on speaker."

"Fara, hang on, I'm putting you on speaker." I fiddled with a couple of buttons on the phone. "Hello? Are you still there?"

"Still me, Mother." Fara and I quoted Albert Brooks from the movie *Mother* every chance we got. Sometimes we would put each other on hold just so we could replay the scene where Debbie Reynolds is trying to figure out how to use call waiting and keeps clicking back to her son saying, "Hello? Hello?" To which Albert Brooks replies in his droll tone, "It's still me, Mother." Priceless.

I could hear Mom talking in the background, but couldn't make out what she was saying. "What's Mom saying?"

"Get back, old woman, I'm trying to talk to Ken and Jeffrey."

"Fara, be nice to Betty." Ken still couldn't get used to the relationship Fara and I had with Mom. He definitely didn't refer to his mom as "old woman". "What is she saying?"

"Hold on, she wants me to switch to speaker." There was a pause while Fara fiddled with her phone. "Okay, are you still there?"

"Still me, Mother." Fara and I both giggled. Ken rolled his eyes.

"It's too bad that the two of you aren't as entertaining to the rest of us as you seem to be to each other."

"He's just jealous," Fara said.

"You are on speaker, so I can hear you."

"You're just jealous."

"What is Betty trying to say?"

"It's on speaker, Mom. Just talk and they will hear you."

"I think I know how a speaker phone works," Mom said.

"Mom." Why do calls with my family always go off track so quickly? "What were you trying to say earlier?"

"I said he looks like Elvis!"

Ken and I both burst out laughing and I launched into a rousing rendition of *Burning Love*.

"Why do you sound like Wynonna Judd whenever you try to sing Elvis?" Fara asked.

"No I don't."

"You do. Mom, doesn't he?"

"Well, I certainly hope Wynonna sounds a little better than that."

"Mom!"

"Honey, we can't sing. You know that. When I was a little girl your Uncle Leonard used to tell me that I couldn't carry a tune in a bucket."

"I can sing," Fara said.

"No you can't," Mom and I said this at the same time.

"Yes I can. The kids love my version of *O Holy Night*."

"Oh, Fara, that's horrible. I have to close my door when you start in on that."

"Mom!"

"She's right, Fara. Every time you sing that, Jesus cries a little bit."

"Jeffrey, don't say those kinds of things." I loved to push the blasphemy borderline with my mom.

"Okay," Ken said and pushed away from his desk. "I think I'm going to go find something to eat since clearly we are not going to talk about Jackson."

"Sorry, sorry, sorry, Mr. Grumpy. Let's talk about Jackson." I pushed him back down in the chair.

"Do you think he looks older in that picture?" Fara asked.

"Yes, I was thinking to myself that he's changing so quickly."

"I don't mean different; I mean older."

"I don't understand. What do you mean?"

"I mean older than two months."

"He's a little chunkier, but I don't think he looks older. Why?"

"I don't know. I just think he might be older than they are saying he is."

"Fara, you are crazy." Ken looked up at me. "Your sister is crazy."

"I'm telling you he's older! I bet he is closer to six."

"What?" Ken and I said at the same time.

"Fara," Mom said, "there's no way he is six years old. He can't even sit up in Santa's lap by himself."

"Months, Mother. Six *months* old."

"Why would they lie about something like that?" I asked.

"I don't know. Maybe he didn't get adopted or something and they are trying to get you to take him."

"Are you saying they are trying to send us a used baby?"

"No! I'm just saying he looks older than two months."

Ken let out a long sigh. "This is the strangest call I think I have ever been on and that's really saying something with you three. And we have to go. We've got to get ready for the Guatemalan Christmas party."

"I wish I was going to be there," Mom said. "Those are the cutest babies I have ever seen."

"We will give them a hug for you, but Ken's right, we should go."

"Alright, thanks for sending us the picture. He is very cute."

"Sure, we will send along the next picture we get of our *used* baby."

"I didn't say used!"

"You could at least have said pre-owned," I said.

"And now we are done," Ken said. "We will talk to you two later."

"Bye!"

"Bye!" Ken hung up the phone. "Your family is too much."

"They are. That's why I love them. Hey, are we really going to go to the party?" I didn't know why but I felt weird about attending the Christmas party.

"Yes, we are going and there's no talking your way out of it. If we don't go you are just going to lay up there on the couch all day and play video games. Besides, it will be fun."

"I know, but sometimes I feel like we are mooching off of other people's kids. And it makes me jealous to see the parents who have just brought their babies home, and then I feel guilty for feeling jealous."

Ken just stared at me. "Get dressed. We're going."

***

We pulled into the parking lot, but neither one of us made a move to get out.

It had been over two months since Jackson had been officially placed with Ken and me. Despite what everyone said, I was convinced that he would be home by now, home in time for Christmas.

A two-month turnaround was unheard of, but somehow I had it in my head that Ken and I would be different than everyone else. I was completely convinced we'd be helping him rip the paper off of his presents on Christmas Day. Now that we were just a week or so away, I was forced to admit that it didn't look likely. This realization had put me in a funk and I couldn't find the strength to get excited about the holidays. We were supposed to drive to Kentucky to spend time with our families, but I honestly just wanted to spend the time off from work curled up on the couch playing video games.

"What are you thinking about?" Ken asked.

"Nothing."

"I know that look. Come on, what's going on inside that big ol' brain of yours?"

"I don't know. I just feel kind of blah. Which is weird,

because you know Christmas is my favorite."

"I do, so why do you feel blah?"

"I was hoping Jackson would be here."

"Honey, there was no way that was ever going to happen. I've been trying to tell you that for weeks."

"I know. I just felt like—I don't know. I guess I was hoping for a miracle."

"We have our miracle. Jackson is our miracle and he is amazing."

"I know, but it's his first Christmas and I don't want him to be alone."

"He's two months old. He doesn't know it's Christmas. And he's not alone. He will be surrounded by everyone at the orphanage."

"But I will know. I just wanted him here with us in time for the holiday. And please don't call it an orphanage. That just gives me *Oliver Twist* shudders. Can we think of it more like a day spa? Or maybe a high-end sleep away camp?"

Ken put his hand over mine. "He is going to be home soon. And we are going to have lots of Christmases together. Remember what your dad said when we told him we were adopting?"

I smiled. "Yes, he wanted to make sure we knew that you can't give them back. That kids are forever."

"Exactly, so a few weeks here or there is not going to make a difference. Not when you compare it to forever."

"You're right. I just need to stop obsessing over when he is coming home."

"It won't be long. Now, let's go inside. This will be good for us. I think you are going to have a great time."

"Let's do it." We stepped out of the car and walked to the front door.

The Guatemalan Christmas party was being held at the YMCA in Grapevine. Karen, who was organizing the event, knew a couple of folks on the staff and they had donated the space for the party.

We were greeted with hugs and hellos when we walked into the room. The space was crawling—literally—with kids from Guatemala. There were babies, toddlers, little kids and even a few teenagers. It was both heartwarming and heartbreaking. I desperately wanted Jackson to be a part of it all.

We looked around at everyone and nodded to some of the parents we knew best. I was excited to see that Debbie and Melissa were there. They were a few months behind us in the adoption process. I reminded myself that we were lucky. At least we had been placed with a child. There were plenty of people in the room like Debbie and Melissa who hadn't gotten the email yet and were still waiting on a placement.

I made a point of catching the eye of the couple who had sent us the picture of Jackson with Santa and mouthed, "thank you." They smiled and nodded. Everyone did their part to support each other. Sending and receiving pictures was a rite of passage. I was looking forward to being able to take pictures for someone else when it finally came time to bring Jackson home.

From across the room Karen gave us a little wave, finished her conversation, and made a beeline directly to us.

"I need your help," she said in between hugs.

"Sure," Ken said. "Do you need us to help set something up?"

"It's a little more serious than that. Follow me." Karen

turned and marched out of the room. Don't let anyone tell you that gay men have the market cornered on drama. Give a lesbian a little responsibility and watch the fireworks fly. Karen was running this party like a field marshal in the midst of battle. Ken and I shrugged our shoulders at each other and took off after her.

"In here, guys," Karen called from the office behind the front desk.

We lifted the partition and walked into the office.

"Oh my God," I said. "Is that what I think it is?"

"It is if you think it's a Santa costume. We have ourselves a little Santa emergency."

"What's going on, Karen, and how can we help?" Ken was such a do-gooder. I had a feeling I knew where this was going and I wasn't thrilled.

"Do you guys know Brian and Mary?"

"Sure, they just sent us a picture of Jackson."

"Right, they just got back from Guatemala with baby Juan. So cute."

"We haven't seen him yet, but we can't wait. How old is he?"

"He's right around six months old."

I gave Ken a look. I wasn't waiting for Jackson to be six months old before we brought him home.

"Anyway," she continued, "Brian was going to play Santa, but now that they have Juan with them, he'd really like to be able to take pictures of the baby with Santa. So we are Santa-less."

"Sounds like a Santa crisis," I said.

"Jeffrey can do it."

"Fantastic! That would be a huge help. I know Brian would really appreciate it."

"Wait, what? I can't play Santa." Ken and Karen just stared at me. "Look at me. I'm a pocket gay."

"What's a pocket gay?" Karen asked.

"Ignore him, Karen. He will be a perfect Santa." She stood there for a second looking between Ken and me. "Seriously, we've got this."

"Okay, well, the costume is in that bag on the floor there, just put it on and I will come and get you in a few minutes."

"We'll be ready."

"Thank you, guys, so much for this." Karen leaned in and gave us a hug and left the room, closing the door behind her.

"I can't play Santa."

"You will be a great Santa. You'll be fun and the kids will love you."

"Ken, look at me. I am a tiny person. Why don't you do it?"

"Because you will do it better than me. Now take off your pants and let's get you in this costume."

"I'm not stuffing myself. That is off the table. You seem to be determined to get me to relive my fat childhood. No way. If I do this, I'm going to be a thin, sexy Santa."

"Just take your pants off before I smack you." I took off my pants and shirt and slipped into Santa pants. The material was not pleasant.

"These look like clown pants."

"They look great," Ken said, trying to keep from laughing.

"They look ridiculous. They are like a size—ginormous. This is crazy."

"Put the top on."

"The top? You mean the shirt? You are so gay."

I slipped on the shirt. "How am I supposed to keep this from falling off?"

"Here, try the belt." Ken handed me a big, black plastic belt. I wrapped it around my waist and buckled it.

"What do you think?"

"You look a little like Mariah Carey on the cover of her Christmas album."

"Really? I can live with that. Where's the wig?"

Ken dug around in the bag and pulled out a hat. "No wig, the hair is attached to the hat."

"That is just wrong. Give it to me." I slipped the hat on my head and white curls cascaded around my shoulders. "I need a mirror."

Ken grabbed my hand. "Trust me, you really don't."

"But you said I looked like Mariah Carey."

"Honestly, you look a bit more like Bea Arthur from the Christmas special of *Golden Girls*."

"Just hand me the beard and let's get this over with."

Again Ken dug around in the bag and came out with a ratty looking beard. He handed it over to me. It had two little hooks that went behind each ear to hold it in place.

"Nasty!"

"What?"

"The mouth area is wet! This is a used costume." Ken couldn't hold back the laughter this time. "I hate you."

"I love you, sweetie. You really do look awesome. The beard makes the outfit."

"Did you not hear me? The. Mouth. Area. Is. Wet." There was a light knock on the door. "Come in," we both called.

Karen opened the door and stepped into the room.

"Look at you! Do you want a pillow?" Something in my look must have caused her to reconsider. "Never mind. You look adorable. The kids are going to be so excited. Are you ready?"

"As ready as I'll ever be."

Karen took my hand and led me out of the office and back into the assembly room. "Hey everyone," she shouted as we walked into the room, "look who I found!"

There was a rumbling around the room and some of the older kids clapped their hands or pulled at their parents, making sure they saw who it was. I noticed the teenagers trying to hide smiles behind their hands. This was probably their first experience with a gay, slim, sexy, Mariah Carey wannabe Santa.

I could tell that some of the younger kids were nervous and hanging back so I did the only thing I could: I pasted on a big, cheesy smile, threw my head back and let loose with a very jolly ho ho ho.

I spent the next couple of hours or so talking with kids, posing for pictures and handing out gift bags. Karen had put together the bags and they were pretty amazing. Nestled amongst the usual assortment of holiday treats were two or three handmade gifts from Guatemala. There was a little doll, a fabric star for the tree, and something that looked like it might be a musical instrument.

After the last bag had been handed out, Karen announced that Santa had to get back to the North Pole. She took my hand and helped me maneuver through the room, which was a good thing since my hat/hair combo kept sliding down over my face and made it hard to see.

Once we were safely tucked away in the office, she gave me a big hug and thanked me again. I pulled off the beard and hair/hat combo and plopped into a chair. I felt like I had just finished a marathon. Being Santa was a lot of work.

"Jeffrey, you were amazing. You really played it up."

"I knew he would, that's why I made him do it." Ken looked particularly pleased with himself, but he was right. I can't walk away from a role like that. Santa is the role of a lifetime, right up there with Scrooge, which, for the record, I played in both high school and college productions of *A Christmas Carol*.

"You are the amazing one. Those bags were the best. How did you manage to get all of that done?"

"Jeffrey is right. Those gifts from Guatemala were really cool."

Karen waved her hand in the air. "It's not a big deal. I worked with the folks at Casa Antigua to collect all the stuff I needed."

"Can we contribute to the cost?" Ken was so good at these things. My mind was on the food. I wondered if there was any left for Santa. I don't know about a skinny Santa Claus but nobody wants to deal with a hungry Santa.

"It really wasn't much. Don't worry about it. Plus, you guys have more than done your part with handing them out. Jeffrey, you basically missed the entire party."

"Missed the party? I was the party! Seriously, I had a lot of fun."

"I'm glad. Can you just stick the suit back in the bag for me? I have to get it back to the rental place tomorrow."

"No problem."

"Oh, but before we do, there is one more gift bag we need to hand out."

"Sure. Let me get my Santa drag back on." I reached for

the hair/hat combo. I wondered if I could get away with a clean shaven Santa for this last child.

"Actually, you are not going to need it." Karen reached into her desk drawer and brought out another gift bag. "This one is for Jackson." She brought the bag over and handed it to me.

"Oh, Karen." That's all I could get out. If I tried to say anything else I knew I was going to start blubbering.

She gave us both a little hug. "I know you two wanted him to be here for this. We have all been there and I promise you, once you get him home, it won't matter to you at all."

"Thank you. I'll put the suit in the bag and we will come in there and find you before we leave."

"Perfect. And grab something to eat—if there's anything left."

"I made him a plate and hid it." Of course he did. Ken is a natural provider and was going to make a great father.

"See you in a bit."

Karen closed the door behind her and Ken pulled me up out of the chair and gave me a big hug.

"Are you seriously putting the moves on Santa?"

"I can't help it; he's so cute."

"He works out ya know."

"I can tell." Ken gave me a couple of quick kisses. "Thank you for doing that. I knew that you would be amazing."

"It was fun. The different reactions from the kids were pretty cool. Some of them really made me work for it."

"That was really sweet of Karen to put a bag together for Jackson."

"It was."

"It's almost like he was here." Ken stepped back so that I could get out of the Santa costume. "So are you feeling a little better now?"

"I am."

"Good. Me too. She's right, you know. Once we have him home with us none of this will matter."

"I know."

"Okay, well, get dressed so we can go say goodbye to everyone."

"Um, and I still need to eat."

"Okay. I'll go snag the plate I hid for you and meet you in there."

"Okay."

"See ya in a second." Ken opened the door to the office.

"Hey Ken." He paused and turned back toward me. "There is no way I'm waiting six months to bring Jackson home."

Ken laughed. "Okay. We will have him home before six months rolls around."

"Promise?"

"This is completely insane. There is no way I have any control over this at all but, yes, I promise."

"Great. Now pull the door closed. People are seeing a whole lot more of Santa than they ever bargained for."

Ken pulled the door closed and I continued to get undressed. Whether he knew it or not, I planned on holding him to that promise.

2002

CHAPTER SIX

Dallas, January, 2002

Ken was on the phone with Cathy and it didn't look like there was good news. Cathy wasn't the type to call without a reason. I had called her dozens of times in the last few weeks to check on the progress in Guatemala and I always got the same answer: When I have something to tell you, I will call you. Perhaps she thought that telling me that would somehow shame me into not pestering her for updates; it did not.

If a few days went by without any news, I would pick up the phone and call her even though I knew what she was going to say. It was my not-so-subtle way of reminding her that we were still here and that we were still waiting. To his credit, Ken didn't play these kind of mind games with Cathy, although he didn't exactly discourage me from doing it.

Jackson was going to be three months old in a matter of days, so another one of my self-imposed deadlines was quickly arriving. At times it seemed like the days were flying by and at other times each hour was a lifetime. I had described the international adoption experience to some friends who were looking at their options as a high-speed car chase in mind numbing slow motion. All of the movement seems frantic, but progress toward your goal is slow. You begin to feel as if you are simply along for the ride, strapped into the passenger seat, completely powerless to affect the outcome. All you can do is keep moving forward one tedious day at a time, all the while hoping that the ride eventually gets you to your destination.

They ended up going with an open adoption. When they told me it occurred to me that perhaps I wasn't the best resource to talk to in my current frame of mind, although everyone kept assuring me that my reaction wasn't unusual.

All adoptive parents struggle under the weight of the system, but it's even harder for gay parents. So many gay and lesbian parents crash and burn, or lose their way. They get sidetracked by red tape, or by money, or by some small-minded case worker who thinks they are acting in the best interest of the child by not placing them with a gay man or a lesbian who will actually care for them. Staying the course requires faith. The bottom line is that adoption is one long act of faith and devotion.

For us, Ken was the source of that faith. He had cut a path through the adoption red tape like an avenging angel, like the world's most efficient project manager with an IV drip of caffeine permanently strapped to his side. That's why the frown on his face had me concerned.

Ken wasn't supposed to frown. For months he had talked me off of every ledge, assured me things were going to work out and scolded me when I pushed too hard. I knew that, if Ken lost his faith, we were going to be in a world of trouble.

As soon as he hung up with Cathy I pounced. "What's happened? What did she say?"

"Promise me that you are not going to freak out, or try to call her back."

"Too late on the first count. I'm already freaking out, but I will make every effort not to call Cathy back. If it comes to it, you can always rip the phones out of the wall."

He gave me a long look, but he still didn't say anything. Was this supposed to be a dramatic pause I wondered. If he was spending this much time selecting just the right words, then something really terrible had happened.

"Ken, you are really causing me to panic. Just tell me what she said."

He blew out a breath. "The judge who is assigned to our case—"

"Oh my God. He found out you're gay and he hates gays! You may have to marry Marti or Fara."

"What? No." He tried to collect himself again before adding, "Not to mention, they are both already married."

"Okay, Julie then. I'm sure she'll do it."

"Please stop talking. That's not the problem."

"Then what is it?"

"His father has passed away."

"Is that all?" I felt a tremendous sense of relief, which was followed by a healthy wave of guilt. "I mean that's terrible for him, but you looked like someone had just popped your birthday balloon."

"The thing is he's going to be taking a leave of absence."

"Okay, so what, they'll just assign our case to someone else?" I still referred to everything in the plural, although as far as Guatemala was concerned I didn't exist. "Are we going to lose a few days while the new guy comes up to speed?"

"Cathy says that is not the way it works."

Ken still looked very stressed and I could feel the panic starting to creep back into my brain. "Maybe you better just tell me what she said."

"She said that our case will go into limbo while he is on leave."

"How long is he going to be on leave?"

"That's the bad part. It's open-ended. He could be on leave for a few days or a few weeks. Even a few months."

"No. That's not going to work for us. We need to get moved to someone else. Let's get Cathy on the phone. You were probably too nice about it." I tried reaching for the phone, but Ken put his hand on top of mine. "*Honey*, let me handle this. I know you hate conflict, so let me talk to her." That much was true, Ken went out of his way to avoid conflict.

"*Baby*, you are not listening. It's out of her hands. This is the way it works in Guatemala. It doesn't matter how much we yell at Cathy; she can't change anything. She's as upset as we are right now."

"This isn't right. He has a US passport. He's technically a citizen of the United States. We just need this guy to review the paperwork so that he can hand him over to us. I'm sorry his dad has died but he needs to take five minutes out of his mourning to review those damn papers.

"I agree, but that's not going to happen. He's already left the city. Apparently, this happened nearly a week ago and it's taken this long for the information to find its way to Casa Antigua and then Cathy."

"God I feel just like Sally Field."

"Sally Field?"

"In that movie, *Not Without My Daughter*. Remember I used to do that parody called *Not Without My Wig*, about a drag queen who was fired but refused to leave the bar without her drag?"

"Not ringing a bell, but I'm guessing this is somehow connected to our situation."

"Yes, in the movie her husband takes Sally and her daughter to visit Iran and then he refuses to let their daughter leave and Sally refuses to leave—"

"Without her daughter?"

"Thus the title."

"Hmm. I really don't see the connection, honey."

I sighed. "Now that I think about it, I suppose it's not really the same. It's just the idea that her daughter was an American and she couldn't get her back home. She's running around Iran like a crazy person trying to get her back."

Suddenly, Ken went very still. "Maybe Sally had the right idea."

"What do you mean?"

"Maybe we should go to Guatemala."

"And try to smuggle him back home? That sounds crazy, even for me."

"No, silly. We aren't going to try to bring him back, but at least we can visit with him. Hold him. I don't know about you but I'm tired of only knowing our son through other people's pictures of him."

Yes, I totally swooned when he said our son. He was right, we had seen lots and lots of pictures. Each new arrival would be carefully inspected for minor changes in our son, and then dutifully sent along to friends and family. This, in turn, would generate a flood of email conversation between us and them: Is his hair getting longer? Look how black his eyes appear in this one! Isn't he handsome? Each picture was like another little stitch into the fabric of our lives that pulled him closer to us; he was no longer Carlos Enrique, an orphaned child in Guatemala, but Baby Jackson. And with each passing picture Baby Jackson became a little more firmly entrenched, not only in our lives, but also in the lives of the people who mattered most to us.

"I think we should go see him. Go make sure that he's doing alright; make sure he knows that we are waiting for him." Ken was already convinced enough for the two of us.

"Let's do it. Can you start looking into costs? The airline tickets are going to be expensive, but I may have enough miles." Before the words were out of my mouth, Ken was already on American Airlines' website, investigating flights.

"You definitely have miles. We've been stockpiling miles for months now."

"And we will need someone to come take care of Patsy. Or maybe we can board her somewhere? Oh, and work. We need to ask for time off from work." The reality of how disruptive this unplanned trip was going to be was starting to sink in. We were planning to fly down and pick up Jackson and then fly right back home. We had always planned for it to be a quick overnight trip. If we were going for a visit and not bringing him back, we were going to want time with him.

"You should go," I whispered. "You should go and make sure he's okay."

Ken looked up at me. "I know; didn't we just decide this?"

"I mean you should go without me. It's so much to plan for and I'm not sure we can both take off work. We just took off for the holidays."

"I don't want to go without you. I'm not sure I can handle it all on my own."

"You can, and if you are nervous you should take your mom with you."

"But what about the cost?"

"Use my miles."

"I don't know. I feel weird about going without you."

"Honey, I want you to go. It will make me feel so much better if you go and make sure everything is okay."

"Really?"

"Absolutely."

Ken stood up from his desk and wrapped me up in a big hug. He gently kissed me on the forehead.

"After that kind of sacrifice I would expect a kiss on the lips."

"I'm just kissing that crazy brain of yours. Without your bizarre, random connections I'm not sure it would have occurred to me to go to him, since he can't come to us."

He smiled at me and gave me a second kiss. This time my lips got a little attention. "Thank you. You really are spectacular."

"Sally is spectacular. I am merely amazing."

"Thank you, Sally," Ken whispered in my ear.

"Okay, mitts off." I untangled myself from his arms. "You've got lots of calls to make. Your mom is going to shit and fall back in it when you tell her."

"Nice image."

I giggled. "You should probably call Cathy and get her involved. Since all the paperwork is in order I can't imagine they won't let you see him, but you have a lot of stuff to get done if you're going to be there in time for his birthday."

"His birthday?"

"Yes, he will be three months old on the 11th of January."

"I know that, but that's next week."

"Exactly, so you better get to cracking." Somehow I just knew that we would have him with us by the time he was three months old. It just didn't occur to me that one of us would have to go to him.

"Are you sure you are okay with not going?"

I wasn't okay, but I knew it was the right thing to do. "I'm sure."

Ken picked up the phone. "Then I better get started."

***

That was how it came to pass that the first time we laid eyes on Jackson in person I wasn't there for it. Ken and his mom left for Guatemala on January 18th, which was a week beyond his three-month birthday, but a remarkable accomplishment nonetheless.

Since all of Ken's paperwork was in order, Cathy assured us he was going to be able to do a lot more than just see Jackson. He was going to be able to pick him up at Casa Antigua and then take him back to the hotel to stay with him and his mom for the entire visit. After waiting for so long to meet him, Ken and his mom were going to spend nearly a week getting to know our little guy in person.

I was insanely jealous of all the time they would get with Jackson. Still, I knew that sending Ken and Joyce was the right thing to do for a number of reasons. Ken was technically the adoptive parent and a part of me was afraid that if I showed up with him they would see the gay all over the two of us and change their minds about letting us have Jackson. I hadn't confessed this fear to anyone but my sister, who shared my healthy sense of paranoia.

I also knew that spending time with Jackson and his mom would mean so much to Ken. Ken's sister had four-year-old twins and I knew he was nervous about how Jackson would fit into the family dynamic. I wasn't worried at all; I knew Joyce would be crazy about him, because she was crazy about Ken. Anything that made Ken happy was going to put her over the moon.

Selfishly, I also hoped that the trip would charge up Ken for the final stretch so that he'd be able to carry us across the finish line. I knew that I was going to have at least four or five total breakdowns between now and when Jackson finally got to come home and I needed Ken's resolve to be fortified.

Deep down, I was also incredibly impressed by my own self-sacrifice. In fact, I felt just a tiny bit like Ann Margaret in that fabulous made-for-TV movie *Who Will Love My Children?*

It's the one where Ann is diagnosed with cancer and spends her last few months finding a home for her ten children. She won a Golden Globe for her performance, and I was fairly certain I would be in line for some similar kind of recognition. I have always had issues with scale.

Ken had promised me that he would call me as soon as he got to Casa Antigua. I had practically been sitting on the phone for the last few hours and when it rang I snatched it up eagerly.

"I'm looking at our son and he is gorgeous."

At those nine words my heart completely seized up. I felt like I had made a terrible mistake by taking on Ann's role. I wanted to be there beside Ken at this important moment. I no longer cared about looking like a great parent who was willing to make sacrifices; I just wanted to be there holding my child. In short, I burst into hysterical sobs.

"I know, honey," Ken said, starting to cry himself. "I'm overwhelmed too."

Ken was sobbing, I was sobbing, and I could hear Ken's mom, Joyce, in the background sobbing. And underneath it all, almost too quiet to hear, was the faintest little cooing.

"Shhhh," I shouted into the phone. "Is that him?"

"Yes, he's so happy. He's smiling and cooing. Here, listen." Ken held the phone up close to Jackson and I pressed my ear even tighter, and I heard it. I heard *him* for the first time. I heard the little nonsensical gurgling noises and cooing of a perfectly happy, healthy, normal baby boy.

And in that moment I really did understand the sacrifices we are willing to make for our children. When Ken got back on the line I didn't tell him how I had made a terrible mistake. I didn't tell him that I felt lonely and that I wanted to be there too. I told him to hold our son as long and as often as he could over the next few days. I told him to take lots of pictures and then to come home safely to me. I told him that I loved him. I told him that I finally understood Ann's sacrifice.

"And sacrifice?" he asked, mishearing me over the crackly connection. "What's *and sacrifice*?"

"Nothing sweetie," I said. "We must have a bad connection."

"Okay, well we should go. The doctor is here and he's going to give Jackson a little mini physical and talk to us about his overall health. Not that there's anything to worry about, he's already told us Jackson is in perfect health. I think it's just a formality."

"Don't keep him waiting," I managed. "Give him a kiss for me. Er, Jackson, not the doctor."

"I figured," Ken laughed. "Goodbye, sweetie, see you in a few days."

"Goodbye."

I clicked off the phone and laid it on the desk. What was an instrument of magic a few seconds ago was now a reminder of the distance between me and my boys. I climbed up the stairs, pulled off my clothes and crawled into our big, empty bed. I whistled for Patsy, who jumped up in the bed, gave me a quick lick on the face and settled in next to me with a contented sigh.

"Don't get used to this, Little Miss," I told her. Patsy cocked her head up at me and tried to look grateful, but she couldn't quite pull it off. It's a look that was foreign to her. She had ruled the roost for so many years now that she didn't give my threat much more than a sideways glance. *Enjoy yourself, old girl,* I thought to myself, *your reign is coming to an end. You've got some interesting days ahead of you when Jackson comes home.*

"Please let it be soon," I whispered to no one. Despite the fact that I had an 80-pound dog laying practically on top of me, I felt alone and disconnected. So I did what any self-respecting ingénue would do in my situation. I grabbed a box of tissues beside the bed, and started a nice, long, three-day cry.

CHAPTER SEVEN

Dallas, January, 2002

On the day Ken was due to arrive back from his trip to
Guatemala, I got to the airport early. Two hours early to
be exact. The bed sheets were covered in dog hair and dried
tears and I couldn't stand another minute in the house by
myself. To put it more bluntly, I couldn't stand myself
another minute. I was sick of my own company and the
endless internal conversations I was having about all the
things that could go wrong with our adoption. I had half-
convinced myself that Jackson would be walking by the
time we finally got him home. In short, I needed to get out
of my own head and into the world. What better place to
wade into humanity than the Dallas/Fort Worth Airport?

After circling the terminal a number of times and
realizing I had way too much time to kill, I pulled into the
parking garage. I opened the door to get out and noticed
that my baggy sweats would not be out of place on a
homeless person. Glancing at my shirt, I could almost use
the stains to map out my food binges from the last few
days. When had I last showered? Suddenly, I was exhausted
at the idea of trying to function in public. I slipped back
inside the car and closed the door. Although I had been
chasing sleep for the last few days at home without much

luck, within a few minutes of shutting off the engine sleep found me and I was out. The sound of a ringing phone woke me up. It was Ken and he was wondering where I was. Only I could arrive at the airport two hours early and still end up being late. I started the car and raced over to the terminal to pick him up.

As I pulled into the passenger pickup zone, I could see Ken standing on the sidewalk, scanning the crowd for me. I parked right in front of him, popped the trunk, hopped out of the car and started loading his bags. I was hoping that my hyper-efficiency would make up for having made him wait while I catnapped in the parking garage.

Once we were both settled in the car I caught Ken giving me the once-over. His eyes went a little wide, but to his credit he didn't point out the stains on my shirt or my hobo-esque sweats. Instead, he leaned over and gave me a big kiss. He was practically beaming.

"I'm so happy to see you and I have got tons of pictures for you," he said. "Oh, and my mom videotaped the checkup with the doctor so you can hear everything he had to say. Although I didn't understand most of it. His accent was pretty thick. Most of the time I just smiled and nodded because I didn't have a clue what he was saying. Hopefully, he wasn't giving me bad news. If he was he must think I'm a really terrible person, because I just kept smiling like an idiot."

"I'm glad to see you too," I said. "I've been going out of my mind on my own and I can't wait to see the pictures." Instead of putting the car in gear and heading home, I leaned over and gave Ken another big hug, holding on tight for a few extra seconds. When I pulled away my eyes were misty.

"Wow, two hugs and a kiss? You must have really missed me. Maybe I need to go away more often if that's what's waiting for me when I get home. Speaking of home, let's get going so I can show you how much I've missed you." Ken wagged his eyebrows a couple of times. "But perhaps we will get you in the shower first—"

"Listen, I think I need to go to Guatemala." The words were out of my mouth before I could stop them.

Ken just stared at me. "Right now?" he finally asked.

"No, silly, not right now. Right now I just want to get you home and take a look at the pictures, watch the video and snuggle up in bed with someone who doesn't shed."

"I didn't hear shower in there anywhere."

"Okay, yes. I could probably stand a little freshening up; it's been a long week. But I'm serious, I need to go to Guatemala."

"I'm just kidding about the shower. Mostly," he added with a grin before turning serious. "Honey, what's going on? What's this all about?"

I thought about coming up with some excuse to make me sound less pitiful, but I knew Ken would ultimately get the truth out of me so I decided to save us both the trouble. "I guess I didn't realize how left out I was going to feel when I suggested you take your mom and not me," I said with a sigh. "Not that I'm upset that she went. I'm really glad she got a chance to go."

"Me too. She's gaga over Jackson already."

"How could she not be?" I asked. "He is adorable. At least as far as I can tell from *here*."

Ken let that *here* set for just a minute. "You know he will probably be home in less than a month."

"Probably. That is the key word. But it could just as

easily be two months, or even three and that's too long. That's longer than I'm willing to wait. We've done everything right, but I have no confidence in the Guatemalan government's ability to hold up their end of the bargain."

"You're right. There are no guarantees," Ken said. "If you want to go, I think you should go. Maybe you should take your mom. That way we will have both of the grandmothers covered."

"I'd love that, but I am afraid they won't let Mom and me take him to the hotel like you and Joyce did since I'm not legally connected to him in any way." I tried not to sound upset, but my voice wavered a little bit as I said the last sentence.

Ken reached over and grabbed my hand, giving it a little squeeze. "I hate that. I promise you that we are going to fix that as soon as we can. Despite what's on file in Guatemala, Jackson is just as much yours as he is mine."

"I know, but if you think me turning up to visit him will jeopardize anything in any way then I won't go."

"Honestly, I don't think they care. We saw two gay guys visiting their son while we were there." Ken fell quiet and I could practically hear the cogs turning. "It's a lot of planning, especially since I just took off time from work to go. And, of course, there's the unexpected costs. But you know me, I don't worry about the money. God I wish one of us could speak Spanish. Then we could probably talk to someone at Casa Antigua and ask them if they would let you and your mom take him."

"Sorry, I took French in high school. It seemed fancier at the time."

"Why am I not surprised?" Ken said.

"Listen, I know it's terrible timing and it's probably going to cost us a fortune. And I'm really sorry if I'm being unreasonable, but I just can't stand the idea that he has only met one of his dads; he only knows half of his story. Maybe we can use the rest of my airline miles if there are any. And I can make all the arrangements. You won't have to do a thing except escort me down there." I realized that I was starting to ramble; Ken must have thought so too since he suddenly leaned across the seat and gave me a little peck on the lips, stopping my long list of justifications.

"Ssh," he said with a grin, "stop talking and start driving. It looks like we have another trip to Guatemala to plan."

***

Although I had volunteered to do it, Ken spent the next few days working on the travel arrangements. I probably should have felt guilty, but he seemed to be enjoying finding ways to get us to Guatemala and back without spending any money. I had a feeling I was going to end up stuffed into one of those little dog carriers.

Since Ken was managing the travel, I was assigned the task of trying to spring the two of us from work. At first I thought about making up an elaborate story involving organ transplants and mistaken identity, but in the end I decided to just stick with the truth: We didn't know when Jackson was coming home and I couldn't go by myself, so Ken needed time off to accompany me to Guatemala. To his credit, our boss gave us both the time off without any complaints. He even offered to put it down as comp time, so that we could save our vacation days.

With my task accomplished and Ken deeply involved in investigating some convoluted route through Miami that would potentially save us a lot of money, I decided to call my mom and give her the latest update. I hadn't told anyone in my family about my little meltdown or that we were making a return trip to Guatemala. I figured if anyone was going to make me feel better about myself and my sudden neediness, it was Mom.

"Hello."

"Hey Mom, it's me. Did you guys get the pictures Ken took in Guatemala?"

"We did. Jackson is so cute. I'm jealous of Joyce, although I'm not jealous of her video taking skills. At first I thought we would be looking at her thumb for an hour."

"I know!" I said with a giggle that almost turned into a snort. "I was actually shouting at the screen, 'Move your thumb! Joyce, move your thumb!'"

"I thought your sister was going to snap when we watched it."

We both laughed at the same time. "You know your sister," Mom said. "She always thinks she can do anything better than whoever happens to be doing it at the time. She kept saying that if *she* had been there the video would have been so much better."

"I can hear her now."

"When Joyce finally moved her thumb I don't know if we were more thrilled to be able to see the baby or that Fara would finally shut up. She was actually becoming more annoying than the thumb." The conversation settled into a comfortable silence as if Mom could sense I wasn't calling to talk about the video, Joyce's thumb or my sister's strong belief in her superior camera skills.

"So listen," I began. "I want to run something by you, to see if you think I'm being ridiculous."

"I'm not sure I'm the best judge of that."

"Well, take off your mom hat and try to think about what I'm about to say objectively."

"Okay, the mom hat is off. Now, what's going on?"

"Okay, here goes—first, do you need to go check your hair? I know how you feel about hat hair."

"Check my hair? I wasn't wearing an actual hat. Oh! I get it. Stop stalling." She knew me too well.

"With this whole dead dad delay—"

"Jeffrey! Don't say it like that," Mom interrupted.

"Sorry, with this *delay* we don't have any idea when Jackson is going to get to come home and so we, actually it's more me than we, have decided to make another trip to Guatemala."

"What! And Ken is going again?"

"Yes. He has to, since he's the actual adoptive parent. I don't have any legal connection to Jackson, so I'm afraid they wouldn't let him come to the hotel with just me."

"Is Joyce going again?" Mom asked.

"No, why?"

"Well, I thought I might go with you, if you don't mind." She paused a second before adding, "It would really help to put Fara's mind at ease."

"Huh? How does you going with us put Fara's mind at ease? Is she that desperate to get you out of her hair?"

"No! I wasn't going to say anything, but it's the pictures. The ones Ken took. She has been studying them closely and she is convinced Jackson is much older than what you are being told. She says there is no way he's only three months old."

"Mom, it's all of that black hair. It makes him look like a little man."

"Well, it's official, we don't have enough frequent flyer miles for free tickets. So that means we are probably looking at March instead of February," Ken said. He had apparently picked up the other extension. "And who's a little man?"

"Jackson," I replied. "Fara has convinced Mom that he's old enough for a learner's permit."

"Jeffrey! That's not true."

"Betty! He's a tiny little thing—" Ken began.

"Jeffrey is exaggerating. She didn't say he was a teenager; she just said that he's not three months old. She thinks he is probably more like seven months old."

Ken poked his head around the corner and covered the phone with his hand. "Your family is crazy." He took away his hand. "Betty, I've seen him in person. Remember?"

"Ken, what do you know about babies?" my sister asked. She had apparently picked up the extension at her house. "He has a mustache."

"The doctor said that's typical for babies from Central America. It will all fall out eventually. It's some kind of womb thing."

"Womb thing?" my sister asked. "Ken, I think Mom and I know a little bit more about wombs than you two. I'm telling you the kid has mutton chops."

"Okay you two," I said to Mom and Fara. "Can I just point out that when Ken and Joyce planned their trip, I'm pretty sure she didn't compare our son to some kind of miniature Elvis."

"Again I will remind everyone that there's nothing wrong with Elvis," Mom said. "Besides, I want to see my grandson. Joyce got to see him and now it's my turn."

"Is that what this is about?" Ken asked. "Of course we'll

get you a ticket. We'd love to have you come with us."

"No kidding," I added. "We are going to need someone to change the poopy diapers."

"What about the aunts?" Fara asked. "Why are the grandmothers getting all of the perks?"

"Fara you've got kids of your own to handle. You couldn't get away from them anyway."

"Mom could stay with them and I could go." Fara sounded very pleased with her solution. "It's a double bonus, I'm more fun than Mom and I'm sick to death of my kids. Everyone wins."

"Forget it, Fara," Ken said. "Betty's going and you are staying."

"That was way harsh, Ty," Fara whispered.

"*Clueless!*" Fara and I both squealed at the same time.

"Fara—get off the phone. Betty—stay on the phone so we can figure out the details. We have to get you here before we can get you there."

Fara said her goodbyes and we spent the next thirty minutes ironing out the details. Adding Mom to the agenda definitely upped the complexity. When we finally got it all figured out it looked like this:

Mom would make the two-hour drive to Louisville and then fly to Dallas. From there, the three of us would fly to Guatemala, via Miami. If you have any kind of head for geography, you can quickly see that this route didn't make any sense. But Ken had assured me that this was the absolute cheapest way to get everyone there that didn't involve drug smuggling, pet carriers or trying to pass me and Mom off as unaccompanied minors flying home for a funeral. Yes, I had him check. At this point in the game we were pretty desperate and nothing was off the table.

Ken had worked so hard on his agenda that I decided not to point out that we seemed to be flying east to go west or that Mom was driving east to fly west, to fly east to fly west. I decided to hold my tongue and not list the thousands of little ways that this plan could go horribly wrong. I decided for once in my life to just go with the flow. As it turned out, going with the flow was vastly overrated.

CHAPTER EIGHT

Dallas, March, 2002

On the morning of our flight, a major flaw in our plan revealed itself. Ken had booked Mom's tickets as two separate trips to save money. This meant that she had one round-trip ticket from Louisville to Dallas and a second round-trip ticket from Dallas to Guatemala City.

In the post 9/11 world, flying in on one flight and then taking another flight was harmless on paper, but in reality it set off a bunch of red flags and turned out to be a big challenge. To begin with, Mom's flight from Louisville was delayed. Since we had booked the next flight as a separate ticket, she didn't have any kind of protection. If she missed our flight to Miami she would likely end up spending the weekend in Dallas with Marti and Greg. Not a bad option, but not what we had planned. Mom was dispatching minute by minute updates to me while Ken and I waited at DFW airport. We had gotten there ridiculously early so that we could meet Mom at her gate and then walk with her to the International Terminal for our flight to Miami, and then on to Guatemala City.

"Her flight out is still delayed," I said as I pocketed my phone. "She's a little panicked."

"Your mom will end up in a Guatemalan prison."

"Shut up. She'll be fine. If she does miss the flight to Miami they'll just have to put her on a later flight. I've told her that she needs to be prepared to cry and maybe claim that I have her medicine with me and she will die without it. One of those has to work and then we will simply wait for her at the airport in Guatemala City."

"Uh-huh. And what about all the big men with big guns who don't speak English?"

"I am trying to stay positive!" I realized that if I was the one trying to stay positive then things were seriously screwed. "You're right; this is a total nightmare."

A few hours later, Mom touched down in Dallas with twenty minutes on the clock. Although I didn't witness it, she says she moved through the airport just like OJ in that old commercial. Her cheap little roll aboard blew a wheel somewhere along the way and she ended up dragging it behind her. When people got in her way she shouted some cryptic message about running to her grandchild, and threatened to emulate the latter day OJ if they didn't clear a path. All I know is that by the time she got on our plane she was positively glowing. And not in that comforting, grandmotherly way. No, this was more like the way Lance Armstrong looked as he pedaled up the final hill in the Tour de France—red-faced and exhausted.

"They need to turn the heat down in this freaking airport," she said and collapsed into her seat.

"Betty, why didn't you take your coat off?" Ken asked.

"Oh, I don't know, Ken. Why didn't I stop and have a leisurely breakfast?"

"Well—"

"Ken, when that plane landed I took off like a bat out of hell. I'm not sure, but I believe I ran over an elderly woman on a walker two terminals back. I was a little too busy to stop and take off my coat."

"Well, the important thing is that you're here now and you won't end up in a Turkish prison like Brad Davis," I said.

"Turkish prison?" Mom asked.

"*Midnight Express*," Ken said.

"Ken and I were just talking about how you'd end up in some dank jail cell with a bizarre stranger, like Brad Davis and John Hurt. Or like *Kiss of the Spiderwoman* with William Hurt."

"I love the Hurt brothers," Mom gushed.

"Of course you do," I said, not bothering to correct her family tree. "I'm sure the worst of it is behind us now, so let's all relax and enjoy ourselves. You know the old saying that a bad start makes for a good finish."

They both stared at me. "You just made that up, didn't you?" Ken was on to my tricks.

"Maybe, but I think it could catch on quick. It appeals to the underdog in all of us."

"Or to the fat kids who turned into smoking hot studs."

"Ken!" Mom and I said at the same time.

"Do not talk about my chubby years. How many times do I have to tell you?"

"You weren't chubby," Mom said. "You were h—"

"Don't say it, Mom. Do not say it or I will snap like a dry twig."

"I won't say husky if Ken promises to stop referring to you as a smoking hot stud. That's more than I care to know."

"How about we all just watch the movie until we get to Miami?"

"Oh, what's the movie?" Mom asked.

"If you're lucky, Betty, it will feature one of the Hurt brothers."

I looked across Mom to Ken and mouthed, "They're not brothers."

"It was a joke," Ken said.

I fixed Ken with one of my patented steely glares. "I've told you before that you are not funny." Mom giggled. "Neither are you, old lady. Now, everyone, headphones on. It's movie time."

CHAPTER NINE

Guatemala City, March, 2002

The rest of the flight was uneventful, which helped us to prepare for the chaos of the Miami airport. Originally I thought that Miami was a layover, but I was wrong. It turned out to be a complete plane change. In a totally different terminal. We lost Mom no less than three times just trying to get from one gate to the next. It didn't help that she was one wheel short on her luggage or that the instructions were given in every language except English. I had managed to travel to Tokyo for a six-week business trip without incident but I was completely undone by the Miami airport.

We did finally get on the plane to Guatemala City and things seemed to be settling down as we flew west toward Central America. Maybe my prediction of a rocky start making for a smooth finish (oh, that's even better) was going to come true. We landed in Guatemala City a few hours later. I was able to talk Mom through customs at the airport in Guatemala without either one of us getting shot. I think her broke-down suitcase might have helped her cause a bit. Nothing screams I'm not a rich American tourist like a three-legged suitcase bought on clearance at Walmart. When we finally emerged from the oppressive atmosphere of the airport it was a bright and beautiful day. Or at least that's what our driver Juan told us as he eagerly pumped our hands, grabbed our bags, and asked us to follow him.

"Welcome! It's a bright and beautiful day," he said, throwing his arms open wide as if to say, ta da!

The reality was that the sun was obscured behind the permanent haze that hangs over Guatemala City. As Juan snaked between cars, Mom grabbed Ken's arm and whispered, "Is he safe?"

"Of course," Ken replied. "Juan works for the adoption agency. He meets all of the parents at the airport and drives them to Antigua. People on the forums love him. He's wonderful!"

"This way, this way," Juan instructed. "Señora, do you need some help?" he asked Mom.

"Oh no, I'm fine," she said with a little smile. Juan managed to snag Mom's bag without breaking his stride.

"Did you hear what he called me?" she whispered to me excitedly. "Señora."

"It's not a title, Mom," I said. "It just means lady. As in Hey Lady! Move your ass!"

By the time we had gotten to the car, Juan had somehow managed to get all of our bags in his trunk and circled back to Mom and me. I didn't check, but it wouldn't have surprised me if he had magically repaired Mom's broken wheel. He was that efficient.

"This way, señora," he said, gently draping his arm around Mom's shoulder as if she was some sort of precious cargo.

"I like him," Mom mouthed to me over her shoulder.

Guatemala City is a bit like Cirque du Soleil, but a

Cirque du Soleil where all of the performers are drunk and/or crazy. There are so many things that compete for your attention that you end up with your head swimming and your senses completely overloaded. For starters, the city is very large and sprawls out in all directions. And while there are signs of poverty and political unrest everywhere—Ken wasn't kidding about the big men with big guns—there's also large scale advertising for Coca-Cola, McDonald's and high-end shopping.

And then there are the public buses, which look like they were abandoned by some elementary school in South Texas, driven across the border to Mexico and freighted to Guatemala. It's very unsettling to see school buses careening down the interstate, jam-packed with commuters.

Not only are the commuters packed into the buses, but they also cling to the outside. It's true. Once the bus reaches capacity, people strap themselves on to the outside, or stand in the open stairwell, half in and half out of the bus. Amazingly, as we passed these wondrous buses, the daredevil passengers would grin and wave at us. I'd wave back, slack-jawed. At one point Mom grabbed my hand and told me to stop waving.

"If one of them falls off trying to wave at you it will ruin the entire trip for me," she said.

The circus-like atmosphere was a welcome distraction from the traffic and Juan's unique approach to driving. Rather than pay attention to the road, he would frequently turn around and talk to the three of us about the changing landscape around us. Since he talked with his hands, this meant that there were long moments when Juan was not only facing the backseat, but both of his hands were off the wheel and gesturing wildly as he pointed to a new shopping mall or a soccer stadium.

"Don't worry," Ken whispered, "we are nearly out of the city."

"Thank God," Mom managed to say through the fake smile she had plastered on her face to try to hide her growing sense of terror.

True to Ken's word, the city quickly fell away to beautiful, rolling hillsides and the interstate became a modest, two-lane road that led to Antigua and Jackson.

As the last bit of Guatemala City disappeared behind us, Mom and I both tried to unclench. Some instinctual thing had caused both of us to tighten-up all of our muscles, gird our bowels, and brace for impact as we flew through those crowded streets and highways. Now that we had survived the exit from the city, we were trying to regain our equilibrium. As it turned out, the ride wasn't quite over yet.

Rather than slowing down once we escaped the city, Juan decided to speed up. This despite the hairpin twists and turns of the two-lane road we were traveling and the fact that some of our fellow travelers were in wagons. Wagons that were being pulled by the world's oldest and most exhausted horses. Juan would race up behind these wagons and then whip over into the other lane at the last moment, only to whip back into our lane after he zoomed past them. All the while he kept up an endless babble of information, while the three of us rolled around in the back seat like groceries from a capsized bag.

"Seat belt," I whispered to Ken at one point.

"There aren't any," he replied.

"Mother of Jefferson Davis!" I cried. Ken gave me a confused look. "*Auntie Mame*," I whispered.

As we got closer to Antigua the roads became increasingly narrow. By this time Mom and I were clinging to each other, white-faced and white-knuckled, as Juan increasingly ignored the traditional approach of picking a lane and driving in it. He compensated for the narrowing roads by driving right down the middle of the highway. This allowed him to take the curves with more speed. When vehicles would approach from the other direction and blare their horns, Juan would jerk the car into our lane until they had passed safely by, and then jerk the car right back to the middle of the road.

"Please tell him we are not in a hurry," Mom frantically whispered to Ken and me.

After countless cab rides in New York, we knew that communication between driver and rider was a one-way affair. While the driver might jabber endlessly in thickly accented English, any attempt to talk back to them would be met with looks of confusion. I was half convinced that Juan didn't speak English at all, but had merely memorized his monologue. I knew from personal experience that this was not that hard to do. I had once taped *Valley of the Dolls* off the television using my portable cassette player and memorized the entire movie. Since I was only seven or eight, I didn't really know what the words meant, but I knew they were very important. It's not every eight-year-old who can deliver, "Thanks. I've already turned down the part you're playing," with perfect Helen Lawson aplomb.

When we finally arrived at the hotel, Juan hopped out of the car and had our bags stacked up for the hotel staff before the vehicle had come to a complete stop.

"Ah, Mr. Ken," he said, clearly distressed. "We are too late. Casa Antigua is closed for the night. Well, we try," he said with a broad smile. "Tomorrow is fine. Yes? You rest tonight and tomorrow—baby."

"That's fine, Juan," Ken said. "Thank you for trying to get us here in time."

Ken lingered curbside to pay Juan and help the bellboy organize our bags while I ushered Mom into the hotel lobby. I could tell the ride had taken a lot out of her, so I attempted to cheer her up.

"See Mom," I said, "Juan was just trying to get us here in time to see Jackson tonight. Wasn't that sweet?"

"That man is the devil."

"Oh, it wasn't that bad."

"That bad! Jeffrey, I blacked out at one point."

"Yeah, was that when he was pointing out the volcano?"

Three large volcanoes loom over the city of Antigua. To the south, the majestic Volcán de Aqua rises up nearly 13,000 feet into the air. Juan was explaining how the locals referred to the volcano as Hunapú, but that it was renamed after a mudslide from the volcano covered the old capital. Twisting around in his seat, he pointed out Acatenango and Volcán de Fuego to the west. Fuego, he explained, meant fire.

"Look!" he had demanded. "Do you see the smoke?"

We did, but more importantly we also saw that the highway dropped off to a steep ravine on either side of the road. Without a guardrail between us and the ravine, we'd come frightfully close to the abyss.

"Yes. It's too horrible to think about," Mom said. "But I suppose that fire volcano really was something to see."

"That's the right attitude," I assured her, "besides, the worst of it is behind us now. Tomorrow we'll get Jackson and we'll forget all about the bumpy ride to get here." Mom gave me a little peck on the cheek as Ken arrived with the keys to our villa.

The adoption agency used the same hotel for all visiting parents, so the staff was accustomed to and accommodating of the unique needs of freshly minted parents. They had put us in a little villa efficiency suite that had a nice, big living room, a large bedroom, and a little kitchenette. The room was clean and the property was beautiful, with flowers blooming everywhere in the middle of March. As we strolled past the pool on our way back from dinner, all of the stress of the day seemed to melt away.

After briefly trying to convince Mom to sleep in the bed with me and Ken offering to take the couch, we all collapsed into sleep, anxious for the next morning when Jackson would arrive.

CHAPTER TEN

Antigua, March, 2002

Mom and I were both so restless the next morning that we cleaned the room within an inch of its life. It wasn't dirty to start with but we both needed a way to burn off our nervous energy. In the middle of remaking the bed for the tenth time, I heard a quiet tap on our door.

I bolted out of the bedroom to try to get to the door, but Ken was already there and about to turn the doorknob. In that moment, time did this funny little thing where everything seemed to both slow down *and* speed up. I saw Ken pull the door open and then, suddenly, there were two smiling girls in our room and one of them held a baby. I had been crossing to answer the door, but stopped in the middle of the room. My eyes were able to take in the new arrivals, but I wasn't able to process who they were. My heart was pounding in my ears and I could sense that my mom was by my side.

"He's so tiny," she whispered to me.

With that, everything clicked into place and I crossed the room in long, hurried strides to claim my son, afraid that Ken would take him before I could. The girls had just barely gotten into the room when the one carrying Jackson held him out, indicating for us to take him. I looked at Ken expectantly and he nodded for me to do it. I tentatively reached out to him and he instinctively reached both his little hands out to mine. I scooped him up and cradled him next to my pounding heart.

"Support his head," Mom said, as if Jackson was a newborn, instead of just new to me.

"I've got him, Mom," I assured her.

"I know you do, honey."

Although I had used the word *overwhelmed* my entire life, my first few hours with Jackson were the first time I really understood what it meant. I can honestly say that my first few minutes with Jackson left me feeling completely overwhelmed and overcome with emotion. At some point I may have cried. I know I smiled. I could actually feel the smile stretching across my face. I couldn't have stopped it even if I wanted to. Mom and I couldn't get enough of Jackson; he was so much smaller than his picture, but his personality was so much bigger. With black hair, black eyes, and a toothless grin that came easy, he had captivated the two of us.

Eventually my thoughts turned to more practical matters, like the care and feeding of our son. The girls who had dropped him off had left Ken with a grab-bag of goodies and undecipherable instructions. It would seem that, since Ken had visited last, Jackson had progressed from a formula-only diet to solid food.

"That can't be right," Mom said, as Ken relayed the instructions he'd been given. "It seems a little early."

"Betty, that's because we haven't been with him. Remember he's five months old now. They told me to walk into town and buy baby food. Look, they even wrote down the name of the store and what I was supposed to get," he said showing my mom a hastily written note.

"Give me that," she said, perusing the note. "How on earth are we supposed to read this?" she said after a moment.

"Mom, we just have to trust that these women"—I had decided to promote them from girls for Mom's sake—"know what they are talking about."

"Women? They were twelve," Mom said. "I still think he is too little for solid food."

"Let's just take things one step at a time," I suggested. "Right now Jackson needs a bottle. Ken, can you get one of the bottles out of the bag we packed? Mom, can you see if you can figure out the formula?"

"Where's the bottled water?" Mom asked.

"Mom, he's from here. He can actually drink the tap water."

"Are you sure?"

"Yes, he's had it his whole life."

Ken returned with the bottle and Mom used it to mix up the powder and water. Once mixed, she popped open the microwave to warm up the bottle. Except the bottle was too tall to fit in the microwave. Ken had invested in some high-tech bottles, guaranteed to prevent gas. They looked amazing. In fact, I was considering trying one out myself. But they were very tall.

"It doesn't fit," Mom said.

"What? Give me that," Ken said, snatching the bottle from Mom and attempting to wedge it into the microwave.

Jackson and I sat perched on the couch. Despite the fact that he was hungry, he seemed amused by the little human drama that was unfolding in front of him.

"Oh, for God's sake," I said from my throne. "This is

like watching an episode of *Laverne & Shirley*. Just pour it into a glass, heat it and transfer it to the bottle."

"Smartass," Ken said shooting me a look.

"Language!" I said with a grin, indicating the baby.

The bottle crisis averted, the rest of the morning flew by in a flash. Literally. Not only were we enjoying our first day as a family, but we were also determined to document every single moment with photographs.

Eventually, the photo session spilled out of the room and into the quaint little courtyard of the hotel property. At one point I spied some beautiful bougainvillea blooming along a particularly picturesque wall.

"Over there," I indicated to Mom and Ken.

They traipsed over to the spot I'd pointed out. "Ken, you hold Jackson, and Mom, you squeeze in close to the two of them," I directed. I watched as the tableau I pictured in my head slowly came into focus.

"Oh, that's perfect. The flowers in the background are just perfect. Now hold still."

"Take the picture," Mom said with a tight grin.

"Hold on, I'm trying to get the right angle. Mom, please stop moving. Just one more second."

"Take. The. Picture," she said and her tight grin had graduated to clenched teeth.

"Hold still!" Despite my instructions, Mom continued to shift around uncomfortably, and then suddenly Ken screamed.

"Holy shit!"

"Ken! Watch your language, dirty bird," I scolded. And then all hell broke loose. Ken and Mom began to hop around and swat at their legs.

"Fire ants!" Ken squealed.

"Watch the baby," Mom pleaded.

I ran over and snatched Jackson out of Ken's hands and began inspecting him for damage.

"They didn't get to him," Ken said. "They were just making their way up my leg."

"Mom, are you okay?" I asked. She was still absently slapping away at ghost ants.

"I'm fine. I'm fine."

"You won't be in a little while," Ken warned.

"Why?"

"Well, because fire ants burn, and then they itch. Really itch. Until you want to tear the skin off your body."

"Oh! He's exaggerating, Mom," I said. Of course I knew he wasn't. Fire ants are one of the ways we know that God can be cruel. "Let's walk into town and pick up Jackson's stuff and then we can just hang out by the pool for the rest of the day and relax." I was determined not to let my visit with Jackson turn into an episode of *The Three Stooges* so I resolutely marched Ken, Jackson and Mom out of the patrolled gates of our hotel and into the belly of Antigua.

Antigua is a tiny little gem nestled in the central highlands of Guatemala. Despite years of political unrest, the city has managed to hang on to much of its charm. With its well-preserved, Spanish, Mudéjar-influenced Baroque architecture and spectacular ruins of colonial churches, the city was charming and romantic, the open-air markets were lively and colorful, and there were any number of tiny galleries and shops tucked away on cobblestone streets. I had read (and memorized) that information in a travel guide before we left and effortlessly recited it to a less-than-impressed Ken, Mom and Jackson.

Antigua is also world-renowned as a language center, so

there are lots of people from around the world walking its streets, eating in its cafes and soaking up the local culture. This makes Antigua feel safe, in a country that can be dicey. For reference, keep in mind that Guatemala is right next door to Honduras. The two countries share a complex history of violence, political unrest, and Catholicism. This last point was particularly evident to us as we had arrived during "Easter Week."

Not surprisingly, the address that the nurses (yes, I had now promoted them both all the way up to nurses) had scrawled on our shopping list did not take us to one of the quaint little places situated on those charming cobblestone streets. No, instead, we found ourselves looking at a little bodega that would not have been out of place in Queens, NY. It was plunked down in the middle of a busy intersection and was clearly intended for locals and not tourists.

The clerk was safely secured behind bulletproof glass and bars, which made communication a challenge. After much gesturing and passing our little list under the protected glass, we finally managed to collect all of the items we'd been instructed to pick up for Jackson.

"Does this look familiar, big boy?" I asked, holding up a jar of baby food with an indecipherable label to Jackson.

"Coo," he gurgled.

"Okay, good enough for me. Let's roll, people."

We made our way back to the hotel and the rest of the day passed without incident. Jackson seemed content with food in his belly and the pool was both warm and sparsely populated. We took turns floating him in the water and catching catnaps on the comfortable chaise lounges. It really did feel like our rough patch was behind us and we were all looking forward to a couple of lazy days lounging at the pool and getting to know Jackson.

Eventually, we drug ourselves back to the room, freshened up and headed to dinner. Not only was the food delicious, but the waitstaff took turns dancing Jackson around the dining room while we ate. They all seemed drawn to the little guy with the big dimples. Things really couldn't have been more perfect. The three of us were well fed and comfortable and Jackson was being treated like a celebrity.

"Are we ready to head back?" Ken asked.

"Yes," Mom said. "I don't think I could possibly eat another bite."

"No kidding," I added. "You may need to roll me back to the room. Me and Jackson. Look at his belly. I swear it's gotten bigger since we've been here."

"No wonder," Ken said. "Did you see how he went after that food? I nearly lost a finger."

"Hush up about my grandbaby," Mom scolded us. With that she picked up Jackson from my lap and whispered something in his ear.

"What are you telling him, Mom?" I asked.

"I'm telling him not to pay a lick of attention to the two of you."

With that she turned on her heel and led the way out of the dining room. A few of the patrons caught our attention and smiled and spoke to Jackson as we left the room. Mom positively beamed, as any proud grandmother would. Back in the room, she insisted that we see if Jackson wanted a little bit more milk before bedtime. This, despite the fact that he looked like he had a balloon stuffed under his onesie.

"I think he's fine," I said.

"Let's just see," Mom said.

"Okay."

I set about warming up a bottle using the complicated transfer system we had devised. After triple-checking the temperature, I passed the bottle to Mom. Jackson was sitting on her lap, and his little eyes seemed to light up when he saw the bottle. Before she could even get it in his mouth he was moving his head toward the nipple.

"See," she said. "I told you he was still hungry."

We settled into a contented silence. Mom fed Jackson his bottle while Ken and I slumped into each other on the couch. The whole evening was taking on a dreamlike quality and I realized that I was really tired. With very little effort, I could have fallen asleep right there—no need to even undress and get into the bed. Maybe Mom and Ken should take the bed, I thought. That way I wouldn't even have to move. I was even prepared to forgo brushing my teeth.

"Betty!" Ken shouted. I nearly jumped out of my skin. His voice was overly loud in the quiet room.

"What is that on your leg?"

"Where?" Mom asked.

"Right there. On your thigh, and your calf."

"Oh. My. God." I squealed fully awake at this point. "It's shit! Mom, Jackson has—"

"Diarrhea!" she finished for me.

The room went into complete chaos. Or rather, Ken and I became chaotic around my poor mom, who sat quietly, covered in shit, trying to both comfort Jackson and prevent the poo from getting on the carpet. My first thought was to grab paper towels, napkins and other assorted clean-up items. I stood staring at Mom with two dishtowels in my hand.

"It's no use," I said. "There is just too much of it. Not even the Bounty guy himself could tackle this job. You two need to get into the bathroom and get out of your clothes."

The next few minutes were touch and go. Ken and I walked/carried Mom and Jackson to the tiled bathroom, carefully trying to avoid getting poop on the carpet or on our persons. Once in the bathroom, Mom closed the door with a grim look.

"Just toss everything into the tub," I yelled through the door, "and I'll take care of it. Out of the corner of my eye, I could see Ken on all fours inspecting the carpet, a wet dishtowel at the ready. Hansel and Gretel-like, he carefully retraced Mom's stumbling steps from the living room to the bathroom.

"I don't think it got on the carpet," he announced.

"I don't see how that's possible, it was like a river of shit running down her leg," I said with a shudder.

"Oh, relax would ya? It's just poop," Ken said.

"No, it's not 'just poop', it's a lot of poop with the consistency of soup. It's poop soup. That's what we have going on here. Poop soup. Saying this is just poop is like saying Hitler was just another tyrant."

At that moment, the bathroom door swung open and Mom and Jackson stepped out, wrapped in towels. "Don't talk about Hitler in front of the baby," Mom said.

Ken widened his eyes at me. I shook my head at him as if to say, "Don't ask."

"Did you manage to get him clean?"

"Yes, I got him under the shower with me," Mom said. "You do not want to know what was hidden away in the folds of fat on his legs. I left the dirty clothes on the floor in there. Let me get a clean diaper on Jackson and then I'll clean it up."

"No, I'll do it," I said. Mom and Ken's eyebrows both shot up. "Hey, this is what it's all about, right? Mom, you take care of Jackson. Ken, why don't you take one of the jars of baby food to the front desk and see if you can figure out what it is? Meanwhile, Hazel," I said, indicating myself, "will take care of the carnage."

"Coo," Jackson giggled.

"You, mister, are on thin ice," I said.

"Coo," he said. Another toothless grin and chortle.

"Oh, I'd be happy too, if I just did that. But now is not the time to rub it in my face."

"Ga ga ga gagagga ga," he said.

"Alright, you win." I smiled and gave him a little kiss on the nose. "Now, where's the mop?"

"No mop," Ken said, "but I found these." He held up a fresh roll of paper towels. I snatched them out of his hand and hugged them closely to my chest. "And this," he said, producing a plastic garbage bag. Again, I quickly snatched it from him.

"I'm going in, people," I said. "If I'm not out of there in thirty minutes, send in reinforcements." With that I closed the door and began to methodically clean up the bathroom and scrub out the soiled clothes using a combination of shampoo and soap. At one point my progress was momentarily interrupted by the flash of a camera. Apparently, Mom had thought to memorialize the moment on film.

When I finally emerged from the bathroom, Jackson was asleep and Mom and Ken were sitting serenely on the couch, watching *Remington Steele* in Spanish on the little 13-inch television.

"Meat," Ken said.

"Meet what?" I asked. I dropped down into the chair, but hopped right back up when I realized it was the scene of the crime.

"Don't worry, your mom has been over the entire room, one sniff at a time," Ken said. "She has crawled around on her hands and knees sniffing everything like some crazed bloodhound. She's given it the all clear. This is a poop free zone."

"Oh thank God," I said and collapsed back into the chair.

"Now, who are we meeting? I'm exhausted."

"Not meet. Meat, M E A T," Ken said. "The baby food was pureed meat."

"Meat!"

"Yep, meat. 100% meat." Ken shuddered at the thought. "I don't even think I could eat that without shitting my pants."

"Nice visual," I said. "And that's one you'll be cleaning up on your own. Hazel is done for the night."

"I knew something was off about those nurses," Mom added. "Everyone knows a baby that is barely five months old isn't ready for solid food! Well, I've thrown it all away. From now on we are going to do it my way. We've got plenty of formula, and I saw lots of things on the buffet tonight we could give him for a little variety. We can cut up a banana, or give him a little taste of mashed potatoes."

"You're the boss," I said. At this point I was too tired to argue. "Turn down the volume and translate, Mom. I know you've seen this episode a dozen times." Her Pierce

Brosnan fetish was well known. Mom immediately started to fill Ken and me in on the case that Laura Holt and Remington were trying to crack. I half listened and half dozed. At one point I must have fallen asleep, because Ken was gently shaking me awake and helping me get into bed. Over my shoulder I could see Mom settling in with *Who's the Boss?*

"Goodnight," she called.

I stopped my slow shuffle toward sleep long enough to turn around and give her a kiss goodnight.

"Goodnight Mom," I whispered. "I love you."

"I love you too." She smiled.

"Don't stay up too late."

"I won't," she said. "I'm just going to read for a while until I get sleepy."

The familiar site of my mom curled up with a book while the television hummed quietly in the background was comforting to me. I floated off to bed, surrounded by the sudden sense of warmth and safety at seeing Mom doing what she did—what she'd always done—in this unfamiliar setting. *Moms are constant*, I thought to myself, *I want to be constant.*

Once in bed, my hands stretched across the cool sheets instinctively looking for a source of warmth. In the dark they slipped under a pillow that seemed to have lost its sense of direction, and was laying sideways, human-like, instead of in its rightful place at the top of the bed. On a mission, my hands crept further.

With a shock, I felt the warm little lump of my son, safely secured in the middle of the bed with a pillow on either side. Mom's doing, no doubt. I gently moved the pillow out of the way and pulled Jackson in close.

In the dark, I kissed his forehead, and moved my mouth to just above his ear and quietly sang him a lullaby. He sighed in his sleep, not minding my off key performance.

The next morning I awoke with Ken beside me and Jackson laying on his belly, on my chest. At some point during the night I must have been fearful of Ken's flying elbows and pulled Jackson on top of me and shielded him in a bear hug. I also realized that my back was killing me and that my neck felt stiff. In an effort not to disturb him, I had laid as still as a statue all night. This would foreshadow many nights of holding myself perfectly still, my arm asleep with pins and needles, so that he could be comfortable.

"Good morning," Ken said. He snuggled in close to the two of us.

"It is good, isn't it?" I said. "In fact, it's great. Let's go out and enjoy it with our son."

"God I love it when you're sappy."

"I know, but don't get used to it. The bitterness is always there, just under the surface. And occasionally it bubbles up. But not today." I gave Ken a little kiss on the cheek and pushed him out of the bed. He tumbled out and toward the bathroom, and the shower.

"Good morning," Mom called from the living room.

I wasn't the least bit surprised that she was already up and showered. She had the maddening ability to be the last person in bed and the first one up. I wasn't sure she ever actually slept.

"Good morning," I said.

"Is Jackson awake?"

"Yes, but he's not saying anything. Maybe he's embarrassed about the poop incident. Are you embarrassed, butterbean?"

"Coo."

"Is that your answer for everything?"

"Coo."

"Here, hand him to me," Mom said. She'd crept quietly into the room and was standing with both arms outstretched, waiting for Jackson. I sighed and handed him over.

"Good morning, cutie," she began. The conversation quickly became a two-way love affair between the adored and the adorer. I pulled a pillow over my head and opted for a few more minutes of sleep. Eventually, Ken forced me to get up and get showered so we could head to the dining room for breakfast, which was every bit as delicious as dinner the night before. Mom smashed up little bits of a banana for Jackson to eat with his milk. Because we had slept in we were the only people eating breakfast and the waitstaff kept stealing Jackson from us to take him for a stroll around the dining room.

After breakfast we walked to the front desk to see if they could recommend something close by we could do to give our legs a stretch. "You are in for a treat today," the girl at the front desk explained to us. "Today is the parade of flowers."

We didn't know this when we were planning our trip but Easter is a very big deal in Antigua. Each year there is a procession through town that illustrates the twelve stations of the cross. Along the route, people create elaborate tableaus out of flowers and colored sawdust. The streets are covered with them; each arranged artfully to represent something important to the holiday. Looking down on these creations, you would swear you were looking at a painting. They were incredibly beautiful.

Once they have been meticulously put together, the parade marches right through the middle of town, completely trampling the flowers underfoot. The contrast between the tableaus and the scenes depicted in the procession was startling. Watching it, we felt like we had stumbled on some ancient pagan cult. Ken was a little more in tune with this Passion Play, as he was raised in the Catholic Church and attended Catholic school. Mom and I were dazed and confused by it all.

While it was happening the parade seemed to have cast a magical spell over the entire city. The noise and shuffle of the city and its people were momentarily quieted and a reverence took hold of the crowd. Onlookers cried or crossed themselves as the procession solemnly marched by. My mind was on the flowers. It seemed like such a pity to waste so many of them. Wouldn't it be more practical to just use plastic flowers? It would be someone's duty post-parade to sweep and bag them up for next year's shindig.

Once the procession had finally passed, the spell broke and Antigua was once more a bustling hive of activity. Children with brooms descended from their hiding places to sweep the streets of the crushed flowers, and tourists, like the three of us, turned their attention to lunch or shopping. Since it was our last afternoon in Guatemala we decided to spend our time walking through the city's open air market. Mom wanted to buy gifts for my sister and her kids and Ken and I wanted to buy some Guatemalan toys to take home for Jackson as keepsakes.

Mom was convinced that she was going to end up paying $1,000 for a t-shirt because she couldn't keep the exchange rate in her head. Luckily, the shopkeepers were more than happy to accept our American dollars, so there was no need to do complicated math to figure out what you were paying for something.

Mom was delighted to find t-shirts for the kids at the rate of three for five dollars. At one point we came across a shop where an old man was making shoes. Mom spent fifteen excruciating minutes trying to figure out if she should invest in a pair of handmade leather sandals for herself for $15, and whether, if she should invest, she should attempt to get them for a lower price. After finally deciding to buy them, she turned to me and whispered, "How much should I offer him?"

Ken, who had grown bored, slapped a ten and a five down on the counter, snatched up the sandals and growled, "Let's go," to Mom and me.

Dinner at the hotel passed without incident. The staff was warm and friendly to us and Jackson got several tours of the dining room on the hip of one server or another.

Better still, his diarrhea seemed to have stopped. In fact, our entire system had finally become routine. Bottles were prepared, diapers changed, and naps taken with remarkably little stress or fuss.

Nonetheless, a certain gloominess hung in the air. We were all aware that only three of us would be making the return trip home the following day. While none of us talked about it aloud, the truth was that all of our hearts were breaking at the thought of handing Jackson over to the orphanage and heading back home without him.

We got an early start the next morning. We had to get Jackson back to Casa Antigua and then start the long (and likely perilous) trip back to Guatemala City to catch our respective flights home.

Because of where it's positioned relative to the mountains, Antigua's mornings are chilly and damp in March. That morning, a light fog hung in the air, lending the entire exchange an atmospheric pallor worthy of Hollywood. Standing outside the gates of the orphanage with Jackson wrapped up securely in a blanket, and all of his worldly possessions in the brown paper bag he came with, it felt like we were abandoning him.

"This is terrible," Mom finally muttered.

"It is," I said. "It is."

There was no talk of "it's only a few more days," because we all knew that the time between now and when he came home to us was something we had no control over. Instead, we all took turns holding him; each one whispering a secret message in his ear.

For his part, Jackson was still upbeat and positive. Our mood hadn't impacted his big, toothless grin and his constant babble of baby talk. He seemed to have more confidence in the system than we did.

At long last, Juan gently pulled us away from Jackson and to his waiting car. Glancing at his watch, he told us that we 'really must go now', and that Jackson is 'good', he is 'safe'. He finally got the three of us settled in the car, but before he started the engine he turned around and said that he had something for us.

The three of us were still distracted in the backseat, and kept looking over our shoulders at the nurses who were waving goodbye. After what they must have felt was a reasonable amount of time, they promptly turned around and disappeared through the gates of the orphanage with our son. I suppose they had learned from experience that parents will never leave as long as they can still see their child.

Juan cleared his throat to get our attention. "Here you go, señora," he said to my mom. Over the seat he handed her a bulky little package, wrapped in tissue paper. She took the package and folded back the tissue to reveal hand-carved letters that spelled Jackson.

"My family and I made them for you," Juan said. Each of the letters were brightly painted and decorated with drawings of animals and whimsical creatures. "These remind you of him."

Juan started the car and we began the long journey home. And while Juan's driving was just as terrifying on our return trip as it was on our arrival, this time we didn't seem to notice the danger. Maybe it was because this time we each had a talisman to keep us safe.

Mom clutched the letters JA, while Ken held on tight to CK. And me? I clung desperately to SON and prayed that it wouldn't be long before I could trade in the wooden letters for the real thing.

CHAPTER ELEVEN

Miami, March, 2002

Once more, the Miami airport was a study in frustration. Although it was not a particularly large airport, it was bursting at the seams with people. And most of them did not seem to have a clue where they were going. I'm sure they thought they knew where they were headed when they arrived, tickets in hand, resolute in their ultimate destination. But somewhere between their arrival and that destination things had gone awry in Miami. Perhaps the babble-like cloud of chatter that rose up from the weary travelers and hung in the air like a reality distortion field was to blame, but everyone seemed especially grumpy. We fit right in.

Into this sea of ceaseless chatter, the three of us waded, but only two would emerge. As international travelers, you must claim your baggage at your first port of entry into the United States, and then re-check it to your final destination. It's an incredibly confusing process in the best of circumstances, and the three of us were each both emotionally and physically exhausted; our hearts and minds were still in Guatemala with Jackson. I'd like to think that's the reason we ended up losing my mom.

This zombie state is actually very conducive to the

whole process of claiming and re-checking your luggage. If you don't think, it's so much easier. Just trust the wisdom of crowds and soon you'll find yourself at your gate, ready for your next flight. Unfortunately, no one told her about this herd mentality.

"Where's your mom?" Ken asked as we settled onto the hard plastic bench.

"What?"

"Your mom?"

"She's," I said, looking around, "well, she's— She's apparently lost." I snapped open my cell phone and dialed mom's number.

"Hello," she whispered.

"Where are you and why are you whispering?"

"It says no cell phones are allowed here. I'm in customs."

"Customs? Wait, what?"

"Yes. Are you two in front of me? I can't believe—"

"Ma'am, cell phones are not allowed in the line," someone interrupted.

"I have to go," Mom whispered.

"Wait! Get out of that line. Are you in the nothing to claim line?"

"No, I have bags with me."

"That's not what it means. Just get out of that line, and go to the nothing to claim line. Check your bags, and get your butt over here."

"What? But I do have stuff to claim. I have my toiletries and I don't want to lose those."

"Shush. You can keep all your crap, just get out of that line. Trust me, Mom, you are about to get the rubber glove treatment."

This last part was met with complete silence. "Mom? Did I lose you?"

"I've switched lines and I'll be right there. No toiletries are worth getting probed for."

"Mom, no, you can keep your—Mom? Mom?" I snapped the phone closed and turned to Ken. "This is the trip from hell."

"It's not that bad, but I am starving. I can't believe they didn't give us food on that flight. I've got to go find a snack or I'm going to pass out."

I craned my head around and looked up and down both hallways as far as I could see. "I don't see a lot of options."

"I'll find something," he assured me. "I think we passed a bar a few gates back. Do you want anything?"

"I'm tempted by the bar, but no. But please grab Mom if you see her."

"Okay. I'll be right back. Don't move." With that he took off in a slow jog toward the bar.

I swung my legs over the metal arm between two seats, stretched out my legs and waited to see if Mom would show up on time for our flight and, if she did, whether she would be without toiletries.

I must have dozed off because when I opened my eyes Mom and Ken were sitting in the seats across from me talking. Ken was working his way through the most disgusting looking nachos I had ever seen. Seriously. Those nachos made State Fair nachos look like a delicacy. The cheese was that unnatural orange that you typically only see from a box of macaroni and cheese. My stomach made a gurgling noise in protest, which must have been louder than I thought since they both turned to look at me.

"Somebody's awake," Mom said. I mumbled something

about resting my eyes and my traitorous stomach made another little rumble.

"Want some?" Ken said, reaching his arm across the aisle and shoving the nachos in my face.

"God no, get those things out of my face." I swatted at the nachos. Ken pulled them back with a little shrug as if to say I didn't know what I was missing. "When did you get here, Mom?"

Ken caught my eye and gave his head a little shake, but it was too late. Mom started explaining how she had managed to get through customs and security by pulling the confused, older, white woman act. I wanted to ask her when she wasn't pulling that act, but I held my tongue. I could tell from the look on Ken's face that this was the second time he had heard this story. But instead of sitting and allowing Mom to tell it, he decided to jump in and help her. He said the best part was that she arrived at our gate on one of those annoying little beep, beep, beep golf carts that shuttle the old and the infirm from one gate to another in airports. I could see the wicked little glint in his eye as he told this part of the story. He knew how I felt about those damn golf carts and those smug bastards who drove them.

I was glad that I had missed the sight of my own mom perched up there alongside a collection of woebegone seniors and their various and sundry walking devices; at the same time I was begrudgingly grateful that she'd made it to the gate before it was time for us to get on the plane, so I made a promise to myself that I would not judge future golf cart riders quite as harshly as I had in the past.

The person at the ticket counter announced that it was time to start boarding the flight. I grabbed Mom and Ken by the hand and pushed my way to the front of the line. I had achieved some crazy executive level status with American from flying for work all the time and one of the perks was being able to get on board the plane while first class was boarding, even bringing a couple of stowaways with me. Another perk was free drink tickets, which I had a wallet full of and intended to make use of on the plane. It was times like this when I really wished I was a drinker, but the next best thing would be getting drinks for Ken and a drink for Mom so they would both nod off and let me read in peace.

About forty minutes into the flight, things were looking good. The drink tickets had been cashed in for margaritas and I was happily reading my book while Ken and Mom watched a movie. It was about this time when Ken leaned across Mom, who had agreed to sit in the middle seat, and tapped me on the arm to get my attention.

"My stomach is a little unsteady."

"Unsteady? What does that mean?" I asked. I dropped my voice until it was barely above a whisper. "Is that code for you have to poop? Please tell me you are not going to poop on the plane." The only thing I hated more than those damn golf carts were people who pooped on airplanes. I just couldn't imagine a scenario where I would willingly be a plane pooper. The shame of walking out and finding a whole group of people waiting to pee—I shuddered when I thought about it.

"No, I don't have to poop," he whispered. "My stomach just feels queasy. Do you have one of those little vomit bags in your seatback? Mine is missing."

"You've got to be kidding me," I began, but stopped short as Ken's face grew visibly whiter in front of me, and little beads of sweat popped out across his forehead and upper lip.

"Hang on, hang on, hang on," I said, rummaging through my seatback. I tried to feel better about this by acknowledging that throwing up was a couple of steps above pooping and golf carts.

After I had taken everything out and still not come up with a bag, I did the only thing I could. I turned around to face the passenger behind me. "I'm sorry to bother you, but do you have an airsickness bag we could borrow? Actually, we probably won't be giving it back," I said with a laugh.

"Honey, I really need that bag," Ken said through clenched teeth. The lady across the aisle from Ken snatched the one out of her seatback and pushed it toward him. "Here," she said. "You can have mine."

Ken gave her a grateful nod and took the bag. The guy behind me asked me if I still needed his bag and I was about to say no when Ken pushed his face into his borrowed bag and started throwing up. A lot. I reached behind me and grabbed the bag and handed it over to Ken. He was trying to close the bag he had already used and pass it off to Mom so he could start in on bag number two.

"Ohhhh, oh," Mom began. "I can't." And then she was dry heaving. My mom was a champion when it came to dealing with baby shit, but she absolutely could not handle vomit.

I unbuckled my seat belt and stood up. "Slide over to my seat."

Mom was dry heaving and wrestling with her seat belt, desperate to get away from Ken. At that moment the flight attendant came over the PA system. "We'd like to remind passengers that the seat belt light is illuminated. If you are up and about the cabin, please return to your seat." I glanced around the plane. I was the only person standing. I looked up the aisle to see the attendant, with the bottom of the phone pressed to her lips, her eyes on me. I smiled sweetly and held up the barf bag, waving it at her. Her eyes went wide as she quickly hung up the phone and began to make her way back to us.

I finally got Mom moved to the window seat and slid in next to Ken.

"Is everything okay?" the flight attendant asked.

"Here. Take this," I said, handing her the two bags Ken had already used. She hurried away with the bags. "And see if you can find me another bag," I shouted after her. Within moments bags began to be passed, tossed and relayed to me from other passengers. For a moment I felt just like *Carrie* when she got her period in the shower and the girls pelted her with tampons, chanting, "Plug it! Plug it!"

"You had to have the nachos," I whispered to Ken, shoving another bag in his hand. He was holding on to the new bag like a life preserver so I didn't have the heart to say anything else. Eventually, Ken's stomach was completely empty. The flight attendant kept ferrying away each bag as he used them and brought him some ginger ale and a wet towel, normally reserved for people in first class to wipe their hands on before dinner.

"Here you go, sir," she said. "I know the seat belt light is still on, but if you would like to go to the bathroom we can make an exception."

Ken gave her a grateful smile and slowly pulled himself out of his seat. Once he got his balance he began to make his way down the aisle to the bathroom, the attendant gently guiding him along.

"It's a good thing he's cute," Mom said when he was out of earshot. "She would have just thrown a dry napkin at us and told us to clean up our mess."

"No kidding," I said. "No ginger ale for us." Mom and I giggled at our own cleverness as we continued to pile on. Eventually, we broke down into full-blown laughter that we tried to stifle with the back of our hands.

The passengers around us were looking at Mom and me like we were horrible people, laughing at the misfortune of our friend. Every time we tried to stop laughing, one of us would come up with another example of the rough treatment we would have received versus the gentle care Ken was afforded. By the end, we had Ken being carted up the aisle by a chorus of singing angels, while Mom and I were forced to pull open the emergency door and vomit into the wind. We were hilarious. At least we thought so.

"What's so funny?" Ken asked when he finally returned.

"You are, honey," I said. "Funny and a little stinky. Have a seat, but you might want to tilt yourself toward the aisle a bit, until you air out a little." Mom and I burst into a fresh round of giggles as Ken took his seat with a sideways glance at us.

"Oh God, don't tell me you two have started that laughing thing." Ken rolled his eyes. "Just so you know everyone around you finds that incredibly annoying."

"Really?" I said. "I had no idea. Thank you for your honesty." This was delivered with a heavy dose of sarcasm and caused another round of giggles from Mom and me.

Ken sighed as if the weight of the world was on his shoulders. "I'm starting to wish I hadn't left first class."

"What! She moved you into first class? That's—"

"Typical," Mom finished.

"Who's laughing now?" Ken said with a grin. "But I gave it all up because I wanted to be with you." He hooked his arm around mine and snuggled in close to me. Within a few minutes he was asleep and slept until we pulled up to the gate in Dallas.

***

"Well, ladies and gentlemen," the captain began, "I have some good news and some bad news. The good news is that we have arrived at our gate early." A few passengers gave a pathetic little woohoo; it had been a long flight and we were ready to get off of the plane. "Don't celebrate yet," he continued. "The bad news is that there is a line of thunderstorms in the area, and they won't let us get off the plane until they move through."

"I have a connection," Mom whispered to me.

"Yes. I'm well aware."

"Should I tell them?"

"They don't care. Besides, if there are thunderstorms, they've likely shut down the airport. You'll be fine. I'm sure we will be off of here in no time." As it turned out, I was wrong.

Arriving at your gate after a long trip and not being allowed to depart tends to make people restless. As the minutes ticked away, the man across the aisle and a few rows in front of us began to sigh deeply and twist around in his seat to stare at his fellow passengers with wild eyes as if to say, "Can you believe this?" After a couple of rotations, he slipped free of his restraint, announced that this was bullshit, and stood up in the aisle.

Ding. "Ladies and gentlemen, please stay seated until the captain has turned off the fasten seat belt sign."

"How about an update?" he shouted in the general direction of the cockpit.

Like a tiny pebble that strikes an unblemished windshield and sends little spider web cracks in all directions, Wild Eyes' question seemed to awaken the other passengers' slumbering discontent.

"Yeah."

"What's going on?"

"How long are we going to be stuck here?"

"I have a connection," Mom added to the growing chorus.

I shot her a glance. "Do not go native on me," I whispered to her. She shrugged. "Well I do!"

In a situation like this the crowd can go from sullen to surly in the blink of an eye. I was already scanning all the emergency exits, just in case I needed to make a quick getaway, when the captain came over the PA.

"Look, folks. We know that you are anxious to get off the plane. So are we. But right now there's nothing we can do. The airport is shut down due to the electrical storm and we are stuck here until they tell us otherwise. Since we are at the gate, I'm going to turn off the fasten seat belt sign." Ding. "If you'd like to stretch your legs, feel free to do so. For those of you making connections, you can relax. Nothing is going in or out of DFW."

Like a bully who had been challenged, Wild Eyes sunk back into his seat with a sigh. "This is just ridiculous," he muttered under his breath. But the voice from on high had stolen all his authority. He was no longer the *Norma Rae* of Flight 1440, but just another loudmouth asshole. I took a moment to turn to Mom and assure her that she would make her connection. The fact that I was inches away from ditching her when things got ugly earlier may have been part of my motivation for trying to make her feel better about the situation. That and I just wanted her to shut the hell up about her connection.

The minutes turned to hours and still we all sat. Mom, who had to work the next day, and still had a ninety-minute flight to Louisville and a two-hour drive home, eventually stretched out in the middle of the aisle with a couple of those paper-thin blue blankets over her and my carry-on under her head. I didn't know whether to admire her moxie or pretend like she was Ken's mother.

I suppose everyone knew she belonged to me, since I had been entrusted with her glasses. Her final words to me were to wake her if Ken even *looked* like he was going to throw up. Meanwhile, Ken seemed to be taking the delay in stride. The serial vomiting had taken a lot out of him— literally and figuratively. Once it was clear we weren't going anywhere, he crawled over me, slumped against the window, and promptly fell asleep.

It seemed I was the last man standing, or, in this case, sitting. I sat in the middle seat, ramrod straight, clutching my mom's glasses, quiet and alert. The two of them had inadvertently created a sort of circle around me. When you added the effect of my overhead light shining directly down on my face, it made me feel like Jesus in *The Last Supper*. Serene and strong in the middle of chaos. Normally I would be muttering under my breath and threatening bodily harm to any and everyone around me, but instead I was thinking about Jackson, wondering what he was up to. Despite the situation, I felt like everything was right in the world, and even with the current stall, my life was at long last moving forward.

After four hours we were finally allowed to depart. As we all tromped down the aisle, the captain came out of the cockpit and solemnly nodded as we walked by. I was shocked to see that this man of quiet authority wasn't much taller than me. For just a moment, I thought about Tina Turner's classic line to Mel Gibson in *Beyond Thunderdome*: "Why you're just a raggedy man."

I held my tongue. Without the wig and the chainmail, I wasn't sure he'd get the reference. And frankly I wasn't sure I could deliver the line in my current state.

Once we were in the airport, we walked Mom over to her connecting flight, which was thankfully in the same terminal. After she got on her plane we collected our bags and were soon in the car and on the way home. I flipped open my phone to let my sister know that Mom was en route, and what time she should expect her.

"How'd it go?" she asked.

"Perfect," I said without hesitation. "It was just perfect."

"Well, I want to hear all about it tomorrow."

"I'll give you a ring. Let me know when Mom makes it home tonight."

"Okay. Love you."

"Love you too." I clicked off.

"You're amazing," Ken said with a smile.

"I know." I grinned and took his hand. "But it's still nice to hear."

I pulled his hand up close to my heart, snuggling it close like a favorite teddy bear.

"I'm going to need that hand to drive."

"Pssh, you've got another one. This one is mine."

"Anything for you, baby. Anything for you."

POPDADDY

As Ken's little black BMW sped toward Dallas, I clutched his hand tightly and thought about the unlikely path we'd traveled to arrive at this moment. Anything for you, indeed.

CHAPTER TWELVE

Dallas, April, 2002

"I don't think Jeffrey should go with you."

Just a few weeks after our second trip to Guatemala, Cathy was calling to tell us that we could go pick up our son. The judge had approved the paperwork, Jackson's passport was ready, and the final step was for us to appear in court in Guatemala to make it all official. Ken had put her on speaker phone, but not before shooting me a look that said, "I told you it wouldn't be long before he would be coming home."

Despite the short turnaround, I felt totally justified in insisting that we make the second visit. I was absolutely certain that if we hadn't taken the trip to Guatemala Jackson wouldn't be coming home until his birthday. Call me crazy, but I knew that my karma was completely shot from some bad choices I made in college and the quickest way to get him home was for me to act (and spend) like he wasn't coming home soon. I also knew exactly how that theory sounded, which is why I kept it to myself. Besides, we seemed to have a bigger issue right now.

"Why not?" Ken asked. "We are both his parents so why shouldn't we both go get him?"

"Ken, it's okay—" I began. It wasn't that I didn't want

to go with Ken to pick him up and be with him when the plane took off and he was truly ours. I did. But I wanted, no needed, him home and safe more than anything else. At this point I was completely vested in the idea that the end justified the means. And the end was getting Jackson home.

"No. It isn't okay," he said, cutting me off. "Cathy, why do you think Jeffrey shouldn't go?"

"Look Ken, I'm on your side. I just want to help you get your son home as safely and quickly as possible. According to the Guatemalan government, you are adopting Jackson as a single parent. That already puts you under a certain level of scrutiny." I was surprised to hear how closely Cathy's reasoning resembled my own. The two of us had butted heads a few times during the process, but I was reminded that, ultimately, she had our best interest in mind.

"But everyone at Casa Antigua has already met Jeffrey."

"Yes, and it's wonderful that he got a chance to see where Jackson is from. But the reality is you are a single man trying to get a six-month-old baby boy out of the country, a country that is coming under increasing pressure about its international adoptions. I'm sorry but we need to play this one by the book, and Theresa—"

"I don't really care what Theresa thinks," Ken replied hotly. Theresa was the attorney who worked for Casa Antigua in Guatemala.

"She's right, Ken," I said before things got out of hand. "She's absolutely right. The only goal right now is to get him home. That means that we, that you," I said, poking him in the chest, "are going to do whatever the hell they tell you to do and exactly the way they tell you to do it so that you can get our son and bring him home to me." I paused to look Ken in the eye. "Okay?"

"But you are being totally marginalized here. You're his parent too."

"As far as you and I are concerned, yes I am. And in my heart, absolutely. But on paper I'm not," I put both my hands up to stop him before he could interrupt me. "One day I will legally be his parent, I know you and trust you to make that happen, but right now I'm not."

"Guys," Cathy began, "If it's any consolation, this entire process from touchdown to take-off is just a twenty-four-hour event. Typically, the adoptive parents fly to Guatemala and arrive late in the afternoon. Theresa will have you in front of the judge early the next morning and by midday the paperwork will be signed and you will be on your way to the airport with Jackson.

"But if Jeffrey was my wife, he'd be going with me. Right?" Ken was like a dog with a bone about this. And despite the fact that he was mad at the wrong person, I felt a sudden flash of love for my guy.

"Maybe. Okay, likely." Cathy sighed, clearly upset by Ken's reaction. "But not always. Sometimes both parents can't make the trip. Sometimes they don't want the added cost. Sometimes one parent can't get off work. Every situation is different." Cathy stopped for a moment to collect herself. "Look, I love you guys and wouldn't be helping you adopt if I wasn't supportive of same sex parents. But this is the world we live in. I don't like it and, Ken, it sounds like you don't like it much either. If that's the case then go get your son, and when you get back work to change it so that the next guys who get the call to pick up their baby can go as a couple."

Ken was quiet for a moment. "I'm fine," I whispered to him. "I really am." And in the most important way I was fine. I just needed to convince Ken that I was okay, so I pulled a classic play out of my handbook and pulled him into a tight hug and added a smidge of sugar to seal the deal.

"Okay Cathy," Ken said when I finally let him go. "We'll do it by the book, play by the rules. But believe me, I do intend to work on changing it, because it's wrong that we couldn't include Jeffrey in the home study and wrong that we can't go together to pick him up."

"Good. I agree one hundred percent. Equal rights take on a new urgency when you have some skin in the game, don't they?" Cathy said. "If it makes you feel any better, it's not just gay men. Single people are forbidden to adopt in some countries. Man or woman. Gay or straight. Just be thankful that Guatemala hasn't cut off adoptions to single men the way China has. At least not yet," she added as an afterthought.

Although she had tacked it on to her sentence, her final words filled me with dread. *Not yet*, she had said. What in the hell did that mean? "Cathy, how soon can we get this done?" I asked with a new sense of urgency. *Not yet*.

"How soon can you get Ken to Guatemala?"

"I'll go pack his bag right now."

"Don't bother, because I'm coming right back home to you," Ken said.

Cathy laughed as the last bit of tension dissolved. "You two never were ones to waste time. I'll start working with Theresa today to get us on the judge's calendar."

"Thanks Cathy," I said. "For everything. I know you've had to deal with the crazy version of Ken and Jeffrey on occasion, but we really are grateful for your help and guidance through this process."

"Don't worry about it at all. Even at your craziest you don't come close to some of the other parents I'm working with. There's a reason I start watching the clock around four to see if it's okay to pour myself a glass of wine." Ken and I both giggled. "Seriously guys, it has been a pleasure and I know you two are going to make wonderful parents. I'll be in touch."

"Thanks again, and go ahead and crack open that bottle. Our lips are sealed." Cathy laughed and said her goodbyes.

Ken hung up the phone and gathered me up in his arms. "I'm sorry," he said. He laid his head on my shoulder. "I'm so sorry." His voice was thick with emotion, and I wasn't surprised to feel tears against my neck. "I'm fine," I said, gently rubbing his back. "I'm just fine," I whispered, and it became a little truer every time I said it. "Please don't worry about this for another second."

"Okay," he said. "I guess I better start looking at flights to Guatemala. Again."

"Oh, don't act like you don't love the challenge. I think I'm going to go upstairs and collapse on the couch and watch TV. That call really took it out of me."

"Sounds good. I will be up in a bit, just as soon as I see if we are going to have to take out a second mortgage to pay for my flight."

"I have faith that you will figure it out," I said. I leaned down and gave him a quick peck on the cheek and headed upstairs. "Don't be too long," I said over my shoulder. "I may or may not be in my underwear." I didn't wait around to hear Ken's reaction, but it wasn't long before I heard him climbing the stairs.

***

"You are a piece of work," my sister said.

"Thank you," I replied. "It's a gift."

I was having my morning coffee and explaining to Fara that we had gotten the call from Cathy last night and that Ken would be off to Guatemala to pick up Jackson before the end of the week.

"And you don't want to go with him?"

"Of course I do, but I'm so busy with work. And Cathy tells us that it's all very fast and very carefully orchestrated. Kind of like a hoedown."

"A what?"

"You know what I mean. Everyone has a very specific role to play and most of the work is done through an interpreter. And there's really nothing for me to do, since Ken is the adoptive parent."

"Uh huh." She clearly wasn't buying what I was selling.

"Hey Fara," Ken said.

"Is there no such thing as a private conversation in this household?" I asked. "I thought you were sleeping in today. I figured you'd be exhausted after last night."

"And now I need to scrub my brain with an SOS pad to remove those words from my memory," Fara said.

"I am still in bed," he said, ignoring Fara's complaints. "And, for the record, I'm not crashing your call. I picked up the phone to check my voicemail at the office."

"Jeffrey says he's too busy to go with you to pick up Jackson," Fara said. "He's lying, isn't he?"

"Completely."

"Ken! My God you are like a one-minute egg. You crack under pressure."

"What pressure?" he said. "Besides, you are lying!"

"And you're not very good at it," Fara added. "So let me guess; they're keeping you tucked away in the closet for this little dance."

"Well, you know the old adage," I said, before breaking into, "Hey! You've got to hide your gay away."

"The Beatles would be so proud," she said. "Now that we have gotten the real story, tell me, how upset are you?"

"I'm not upset at all," I said.

"How upset is he, Ken?" she asked, completely ignoring me.

"He's okay," Ken said. "I'm the one who nearly ripped Cathy a new one."

"Wow, did the two of you change personalities?"

"I know, right? Poor Cathy, I just laid into her, even though I knew it wasn't her fault. We eventually got it all sorted."

"Well, I'm sorry that you won't get to go, Jeffrey. I know you were looking forward to it."

"I'm fine," I said for what felt like the hundredth time.

"He really is," Ken added. "Besides, it's me you should be feeling sorry for. I'm the one who has to fly home with a six-month-old baby. If you are planning a pity party, I should be the guest of honor."

"Sounds brutal," my sister said. "You know whoever ends up next to you is going to be giving you the stink eye when they get on that plane."

"Thanks for not holding back," Ken laughed. "I'm getting off of here and getting in the shower."

"Bye Ken."

"Bye Fara." Ken hung up the extension.

"Okay, seriously, how upset are you?" Fara asked.

"Oh my God! How many times do I have to say I'm

fine? I was upset for like two seconds, but then Cathy said something about adoptions in Guatemala coming under a lot of scrutiny lately and that triggered my panic button. Right now I just want to get him home, and this isn't the first time I've been removed from the official story. Remember, I don't appear anywhere in the home study they sent to Guatemala."

"Don't get me started on that."

"No, let's not, because I haven't had enough coffee to hear that rant again. I should get off of here as well. But listen, will you do me a favor and tell Mom? I'm not up for a do-over with her."

"I will, but you know she will call you anyway."

"I know," I said with a sigh.

"And she will probe you," Fara said very quietly. "She will probe you deeply."

"Nice, thanks for that visual. If you are done with that SOS pad can you please pass it to me now?"

Fara giggled. "You deserved that after that sex comment earlier. And as far as Mom goes, you know how she is. If she thinks you're upset she won't rest until she gets it out of you."

"Why? So that she can be upset too?"

"Exactly! It's a parent thing. You'll see soon enough."

"Okay, but tell her anyway. And please support my story. Maybe if she hears it twice she will believe it."

"Yep," she said. "I will tell her."

"And support my story!"

"Of course. I always support your stories." I couldn't argue with that. She had been the co-pilot for my shenanigans for years. "Okay, I gotta run. The kids apparently need a ride to something or some such. What am I, a taxi? I'll talk with you later. Love you, and congratulations, this is really good news."

"Thanks. Love you too. Bye."

I hung up the phone and popped my cold coffee into the microwave. Sixty seconds and a scorched tongue later, the phone rang again.

"Are you okay?"

"Hi Mom."

***

True to her word, Cathy had Ken on the judge's calendar before the end of the week. The plan was for Ken to fly out on Wednesday afternoon, appear before the judge on Thursday morning and then head straight to the airport, with Jackson and his freshly minted United States passport in hand.

I was thinking the week was going to drag by but instead it felt like someone had pressed the fast-forward button and, before we knew it, Wednesday had arrived and Ken and I were sitting in my new Jaguar outside of the airport terminal. I had traded the Jeep in for the Jaguar in an effort to have a more "family friendly" car.

"I'm nervous," Ken said. "You are so much better at this kind of thing than I am. You should have been the adoptive parent."

"Ken, you're wrong. You are very good at these kinds of things. Not to mention you are also incredibly attractive, and, trust me, that won't hurt."

Rolling his eyes, his big, blue eyes, Ken half-heartedly smiled at me. "You are such a freak."

Say what you will, I thought to myself, *but tall, dark, and handsome never hurt anybody.* Man or woman, I knew that all Ken had to do was stand there looking all modelesque and the judge would hand Jackson right over to him, along with any other babies in the room that he might choose. It wouldn't surprise me if the judge didn't offer to drive him to the airport or ride along with him back home.

"You'll be fine," I said. "Better than that even, you'll be amazing. And according to Cathy, all you have to do is answer a couple of questions, sign all the papers, and then you are out of there. She says it won't take more than a few minutes, and Theresa will be there with you the whole time."

"She better be, since I don't speak a word of Spanish."

"She will, and she does. And she's done this a hundred times before. Just let her guide you."

"I'm still nervous," he said. I reached across the seat and picked up his hand.

"I know, sweetheart, and I would be too." I gave his hand a little squeeze. "Okay, you should go. I wish I could go to the gate with you."

"Me too, but you know the new rules. You can't. I really should get going, it is probably going to take an eternity to get through security." Ken just sat there holding my hand, as if he was trying to find the courage to open the door.

"Okay." I leaned across the seat and gave him a kiss. "Remember, I love you."

"I love you too," he said as he finally opened his door.

"Call me when you have him."

"I will." Ken stepped out of the car and retrieved his bag from the backseat.

"You've got everything you need for the baby?" I asked before he closed the door. I knew he did, we had gone through everything at least a dozen times to make sure Ken didn't end up with a baby and no bottles, diapers, or other baby paraphernalia.

"Everything but you," Ken said with a sad smile.

"Get going then," I said.

I sat there in the car and watched as Ken maneuvered his luggage and diaper bag expertly through the crowd. I could see a few heads turn in his direction as he made his way. There was just something about a man with a diaper bag. With a final glance over his shoulder and a wave, he was gone.

When I couldn't see him anymore I put the car into drive and headed home. A few miles past the airport I swung through a McDonald's drive-through and ordered enough calories to put me in a food coma. Sitting in the parking lot, shoving an endless stream of French Fries into my mouth, I wondered what awaited Ken in Guatemala. Knowing Ken, he'd move through the whole thing with grace and style.

It's a good thing I'm not the adoptive father, I thought to myself. *I'm sure it would turn into a whole cluster*. Yes, I was thinking about the karma thing again. I wondered if there was some sort of cleanse I could get to wipe the slate clean. Sort of like a karma colonic. The visual of that got me tickled and I nearly choked on a bite of my Big Mac. Talk about karma, imagine if I choked to death in the parking lot of a McDonald's on the eve of Jackson coming home. With that happy thought, I started the car, pulled up next to the trash can, rolled down the window and threw a few thousand calories away.

"Get a grip on yourself, fat boy," I said aloud. "It's only twenty-four hours." I eased out of the parking lot and headed back to the interstate. *Just twenty-four hours, and then I can exhale*, I thought to myself. My cell phone rang, nearly

causing me to jump out of my skin. I glanced at the display.
"Hi Mom. I just dropped him off, and, yes, I'm okay."

CHAPTER THIRTEEN

Guatemala, April, 2002

"I have him." Just as he had promised, Ken called me the minute he had signed the paperwork to make Jackson's adoption final. "We just left the courthouse."

"Oh my God, that's fantastic. I can't believe it. I was starting to think it was never going to happen."

"Yep, we are officially parents. Whether we are ready for it or not, Jackson is our son."

"He's the one who better get ready. He has just been dropped into a family full of crazies. How does he look? Can you tell if he has gotten bigger?"

"Uh, no. He looks the same as he did a few weeks ago," Ken said with a laugh. "Talk to Daddy, Jackson." I could just picture Ken strutting through the hallways of the courthouse with Jackson hanging off of his chest in his BabyBjörn with the cell phone pressed to his little ear.

"Coo."

"Still with coo, mister? Nothing new in your repertoire?"

"He's in a great mood, and Juan is going to drive us to the airport in just a bit, so I should probably go—"

"Wait! Ken, you called me *Daddy*. Am I Daddy? I can't believe we haven't talked about this until now. What were we thinking?"

"Well, at least one of us has been thinking about this and, yes, I think Daddy for you. Are you okay with that? Not that we have to decide right this instant. I mean, we can talk about it when I get home."

I was secretly thrilled, because I wanted to be called Daddy, but I didn't want to act like I had just scored big in the name game. It would be just like Ken to realize he'd given up the primo name and try to take it back. "No, I'm good with being called Daddy. But what about you? Are you Dad? Daddy Ken? Oh, I know, how about Big Daddy Ken? Or is that just too Tennessee Williams?"

"Honey! Shush! I'll remind you that this is an international call. Man, you Roaches sure do love to hear yourselves talk." I started to deny it, but what was the point? We really did love the sound of our own voices. "Anyway, that's a big no to Big Daddy. That's borderline creepy. I thought I'd go with Papa. So Papa and Daddy."

"Or Daddy and Papa, if we want to keep it alphabetical."

"Well, that's certainly an important consideration, but let's talk about it later. I really have to go. We are already running a little behind and I'm afraid Juan is going to try to make up the time with his insane driving."

"Yikes! Okay, okay, you should definitely go. We can talk about it when you get home, Papa." I couldn't resist trying it on for size. "I love you."

"I love you too, Daddy."

"Yeah, that's a little yuck, but I'm sure I will get used to it. But go! And good luck on the plane. Oh, and hurry home, okay? Ken? Are you there?" The connection had dropped. Or Ken had dropped it on purpose to stop me from babbling.

After we were disconnected—I was choosing to think the call had dropped—I sat and thought about my good fortune. I couldn't believe I was going to end up with Daddy. Not that there was anything wrong with Papa. There wasn't, but every time I heard it all I could think was, "Eat, Papa! No one wants to see a skinny Santa Claus." I must have watched that cartoon for at least ten Christmases and now I always associated Papa with the idea of porking up. I wanted to share my good news with someone so I snatched up the phone and called my sister.

"I got Daddy," I didn't even bother with hellos or any kind of explanation. It didn't surprise me when Fara instantly figured out what I was talking about.

"Thank God! How did you manage that? I've been afraid to ask. So, what's that make Ken? Is he just Dad?"

"Believe it or not, he offered up Daddy to me. Free and clear. What are the odds? I was terrified of being called Daddy Jeffrey. That's a little too hairdresser for me."

"No, that would be Mister Jeffrey."

"You're right! That's even worse," I giggled.

"So if you have an exclusive on Daddy in all of its various forms, what does that leave for Ken? Tell me he is not insisting on Father. If so I will have to fly down there to remove the stick from his ass."

"Nope. Not Father. He wants to be called Papa."

"As in *Papa, Can You Hear Me?*

"Yes Barbra."

"Wow, I didn't see that one coming. I guess he doesn't know that Papa has a little bit of a fat connotation."

"Because of *The Year Without a Santa Claus*! Right?"

"Yep."

"I don't think he knows that and we aren't going to tell him. Right now I feel like I have totally won the name lottery and the trick is to not let Ken know he got the short end of the stick."

"My lips are sealed. Hang on a second." I could hear her having a separate conversation with somebody in the room, but I couldn't figure out who it was or what they were talking about.

"I'm back. That was Mom. She wanted to know what was going on."

"Oh God! Don't tell her about the fat Papa thing, you know she can't keep a secret. She will end up telling Ken and I will lose Daddy."

"Who do you think you are talking to? I wrote the book on keeping things from Mom. What do you want, old woman?" I was pretty sure that wasn't directed at me. "Okay, I will ask him if you will leave me alone."

"What does she want to know?"

"She wants to know what time Ken is supposed to get home tonight."

"His flight lands around seven. I don't know how I'm going to make it until then." I had already cleaned the house and walked Patsy so many times that she refused to even look up at me when I got her leash off the hook in the garage.

"Oh don't worry, Mom will call you at least ten times."

"No I won't!" Mom had apparently gotten tired of second-hand information and picked up the other receiver.

"Mom?" Fara and I said at the same time.

"Okay, this eavesdropping is becoming chronic," I said. "We've got to get this under control. What if we were discussing putting you in a home or something?"

"Oh she knows she's going into a home. The minute she starts to lose it and walk around the house in her panties."

"Fara!" Mom and I shouted at the same time.

"I'm only kidding," Fara laughed. And for the next hour we laughed about Mom's pending dementia and Ken's odd name choice. It was just what I needed to take my mind off of Ken and Jackson's arrival. Of course, I shouldn't have been surprised. Mom and Fara had always seemed to know exactly what I needed and did their level best to make sure I had it. I really don't know how I would have survived this long without them.

***

"Where are you guys?"

Marti and I had been waiting in baggage claim for about an hour, but we had yet to catch sight of Ken, although, according to the display, his plane had landed twenty minutes ago. I told Marti she didn't really need to drag the baby to the airport this late in the evening, but she was adamant—even if it did mean bringing two cars, because we didn't want to deal with taking Mason's car seat out of her car and transferring it to mine. Trust me, once you get those bastards anchored in you never want to move them. I had already decided that if we got a different car I was leaving the car seat in my old car and paying the dealership to install another one in the new car.

"We just this minute stepped off the plane."

"Well, hurry up. Marti and I are waiting by baggage claim."

"Yes. So you said ten seconds ago when you called me. A baby, bags, and a phone do not mix. Let me let you go, and we'll see you in a few minutes."

Ken clicked off without waiting for me to reply. I remembered that I forgot to ask him how the plane ride was with Jackson and started to call him back, but just then I saw them through the glass, queuing up at the revolving door that led to baggage claim.

Unbelievably, several people encouraged Ken to go in front of them, all the time fussing over Jackson. I could tell from their animated faces that they were completely enthralled by this handsome man and his cute son. Even the ever-present, slightly ridiculous BabyBjörn didn't seem to detract from his appeal. I could practically read their minds from where I stood: Was he single? Gay? Straight? Bitches. I hadn't given much thought to the appeal of a man with a baby, but I guessed it wasn't that different from that of a man with a cute puppy. Great, just what I need, another demographic of people with their sights set on my man.

"Lady with a baby coming through!" Marti grabbed my hand and pulled me through the crowd just as Ken and Jackson stepped out of the revolving door. She made a beeline toward them and then the five of us were in the middle of a group hug. Marti stepped back so I could lean in and give both my boys a kiss. I'm not sure, but I believe one of Ken's earlier admirers gasped behind us. *That's right, sister,* I thought to myself. *You can cross this one off your list.*

Ken offered Jackson up to me and I carefully took him into my arms gave him a little hug, then turned to Marti. "Okay, you came all this way out here, hand Mason to Ken and say hello to Jackson." We did a quick baby exchange and I could see that Marti was talking quietly to Jackson and tears were running down her face.

"Okay, you take him back, Jeffrey, and Ken, give me

Mason. We are going to head home and give you guys some time alone." Marti handed Jackson to me, but Ken hung on to Mason a bit longer.

"Marti, you don't have to rush off. Don't you want to come by the house?"

"Thanks Ken, but we just wanted a quick peek at him tonight. You three should spend your first night on your own."

"If you're sure." Ken handed Mason over to Marti.

"I'm sure. Mase and I need to get home and give Greg all the details, but we are definitely coming to see you tomorrow. That's non-negotiable."

"We wouldn't have it any other way." Ken gave Marti another hug and then she said goodbye to Jackson and me and headed toward the parking garage.

Jackson hadn't made so much as a peep during this entire exchange. "That was Marti and your soon-to-be best friend Mason," I told him. "They wanted to welcome you home. Were you a good boy on the plane? Hmm? Were you a good boy for Papa?"

"Pa," Jackson gurgled. "Paaaa."

I cut my eyes over to Ken. "Pa? What happened to coo?"

"What do you mean?" Ken asked innocently. "He's making all kinds of funny noises."

"Paa pa. Paaa."

"I can see that," I grunted. "Let's get out of here."

With Ken's bag stored in the trunk, and Jackson securely buckled into his car seat, I tossed the car keys to Ken. "You drive," I said and slid into the back seat with Jackson.

Ken started the car and the Manford-Roach family

headed home for the first time.

"I left all of his clothes in Guatemala, other than those he's wearing. The rest I wanted to donate to the orphanage."

"That makes sense. It's not like we don't have a dresser full of clothes at home. Right Jackson? Hmm, you have so many clothes and toys waiting for you handsome."

"Paaaa. Paa. Pa."

"Coo," I countered.

"Paaaaaaa. Pa."

I couldn't believe how I had been played. Here I was thinking I had ended up with the best name ever and Jackson was already calling out Ken's. Repeatedly. "Ken, you really are too much."

"What?"

"Really? Let's see; how did that go? Oh yes, I think we should call you *Daddy* and I think I want him to call me *Papa*? Are you trying to tell me that's a coincidence, Paaa paa?"

"Don't be ridiculous," Ken said, trying to suppress a grin. "I've always wanted to be called Papa. Just like I know you've always wanted to be called Daddy. It's deeply embedded in your white trash roots."

"Oh, don't you try logic with me. I know what you are up to. This is all calculated to make you even more appealing to friends and strangers alike."

"Ha ha ha." Ken snorted from the front seat. "Purely an accident, I assure you."

"Jackson, did you hear your papa? He thinks he's so clever, doesn't he?"

"Paapaaaa, pa pa."

"Daddy. Daaaa deee. Can you say Daddy?"

"Paaa paa pa pa."

"Try this Jackson: Dddaa dddaa."

"Pppaaa ppa."

"No Daddy?"

"Apparently not," Ken said and laughed machine-gun style—ha-ha-ha-ha. He tends to do that when he's particularly amused.

"It's fortunate for you that we have a baby in this car, otherwise I would ask you to pull over just so I could slap you. And not a love tap. A full, open-palmed smack right across your smart mouth."

"Paaa pp pp pa."

"Yeah, yeah, I hear you, motormouth. Paa papa paa. Are you calling for your stinking papa?"

Jackson broke into a huge smile.

"Oh my, that's a lot of gum, mister. Yes it is. Do you like it when I call your papa stinky? Huh?" Jackson continued to grin.

"He seems to like it when I verbally abuse you," I said to Ken.

"Go right ahead. I'll always have the memory that Jackson's first word was Papa."

I fixed the back of his head with my deadliest stare, the one that had been known to cause a mere mortal to dissolve into tears.

"I can't see your hate face," Ken laughed. "My eyes are on the road. The baby's safety comes first."

I narrowed my eyes, to sharpen my point.

Ken glanced up in the rearview mirror. "Jackson, tell your daddy his face is going to freeze like that."

"Paaapaaapaaaa."

"Daaddaaaa," I countered.

This caused Ken to break into a fresh round of giggles. "I hate you, Mr. Manford."

CHAPTER FOURTEEN

Dallas, April, 2002

"What is Jeffrey saying?" Fara asked.

Marti might have been willing to give Ken and me some alone time with Jackson, but my family wasn't feeling nearly as generous. Our phone was ringing as we pulled into the garage from the airport.

I answered it long enough to tell them that we were home and that everything was great. Then I told them we needed some family time and that I would call with a full report in a couple of days. As soon as I hung up, Ken made a quick call to his mom and delivered the same message.

Unbelievably, everyone had given us the space we asked for and now we were living up to our promise and calling them with all the details of Ken's pick-up and what had happened since we got him home. Of course, Fara was the first person we called, because we knew she had the unhappy task of keeping Mom out of our hair and was probably ready to shoot her, or herself.

"He's trying to get Jackson to say Daddy. He's been at it for hours. It's pretty hilarious."

"Doesn't he realize that babies don't talk at six months old?"

"You're on speaker, so I can hear you. And maybe

regular babies don't talk, but I think I'm making some progress with our little genius." I had gone to Circuit City when Ken was in Guatemala to pick up a new phone system that had a better speakerphone. I figured our family would want to hear Jackson and both of us wanted to share all the details with them. "Ready Jackson? Say Daddy for Aunt Fara. Daaa deee."

"Give it up, Jeffrey, he's way too young to understand words. He's just making noises right now. You are wasting your time."

"Paapaapppapaa."

"Was that Jackson? It almost sounded like he was saying—"

"Papa? Uh-huh. He has been saying it non-stop since we got him home. Nothing but PPPAAAAPPA. It's incredibly annoying."

Mom and Fara were giggling on the other end of the phone and Ken was looking particularly smug. Fara finally got her giggle fit under control, "You realize he's not really saying Papa. It's just a coincidence. He's too young to say real words and know what they mean."

"Well, Jeffrey talked really early," Mom said.

"Oh, here we go! Yes, Mother, we all know that Jeffrey was potty trained at nine months, walking at ten months and could drive a car by eighteen months."

"Fara, he was just a tiny little thing and he could recite nursery rhymes by heart," Mom said. "Ask Lydia, she'll tell you." Lydia was my mom's sister, and she was like a second mother to Fara and me.

"No doubt she'll confirm your story about what an amazingly gifted child Jeffrey was," Fara said. "And then you had that other one. The one that couldn't speak until she was nine. What was her name? Oh right, that was me!"

"Don't be ridiculous," Mom said. "You weren't nine. Although you were closer to three."

"Slow much?" I said to Fara.

"The point is, if even the great and powerful Jeffrey couldn't talk at six months, what are the chances that Jackson knows what he is saying?"

"He knows." I refused to let this go. "He and his damn papa have cooked up this little scheme just to vex me."

Ken gently lifted Jackson out of my arms and leaned down to fake whisper in his ear. "And it's working too, isn't it, baby?"

"Okay, back to the business at hand," Fara said. "Let's talk baby shower."

"Fara, we don't need another baby shower. We either got everything that we need at Marti's shower, or we bought it ourselves." For once my sister and mom were quiet.

"Seriously, we don't need a thing," I continued.

"What's Joyce's opinion of this, Ken?" Mom finally asked.

"Oh, she's planning a shower," Ken said.

"Exactly, and so are we," Fara said. "So suck it up and make a list of stuff you need."

"Paaap paaaaap."

"Daaaadeeee."

"Would you just give up on that?" Ken laughed.

"Never!"

"Oh!" Ken said. "Jackson must have really liked that. I think he just pooped."

"Lucky him," Mom said.

"No, no, no," Ken said to me. "This can't turn into

another conversation about your family and their convoluted bowel issues." I just shrugged my shoulders.

"So back to the baby shower," Fara said. "What's the plan?"

"The plan is that we are coming home in a couple of weeks. We'll drive straight to your house for a few days and then drive to my family's house."

"Are you sure you want to spend twelve hours in the car with a six-month-old?" she asked.

"No, but we've spent a fortune on plane tickets and driving is going to be so much cheaper. Plus we'll have a car to make the trip between the two houses." Ken's family lived about ninety miles from my sister's house.

"Okay, we'll get everything figured out," Fara said. "Everyone is excited to meet Jackson."

"Everyone? As in *everyone* in my family?" I asked.

"Of course."

"Even Dad's side of the family?"

"Yes! They'll all be here. Not just Mom's side of the family."

"This should prove interesting," I muttered. "Do they know about me and Ken?"

"They've known you your entire life," Ken said, "they'd have to be blind, deaf and dumb not to know."

This caused a fresh round of giggles. "Ha ha ha," I said. "I'm glad you three are having such a good time."

"Jeffrey, they are really excited," Fara said. "Have a little faith in your family."

"Okay, I'll trust you on this one."

"Good, because you know I'm never wrong."

"I know."

"So we are good to go?"

"Yes, good to go. Now let me go change this poopy diaper."

"Have fun. Love you."

"Love you too."

We disconnected the call with Fara and I took Jackson from Ken. "Why don't you call your mom while I change his diaper?"

"Don't you want to talk to them too?"

"I do and I'm sure they will want to hear Jackson do his Papa trick, but he needs to be changed. You go ahead and get started and I'll be back down once I finish up with him.

"Okay, don't take too long though. My family isn't as crazy as yours, so the conversation won't take nearly as long."

"You just keep telling yourself that, honey." I leaned in and gave Ken a quick peck on the cheek and headed up the stairs to the nursery.

"Remember there are Dixie Cups in his bathroom."

"Thanks for the reminder." One of the first times I changed Jackson's diaper I had taken the dirty one off, and was about to tape up the clean one, when he let loose a stream of pee. I was in the middle of carrying on a full conversation with him and some of the pee went right in my mouth. From that moment on I used a paper cup as a pee guard when I changed him.

"I don't think I could stand to deal with another pee incident," Ken said. "You must have brushed your teeth a thousand times and you still claimed you could taste pee."

I didn't even bother to stop but kept moving up the stairs. "That's because I could, and you know what it tasted like? Tea."

"Dialing!" I guess that was Ken's way of saying he

didn't want to hear my theory on how tea tasted like pee again.

After I got Jackson changed, we came back downstairs and Ken put the phone on speaker. Joyce was thrilled to hear Jackson's voice again and loved that it sounded like he was trying to say Papa.

"Now how did you two decide on who would be called what?"

"Jeffrey really wanted to be called Daddy, so I told him I was okay with being called Papa."

"Ken Manford!" I leaned down close to the speaker to be sure Joyce could hear me. "Your son is a liar, liar, pants on fire! He called me up from Guatemala *after* he discovered Jackson had been programmed to say nothing but the word Papa and suggested I be called Daddy and he would take Papa. Now, he's your son and you know him best, but do you really think that was a coincidence? Or do you think he wanted to be able to say for the rest of our lives that Jackson's first word was Papa?"

"Well—"

"Mom, that's not the way it happened at all. He actually suggested that I be called Big Daddy!"

"Well, that's—"

"Exactly! That's just wrong, so I took the only available name left and it just so happened that was the one word Jackson kept saying."

"First of all he's not actually saying Papa, he's just making noises. Right, Joyce?"

"Well, he's probably—"

Ken jumped in again with another counterpoint and poor Joyce could barely get a word in between the two of us. Eventually, Ken realized that we were doing all of the talking.

"Okay, you need to go or Mom and I will never get a chance to talk."

"Well, if that's the way you feel, I guess I'll be forced to go play my XBOX." I leaned down to pick up Jackson from his blanket. "Come on, Jackson, we know when we are not wanted."

"You can leave the baby."

"Harsh. Okay, I will leave the two of you to talk to your mom about the trip home and I'll just go upstairs by myself and sulk." I gave an exaggerated sigh and did my best to look like I had just been excommunicated for drinking the communion wine.

When I got out of sight, I did a little fist pump and quickly turned on the television and loaded up my game. I had been worried that once Jackson arrived my video game privileges would be revoked. I was thrilled to see that even with a baby in the house I was still going to have time to kill a few aliens.

After an hour or so, Ken and Jackson came upstairs to the media room. Ken promptly walked right over to the TV and switched it off.

"Ken, I'm right in the middle of trying to save the world here." Geez, he could have at least let me save my game first.

"Don't think you fooled me with that little display earlier."

"What?"

"Do you think I fell for that woe is me routine earlier? Oh, I'll just go play my video game upstairs while you and your mom plan the shower."

"Crap. I thought I had found a way to cheat the

system."

"There's no cheating the system. The system knows all." He plunked Jackson down in my lap. "Watch Jackson while I get cleaned up. Marti and Greg are on their way over and I need to get ready."

"What about me?" I looked down at myself and realized I was wearing dad jeans and an old sweatshirt. "I need to get cleaned up too."

"Well, I guess you should have been doing that instead of killing those mutants." Ken turned and headed toward our bedroom. "And change Jackson into something adorable."

"They're aliens," I muttered under my breath. "Come on, Jackson, let's go find something adorable for you to wear. Maybe it will take the focus off of me." That stopped me dead in my tracks. Just a few days in and already I had become that parent with stains on their shirt at Target. I had thought it before, but it was worth repeating: How the mighty had fallen.

CHAPTER FIFTEEN

Fara's House, May, 2002

"Put him in the University of Kentucky sweat suit."

Ken and I had arrived at my sister's house with remarkably little drama. Jackson had sailed through the trip without a peep. The only thing remotely dramatic that happened was we decided to come a day early. When we pulled into her driveway, Fara came running out with giant rollers in her hair and her boobs flying everywhere. I was tempted to shield Jackson's eyes, but before I could do anything he was out of his car seat and into her arms as she went on and on about how *little* he was. Ken and I rolled our eyes. So much for Jackson being much older than what we were told.

"Really? You want him to wear a sweat suit the first time he gets to meet everyone?" Ken said. "I want him to wear something nice." Ken kept rummaging through the suitcase we had packed for Jackson, trying to find the perfect outfit.

I got up off the bed and walked over to him. I leaned into the suitcase and plucked out the UK warm up suit that Ken's mom had bought for Jackson. "Listen, he's about to meet my dad. If you cut that man he bleeds Kentucky blue. Trust me, that UK getup is the ticket."

"Betty!" Ken shouted. "Get in here."

"Is the baby okay?" Mom said, practically breaking her neck to get into the bedroom.

"Jeffrey wants Jackson to wear a sweat suit today for his baby shower."

"A UK sweat suit," I corrected him.

"Ken, you scared me, I thought something was wrong," Mom said.

"Something is wrong. Jeffrey's sense of fashion is very wrong. I'm not putting him in a sweat suit."

"Ken, your mom wears sweat suits all the time," I said.

"Those are not sweat suits. They're—"

"Yes? Go on? They're what?"

"Uh, matching coordinates," Ken offered. "They're pink and velour. And, besides, she doesn't wear them to parties."

"Wear what to parties?" Fara asked, walking into the bedroom. "And why isn't Jackson dressed yet? And why does he look so—oily?"

"I put a little baby oil on him after his bath," Ken said. Now that Fara pointed it out, Jackson was looking particularly supple.

"Define a little," Fara said. "He looks like you're about to cook him or something. Are you sure you didn't use vegetable oil?" She crossed to the bed where Ken was sitting, holding Jackson. "Did you put it in his hair?"

"Just a drop or two," Ken said. "What? That flyaway hair is driving me crazy. I knew we should have gotten it cut before we left."

"Give him to me," Fara said. "We need to get some of that off of him."

"He's fine," Ken said.

"Give me the baby. Now."

"You are so hardheaded! A little baby oil is not going to hurt anything."

"Ken, we have elderly aunts and uncles coming here to see and hold this baby. Right now he would slide right out of their hands. Give. Him. To. Me." She towered, as much as someone who is barely five feet tall can tower, over Ken with her arms outstretched.

With a sigh of resignation, Ken handed Jackson up to her.

"Mom, get those jeans"—Fara pointed—"and that shirt ironed. I'm going to work on the oil slick situation. You two," she continued, "get in the living room and get ready to greet people. And smile. It's a party. Come on Jackson Valdez," she said to Jackson. "I may have to go all Karen Silkwood to get this shit off of you." With that she turned on her heel and walked out of the room.

"She's so bossy," Mom said.

"I told you that sweat suit was a bad idea," Ken said.

"I'm not the one who tried to re-create the Exxon Valdez oil spill," I said.

"Are the three of you doing what I asked?" Fara shouted from the bathroom. "It sounds like you are still standing around with your fingers up your asses and your minds in Arkansas."

"Yes," I shouted back, "everything is under control."

"What does that even mean?" Ken asked. "Why would you have your finger up your ass and your mind in Arkansas at the same time? That's not even physically possible."

"Ken, your mind is not actually *in* Arkansas." He just sat there staring at me. "It's, you know, like a Southern saying. It means you aren't paying attention to what you are supposed to be doing."

"It's definitely not a saying, Southern or otherwise."

"Of course it is. My dad has said that to me my whole life."

"With good reason," Fara shouted from the other room. "Are you three still standing around in there?"

Mom shooed us out of the bedroom and into action. Twenty minutes later, everyone had completed their assigned task and Jackson, Ken, and I were sitting on my sister's sofa, anxiously awaiting my big and boisterous family.

"I never get to hold Jackson," Sydney said. "It's not fair. Alex and Nick get to hold him all the time." Sydney was my sister's youngest child.

"Not today, Sydney," Fara said. "Today Jackson is going to be passed around like a hot potato. He doesn't need you added to the mix."

"Come here, Syd," Ken said. "Sit next to me and you can hold him while we wait for people to get here. We still have thirty minutes or so."

"Actually we don't," Fara said. "Dad just pulled in the driveway. He wanted to get here early to have some alone time with Jackson. Give him to me." She crossed the room in a flash and snatched Jackson out of Ken's hand.

"No fair, Mom. You big baby hog," Sydney complained.

"Sydney hush," she said over her shoulder.

"Look what I've got," she said, opening the door for Dad.

"Well, hello there, partner. You've got your papaw's belly," he said, giving Jackson's belly a rub and laughing his infectious laugh.

"You want to hold him?" Fara asked.

"You betcha, but let me get in here and sit down. Your papaw's old and not in very good shape," Dad said to Jackson.

I hopped up to give him a hug and make room for him on the couch. "Hey Dad," I said.

"Well hello there, son of mine," Dad said.

"Hey Russell," Ken said, giving Dad a hug as well. "How are you doing?"

"Oh, I'm just doing the best. How are you doing, Ken? Busy these days I would imagine," he said with another laugh, and settled himself on the couch. "Okay, hand the little fart over to me."

"Jackson, meet your grandpa," Fara said and gently placed Jackson in his arms.

"Lucky you," Sydney said. "I never get to hold him."

"Sydney!" Fara said. "Go to your room and watch TV or something."

"Oh, leave the girl alone," my dad scolded her. "You better get over here, Red, and sit next to your papaw. That way if anyone gives you any trouble I can personally kick their happy ass." Sydney quickly snuggled in next to Dad.

"Where are the boys?" Dad asked. "Tell them to get out here and say hello to the old man. Hell, I could be dead next week."

"Russell, to hear you tell it you are always at death's door," Mom said. She had a point, Dad had been counting his days since forever, or at least as long as I could remember.

"Hush midget," Dad said with a laugh. "Get out your little medical book and see if we can't figure out what's wrong with me."

"I vote for meanness," I offered.

"Yep. That sounds about right," Dad said.

"Boys!" Fara shouted. My sister is a firm believer in the power of the voice over the legs. She never bothers to close the distance between herself and the person she's addressing. She simply raises her voice. "Get in here and say hello to your grandpa. Now!"

For his part, Jackson couldn't seem to take his eyes off my dad. He'd probably never encountered so much personality in anyone before. And that's saying a lot, considering he had already been exposed to both my sister and me, who have inherited our dad's "never met a stranger" philosophy.

But there's no doubt that Dad is the original. Fara and I are just pale copies who can't hold a candle to him. As if to prove the point, Dad leaned over to Sydney and whispered, "Are there going to be any single, good-looking women here?" Sydney's eyes went wide and she grinned like he had just said the most amazing thing to her.

Mom, on the other hand, is immune to Dad's charm. Whatever hold he might have had on her in the past has long since disappeared. "None that you're not related to," she assured him.

"I see. Well, that does take some of the fun out of it."

Nick and Alex came flying into the room at top speed and ran over and gave Dad a quick hug. Nick explained that he was in the middle of his video game and couldn't quit until he could save his progress.

"*Halo?*" I asked. Nick nodded. "I feel your pain."

Dad didn't seem to know what to do with this information so he turned his attention to Alex. "What do you know, hoss?" he asked.

"Nothing," Alex said with a grin.

"Not a damn thing, huh?"

"Nope. Not a D thing."

"Alex," Fara warned.

"Get over here, boy, where she can't reach you." Alex skipped over to Dad, leaned down and grabbed both of Jackson's cheeks and gave them a little pinch and raced back out of the room.

"He must have some very important business back in his bedroom," Dad said with a laugh.

"Hey Papaw," Nick began, "Dad says you still have your Christmas lights up. Did you want me to come to your house and help you take them down?" Nick was an old man trapped in the body of a thirteen-year-old boy.

"Nah, I've decided to leave them up until Easter, since I barely got to enjoy them at Christmas. Ya'll ought to bring Jackson down to see them. I've got the prettiest little blue lights on the tree in the front yard."

"Papaw, Easter is already over."

"Is that so? Well, hell, I guess you better come down and help me with them next week then."

"Okay. I will see if Dad will bring me to your house next week to help you take them down." Satisfied that he had spent the required amount of time visiting with Dad, Nick slipped out of the room to resume his battle against the alien menace in *Halo*.

"Dad," I asked, "why didn't you get to enjoy your lights at Christmas this year?" Fara shot me a look that said, "Don't go there," but it was too late. I'd already opened up that can of worms.

"Because some little bastard kept cutting my lights,"

Dad said.

"What do you mean?"

"Cutting the wires on my Christmas lights."

"What? On the trailer?" Dad's festive Christmas lights were a source of pride and I instantly became concerned for the little bastard's long-term health.

"Uh-huh, and on my little tree in the front yard."

"Did you catch 'em?" I asked. My family had a strong vengeful streak and we didn't take kindly to anyone messing with our stuff. "Remember that time someone was smashing Fara's pumpkins and she set up her video camera to catch them?"

Dad laughed. "Oh, yes. It is not wise, Son, to mess with your sister."

"Little assholes," Fara piped in.

"Well, I fixed his wagon," Dad said, returning to his story.

"You didn't shoot him did you?"

"Lord no, too much mess to clean up."

"So what happened?" I asked, preparing myself for the worst.

"I hooked my lights up to a 120-volt battery."

"Okay."

"That night I was laying there in bed and I heard the *awfulest* pop!" Dad laughed. "When he cut through those wires with metal, he got hit with 120 volts."

"Did he scream?" I asked.

"Oh, like you wouldn't believe. I got out of bed, opened up the back door and told him that I would see him tomorrow night and that the voltage would be doubled. I haven't had a problem since."

"Dad, you could have killed him," I said.

"Nah, you can't kill someone with 120 volts. But you can teach them a lesson. And you most assuredly can stop them from cutting your lights."

"You have a point," I conceded. "At least you didn't threaten to shoot this one." The previous summer, Dad was having a big BBQ at his house. He lived way out in the middle of nowhere on the banks of the Green River. There was a little dirt road that ran in front of his property that people who have lake homes and campsites used to get back and forth from the highway.

During the BBQ, a handful of teenagers were flying up and down the dirt road at top speed. At one point my dad heard them coming and ambled out to the road and stood there waiting for them. As they approached, he put both his arms in the air and flagged them down.

"Boys, I just want to let you know something," Dad said. "With the way you are driving up and down this road, one of you is going to end up running over one of my grandbabies. And when you do, I'm going to get my shotgun and blow your damn head off."

According to my sister, who was there at the time, the boys stared at my dad slack-jawed. When they swiveled their heads to her, she gave the slightest nod, as if to let them know he wasn't joking.

"Of course they'll put me in the pen," Dad continued, "but you'll still be dead. Now do you want my grandchildren to have to come and visit me in jail?"

"No sir," one of them mumbled.

"Then let's try to keep the speed down." Having said his piece, Dad walked back to his yard and continued to monitor the turkey he was deep frying. "Stop by for some food later if you're hungry," he added over his shoulder.

The teens slowly drove away, barely kicking up a cloud of dust.

"Russell, what would you have done if he died?" Mom asked.

"Well, I guess I would have dragged his body to the river, although he was a big ol' boy. I'm not sure I could have managed it."

"Just call me, Dad, and I will come down and help you dispose of the body," Fara said.

"Fara, do not encourage him."

"Oh Mom," Fara said, "you can't kill somebody with 120 volts!"

"Aren't we supposed to be having a party?" I said, changing the direction of the conversation before Fara and Dad could plan their next murder.

"Dad, come out to the kitchen and help me finish setting everything up."

"One of us can help," Ken offered.

"No, you two stay here with Jackson. People should start arriving in a few minutes."

"Come on, old man." Fara leaned down and helped pull Dad to his feet. "I'm going to put you to work." The two of them headed off to the kitchen, leaving me, Mom, Ken, and Jackson to fend for ourselves. At some point Sydney had sneaked away to watch one of her beloved Mary Kate & Ashley movies. Those two creeped me out and I was just thankful I had an excuse not to have to sit through those videos again.

"My dad is completely insane," I said to Ken once they were out of sight.

"He is," Ken agreed. "But that's what makes him so amazing."

"Indeed."

"I'm not sure he would have cared if he killed that kid, as long as he stopped him from messing with his precious lights," Mom said. As I mentioned before, Mom remained immune to Dad's particular charms.

"You are probably right," I said. "But seriously, what kind of asshole cuts a man's Christmas lights?"

Ken laughed. "God I love Russell so much." He turned and looked at Mom with a curious look on his face. "I have such a hard time picturing the two of you married."

"That one is lost on all of us," I agreed. "I swear they don't have a single thing in common."

"People say the same thing about you two," Mom pointed out.

"Does this mean that Jeffrey is going to be one of those crazy old men who terrorize everyone in the neighborhood?" Ken asked.

"If anyone is going to torture the neighbors it's going to be you. I'll be the one making the apologetic phone calls and baking the forgive me brownies."

Ken laughed and pulled me into a hug. "Well, they say opposites attract, baby," he whispered in my ear.

"Yes, that worked out just great for me and your dad." With that, Mom stood up and wandered out of the room in search of something to do.

Before either of us could say a word, Fara shouted from the kitchen that my Aunt Monnie had just pulled up and that I should run out and see if she needed any help. I yelled back that I was on my way. Before I left I leaned down to Ken. "Sit there and look pretty. If we are lucky no one will realize that two big queens have just adopted a baby."

Ken started to say something back but I put my finger across his lips. "Less talking and more pretty. Be right back with the family in tow."

I met my aunt and her daughter Joyce Ann at the car and led them to Fara's living room where Jackson sat perched on Ken's knee.

"It looks like he has his papaw's belly," Aunt Monnie said.

"It looks better on him than it does Uncle Russell." Joyce Ann was one of the few members of my extended family that we saw on an annual basis. She always made a point to stop by Fara's house with her kids whenever we were in for Christmas. "Hey Ken."

"Hey Joyce Ann, bring your mom over here and let me introduce the two of you to Jackson."

"Jeffrey! Car!" Fara shouted from the kitchen.

"You two go say hello," I said. "It looks like Fara is going to keep me running all day."

I spent the next couple of hours greeting aunts, uncles, cousins and old friends. Most of them pulled me into a big hug, as if I was some long lost relative. Which, for all practical purposes, I suppose I was. It had been years since I had seen most of them and I was surprised at how genuinely excited they seemed to be to see me.

But as soon as they saw Jackson, their excitement at seeing me was quickly overshadowed by how taken they were with him. They couldn't get over how handsome he was. With his dark eyes and brown skin, he certainly stood out in our crowd.

This was also the first time most of them had met Ken. A few of the women whispered to me that he wasn't so hard on the eyes either. It seemed my two guys were a big hit.

Later in the day Ken and I found ourselves alone for the first time. "I think you have undersold your family," he said. "They have been great."

"I know. Either I have created a bunch of false memories or they have really mellowed out."

"Either way, they seem to be totally dazzled by Jackson. His butt hasn't hit the ground since they started showing up."

"Yes, they have been wonderful."

"I told you they would be," Fara said from behind us.

"Fara! Don't you know better than to sneak up on people when they are whispering," Ken said.

"There are no secrets around me. Remember, I hear everything." Fara slipped between the two of us and headed toward the living room.

"Now that we're parents do you think we will start treating everyone like they are our children?" I whispered to Ken.

"I heard that," Fara said over her shoulder as she stepped into the middle of the room and clapped her hands a couple of times.

"Okay people. It's time for baby shower games!"

CHAPTER SIXTEEN

Joyce's House, May, 2002

The rest of the baby shower at my sister's house went off without a hitch. I was a little disappointed that nobody got drunk or broke down in tears and that guns and knives didn't make an appearance. Maybe I would get around to inventing a few false memories to make it more entertaining when I told Jackson about it when he was older.

The next morning, Ashley, Josh's daughter from his first marriage, brought her baby to Fara's house. It was hard to believe that my sister was already a grandmother, especially since I was just now becoming a father. Ashley was very young when Fara and Josh married, and Fara had always treated her like her own daughter.

Evan was just a few weeks old and Fara had bought him and Jackson matching outfits. When we saw how tiny Evan was I started to think maybe it was a blessing that Jackson didn't come home until he was nearly six months old.

Ken and I were laying around in the living room with my family, playing with the babies and putting off the two-hour drive to his family's house. We were still trying to catch up from the long drive from Dallas and Fara was trying to recover from all the work that went into the baby shower. For my family, things were uncharacteristically low key. I should have known it wouldn't last.

Fara suddenly bolted up off the couch. "Hurry! My lesbian neighbor just pulled into her drive."

"What?" I mumbled. I had just given up on trying to stay upright and had stretched out on her big, old, comfy sofa and was in no hurry to move. "I don't think I'm physically capable of hurrying today and why do I care about your neighbor, lesbian or otherwise?"

"Would you move it before she gets in the house and we blow this perfect opportunity? Not to mention you owe me after that Jennifer fiasco." On a whim Ken had flown his sister Jennifer to Dallas in early April to help us get Jackson settled in. Fara was not amused.

"I can't believe you are still bitter about that. And exactly why are we rushing out to see your lesbian neighbor and what opportunity are we blowing?"

"Fara has a crush on the neighbor," Josh shouted from the kitchen. Fara's husband was a man of few words, but he tended to make them count.

"I don't have a crush on her, Josh, but I want her to know that we are gay friendly."

"What am I? Some kind of gay totem?"

"Well, let's see, you drove up in a silver Jaguar, you're wearing a black tank top and you're ridiculously fit for a man of your age. Sounds pretty gay to me. Now let's go," she said, reaching down and pulling me up off the sofa. "You too, Ken! And grab the baby."

"Don't you think you are overselling it just a little bit?" I looked at Ken, hoping he would be the voice of reason here. He shrugged his shoulders. "Doesn't matter to me, we need to get moving anyway."

"Now see what you've gone and done? I was planning on at least another hour of doing nothing but laying here on this sofa and you have gone and lit a fire under Ken's butt."

"I've got news for you, precious, Ken was never going to give you that hour."

"She's right. We really have to get on the road. We have another baby shower to attend."

"Exactly!" Fara said. "Now move it, she won't linger forever."

"This is crazy," I said.

Josh had wandered into the kitchen and was eating a sandwich at 9:30 in the morning. "I don't know; she is pretty hot. And she's a cop."

"Okay gag. Let's get this over with before it turns into some freaky three-way."

"Well, thanks for that visual," Mom said.

"And it would be a four-way," Josh added. "She has a girlfriend who is even hotter." I loved that my family was so comfortable with same sex couples that we could have these kind of super awkward conversations.

Fara looked up at Josh. "First of all, who says we would include you? Second, her girlfriend is a skanky whore."

"Wow," Ken said. "Just wow."

I knew I shouldn't ask, but I couldn't help myself. "Why is her girlfriend a skanky whore? Do you know her from high school or something?"

"She's never met her," Josh said. "She just doesn't like the way she looks."

"That's because she looks like someone Dad would date," Fara said to me. "Flitting around out in the yard in her Daisy Dukes."

"Ouch."

"Exactly."

"Wait, didn't Jeffrey used to wear Daisy Dukes?" Ken asked.

"I was in the eighth grade and was wearing them *ironically*."

"You weren't," Fara said with a sad little shake of her head. "And it was terrifying."

"Moving on—let's get your gay on. You know I love to share the magic of me with others." I drug myself up off the couch and extended a hand to Ken so that he could pull himself up. Once he was upright, he leaned down and picked up Jackson off of his blanket. I turned to Fara. "Okay, the prototypical gay family is ready for their close up."

"Finally," Fara muttered and led us all toward the front door. "Don't even think about it Josh," she said over her shoulder.

She pulled open the door and the four of us marched out onto her porch where she came to an abrupt stop. "Well hell. She's already gone in." She turned around and smacked me on the back of the head.

"Ow! What was that for?"

"For taking too long and denying me the chance to grow my gay network."

"Oh well," Ken said. "Now that we are up we should get the car packed and hit the road."

Now it was my time to smack Fara on the back of the head. "Nice job, bag buster, now Ken's going to force me to be a productive human being."

"Bag buster?" Ken looked between Fara and me, waiting for an explanation. "Do I even want to know?"

"I've been banned from ever speaking of the incident," I said to Ken.

"Okay, I definitely want to know. Fara?"

She sighed. "It's a Dad thing. When we were nine or ten, Dad had a Chevy van that he loved more than life itself."

"It had shag carpet on the ceiling and everything," I added.

"It had shag carpet everywhere," she corrected me. "Anyway, Dad took us to the store and told us we could each get a Coke and a snack. Tubby over here got a candy bar."

"Not just any candy bar. I got a Mars bar, because I felt it made me look more sophisticated."

Fara just shook her head. "It didn't. I picked out a bag of Lay's potato chips. Dad paid for our stuff and we all piled into the van to head home. Dad wanted us to wait until we got home before we ate, but we promised him we wouldn't spill anything on his carpet."

"Oh no," Ken said. "This isn't going to end well."

"You guessed it. I couldn't get my chips to open, so I pinched both sides of the bag and gave a little tug and the whole bag just exploded. Chips flew in every direction. I was horrified. Not only had I just lost my snack, but I had gotten chips all over Dad's shag carpeting. That's when he caught my eye in the rear view mirror and said, 'Way to go, bag buster.'"

I draped my arm over her shoulder in mock solidarity. "And the name just sort of stuck until I came up with the much more colorful *thunder thighs* a few years later."

"Weren't you just leaving?" Fara asked. "I kid because I love you, but, seriously, get out."

"Actually we really do have to get a move on," Ken said. "Remember it's an hour later in Louisville."

"You two can start packing while I play with Jackson," Fara said. She held her arms out to him. "Come to Aunt Fara, Jackson."

"Papapppap papapa."

"That's starting to annoy the shit out of me," Fara said. Jackson must have thought that was hilarious because he broke into a big, goofy smile. She took him out of Ken's arms and headed back into the living room while Ken and I started collecting our stuff and piling it into the car. I was starting to stress because the car was already at capacity and we hadn't even collected our booty from Ken's family yet. I hoped that they took my request for small gifts seriously.

Once the car was packed and we said our goodbyes, we buckled Jackson into his car seat and headed toward Louisville. Although we were all crazy about each other, my family wasn't one for teary goodbyes. Sometimes my dad would just get up and announce he was leaving and go. If you wanted a hug out of him you had to really be quick about it. The Manfords, on the other hand, were an emotional bunch and I was already envisioning Ken's mom strapping herself to the top of our car when it came time for us to go home.

After we had been on the road for about a half an hour, Ken turned to me and said, "I'm glad Fara insisted on another baby shower. That was a lot of fun."

"I was just thinking the same thing".

My family had really surprised me. Not my sister and her crew, I knew they were going to be thrilled to death with Jackson, but I had always considered some of my extended family to be somewhere between hillbillies and country folk, and I didn't think they would be particularly open-minded. Not that I thought they were terrible people, I knew that wasn't the case. But I had always hidden a part of myself from them growing up because I didn't think they would be interested in getting to know the unfiltered me. So I figured spending the day with two gay guys and their baby would just be too much for them to accommodate.

As it turned out I couldn't have been more wrong. They were warm and friendly and each of them spent time playing with Jackson, treating him like a real family member. I was a little embarrassed that I had gotten it so wrong.

"I wonder if the parent card somehow trumps the gay card?" I asked Ken.

"What do you mean?"

"I don't know, it's just that it seems the common bond of parenthood is so strong that it makes us more ordinary."

"You think we are ordinary?"

"Not in the bad sense, but in the sense of being typical or everyday. Now we are just two people trying to raise a kid. Before I think people assumed our lives were a lot more exotic."

"That's a laugh. We are about as non-exotic as it gets."

"The funny thing is that we will probably get the opposite reaction from our gay friends. We have suddenly gone from ordinary to exotic."

"Except now most of our new gay friends have kids."

"Good point. It's weird that, until today, I never considered how our identities would change once we became parents."

"Maybe you just weren't being generous enough with

your opinion of your family."

"Maybe," I agreed.

"Does it bother you?"

"Does what bother me?"

"That our identity as a couple or that your own individual identity has been somehow consumed by our identity as a family?"

I thought about it for a minute. "Not in the least. You know me, I stopped caring what people thought the day I slid into those Daisy Dukes in the eighth grade. The only thing I care about is what you think."

"Me too," he said.

"Are you saying that you care about what *you* think as well?"

Ken rolled his eyes. "Shut up and drive."

***

"Can I hold Baby Jackson?"

Having successfully wrapped up the shower at my family's house, packed it all up and driven it to Louisville, we had finally arrived at Ken's parents' house. We hadn't managed to extract ourselves and all of our crap from the car before Ken's young niece began her campaign to hold Jackson.

What is it with kids wanting to hold babies? Does it in some way signal to them that they are all grown up now? I'm not sure, but I can distinctly remember lobbying my parents in exactly the same way when I was nine or ten.

"Caitlyn, let them get in the house first," Jennifer said. Jennifer is Ken's baby sister and lived just a few blocks away from his parents with her husband, James, and her twins, Caitlyn and Ethan.

The twins weren't much bigger than Jackson, although

they would be five on their next birthday. They were born premature, and their first few months were a struggle. But, based on their current energy level, they seemed to be right as rain. They were bouncing up and down, trying to get a peak at their new cousin. *Cousin!* I was totally in love with the idea that Jackson had cousins. Growing up, Fara and I spent more time with our cousins than we did our friends. I knew it would be different for Jackson, since we lived so far away, but I still hoped he would have that bond with his cousins.

"Besides," Jennifer continued, taking Jackson from Ken's arms, "he probably misses me. I haven't seen him in a couple of weeks and aunts outrank cousins, kiddos." There was some grumbling from the twins that Jennifer promptly ignored, giving Jackson her undivided attention.

"Hello, Baby Jackson, it's your Aunt Jennifer. Hello."

"Pppapappp."

"Did you hear that, Caitlyn? I told you he was trying to say papa! That's so cute." I rolled my eyes at Ken and he tried to hide the smirk that seemed to appear every time someone pointed out that Jackson was saying papa.

"Where are Mom and Dad?" Ken asked, completely ignoring my stink eye. I considered hitting him with one of my withering looks, but the truth is I was too tired to pull it off and I feared that he was building up an immunity to them, so I had to save them for times when it really mattered.

"Mom's in the bathroom and Dad's in the basement. Surprise. Surprise," Jennifer said. "Come on, Jackson, let's see if we can find Mamaw and Papaw." Jennifer led the way into the house.

"Mom! Dad! They're here," she shouted. One thing

both my sister and Ken's don't lack for is volume. Maybe it's a mom thing, but my sister can stand perfectly still anywhere in her house and summon her children from the farthest reaches of their rooms. They can be buried under a mountain of toys or plugged into the latest video game and her voice will penetrate through the chaos.

The bathroom door flew open. "Oh! I didn't hear you guys pull up. Have you been here long? Hello Jackson." Ken's mom crossed the room and took Jackson from Jennifer.

"Well, so much for my baby time," Jennifer said. "I think that's my cue to go smoke." She detached the twins from her legs and slipped out the back door for a cigarette. They quickly regrouped around Joyce.

"How was the drive?" Joyce asked. "Did you hit any traffic coming into Louisville?"

"Really easy," Ken said. *It's always easy for him,* I thought, *since I'm the one who does the actual driving.* But I kept this to myself. I always allowed Ken's family a little extra time to get used to my bitterness, since they were much more civilized and pleasant than my family.

"And the baby shower at Fara's, did you get lots of good stuff?"

"It was great, lots of fun," Ken said. "The whole clan turned up. I'm not sure how we are going to get everything home."

"Hey Jeffrey," Ken's dad boomed, coming up from downstairs and blinking at the light. He grabbed me in a big bear hug. "How was the drive?"

"Good, Kenny," I answered. "Are you hiding out in the basement before the craziness starts?"

"You know it," he stage whispered to me, as he sailed

by on his way to the hallway, managing to completely miss Jackson's presence.

"For Heaven's sake. Kenny? Come see who I've got," Joyce said. "And do not even think about turning down that air conditioner. There's going to be a lot of people in here today and I'm already roasting."

Kenny came back into the kitchen shaking his head. "Roasting? Did you hear that, Jeffrey? She's roasting. You better wrap the baby up in a blanket because she has got it like a freezer in here."

"Oh Lord, will you hush and just come look at this baby?" Joyce demanded.

"Hey buddy," Kenny said, crossing the room to Jackson. "Look at all that hair."

"Where's the video camera?"

"I don't know, Joyce. I guess it is downstairs in the basement."

"Kenny! Well, don't you think you should go get it? I want to make sure we get a nice video from today."

"Why don't you go get it?" he said. He turned and headed back toward the basement stairs without waiting for an answer. "She's good at bossing, isn't she?" he whispered to me as he squeezed by. Ken's dad was rarely still for a minute.

"Jennifer do you have your digital camera?" Joyce asked. When she didn't get a reply she managed to tear her eyes off of Jackson long enough to look around the kitchen. "Where is Jennifer? I swear if you want something done in this family you have to do it yourself."

"I think she went out to smoke, but I've got my camera, Mom," Ken offered.

"Oh good! Well come on into the living room and sit

down. Dad was up at five this morning making enough noise to wake the dead and I need to rest before things get busy."

"We should unpack a few things first," Ken said. Of course, he didn't move to actually do anything. In all the years we had been visiting Ken's parents he had never helped unpack. I always schlepped everything in from the car while he sat and visited with his family.

"I'll get it," I said. "You and Jackson can visit with your mom."

"Do you three want to sleep downstairs in Dad's office?" Joyce asked. "You know that futon makes out into a queen-sized bed. Or do you want to stay in the spare bedroom like you always have before? I don't know if that bed is going to be big enough for the three of you?"

"I'm sure the bed in the spare bedroom is fine," Ken said.

Fine? That bed is anything but fine, I thought to myself. It is a study in torture and discomfort. It's one of those daybeds that has a spring-loaded mattress tucked underneath it. You reach down under the skirt, slide out the mattress and then disengage the locks to lift it up and lock it into place. The theory is that once it's locked into place you can push the two pieces together to make a bed, albeit a bed with a giant fault line running right down the middle of it. This means it's impossible to lay in the bed in any normal kind of way. Instead, we always ended up laying sideways, each of us on our own twin mattress, and avoiding the middle for fear of falling through, getting pinched or waking up crippled the next morning.

"I'll put everything in the bedroom and we can figure out the sleeping arrangements later," I offered. "Seriously, you guys go visit." I picked up the few bags we had brought in with us so that I could carry them down the hallway and into the spare bedroom. I poked my head back into the hallway. "By the way, what time are people coming?"

"In about an hour," Joyce said.

"And who's coming?" Ken asked.

"Well, everybody was invited," Joyce said, as if it was the most obvious thing in the world. "But who knows who will actually show up."

On my way back out of the bedroom I had to squeeze around the twins, who were both still clinging to Joyce as she held Jackson. The four of them were seriously jamming up my unloading zone.

"You two get out of the way and let Uncle Jeffrey get by," Jennifer said. She had managed to sneak back in without anyone seeing her. "And you're about to knock Mamaw down. Come on, Mom, let's go sit on the sofa before they tear your arms off and cause you to drop my nephew."

I headed back outside as the Manford clan moved en masse to the living room. "Where are Mike and James?" I said over my shoulder. Mike is Ken's younger brother and James was married to Jennifer.

"They went to pick up the cake," Jennifer answered.

Cake is good, I thought to myself. Perhaps cake would be enough to get me to agree to sleep in the bed from hell. I could tell that Ken wanted to be upstairs with his parents and not squirreled away in the basement.

I grabbed the first load from the car and dumped it on the floor of the bedroom and made several more trips back and forth until I had everything unloaded. On my last trip, Ken looked up at me with a puzzled look on his face.

"Why are you unpacking the gifts?"

"I figured we needed to see what we got here and then repack it all."

"Seems like a lot of work."

"Yes, you look completely tuckered out from the effort you've put into unpacking all this crap."

"I love you, sweetie."

"I'm feeling that love right now," I mumbled under my breath.

"Can you see who just pulled into the driveway?" Joyce asked me. "I hope that's James and Mike with the cake and not people showing up early." I was pretty sure it was James and Mike. It would take a truly brave person to mess with Joyce's schedule. If people started showing up before she was ready she would not be pleased.

I craned my head to look out the window. "Yep, that's them."

Joyce handed the baby over to Jennifer. "I'm going to go get the cake situated and start putting everything out."

"Do you want some help, Mom?" Ken asked.

"You don't have to help, but I would love the company." Ken followed his mom to the kitchen and I heard the back door open, followed by Ken's hellos to James and Mike.

I dumped the last of our stuff in the bedroom. By this point the floor had completely disappeared. Even if we wanted to sleep in there, I wasn't sure how we were going to pull it off.

I headed back to the living room and asked Jennifer if she was okay with Jackson for a few minutes and she told me she was going to take advantage of this, because once everybody got here she wouldn't get any baby time. I told her she was probably right and headed into the kitchen to say hello to James and Mike. As I was leaving, I saw her motion for the twins to come sit next to her on the sofa so that she could let them hold Jackson.

"Hey Jeffrey. How was the drive?" Mike came over and gave me a quick hug as soon as I stepped into the kitchen.

"Not bad at all, but I'm not looking forward to the drive home."

"How long is that trip?" James asked.

"Twelve hours—give or take." James let out a low whistle. "Where's Jennifer?"

"In the living room with Jackson."

"Do you think she will let me hold him?"

"I doubt it. She's already staked her claim for the next half hour or so."

James sighed. "That figures." He headed into the living room to try his luck. It seemed that even James couldn't withstand the charms of a baby.

"We are lucky to have this cake," Mike said.

"What do you mean?" Joyce asked.

"It wasn't decorated at all. I told them we wouldn't take it if it wasn't decorated. At first I didn't think she was going to do it because they aren't allowed to decorate during the day."

"That doesn't make sense," Ken said.

"I know, but that's the rule. I threw a big fit and they agreed to bend it this one time, because I wasn't going to take the cake otherwise. And they gave me ten percent off." Kenny said that Mike always talked the way Kentucky played basketball: fast and furious.

Mike wandered into the living room to meet Jackson, while Ken and I helped Joyce get everything situated. It wasn't long before the Manford clan began to trickle in. Much like my own brood, they were turning out in full force to support Ken and his brand new family. An endless parade of aunts, uncles, and cousins on both sides of his family introduced themselves to me with hugs, smiles and kind words for Jackson.

"Who are all these people?" I whispered to Ken at one point.

"I have no idea." He laughed. "But I think they are all related to me. It's pretty cool though, isn't it?"

"It is," I agreed. "Not to mention all the presents. If I can count on this kind of haul I'm going to let Joyce plan my next birthday party."

"Birthday party?" Joyce said. Where had she come from? This was yet another mom skill I needed to learn, how to just magically appear somewhere. So far super loud voice and teleportation were on the list. I was starting to think that this parenting stuff was complicated.

"Are we already planning Jackson's first birthday party?" she asked.

"Yes," I said without hesitation. "We thought it would be fun for all of you to come down to Dallas for Jackson's first big birthday bash."

"That does sound like fun," she said. "Ken, come say goodbye to your grandpa. He's getting tired and I'm going to have James or Dad drive him home."

"I'll do it," Ken said. "I moved our car to the street when the driveway started to fill up in case we needed to run an errand."

"Are you sure?"

"Absolutely, I don't mind at all."

"Let me go get him moving in that direction," Joyce

said. "It might take a bit."

"Okay, I'll meet you up front in a few minutes."

"Did you just make that up about a birthday bash on the spot?" he asked me. I nodded.

"Wow, that's impressive."

"Thank you," I said. "I haven't mastered loud voice or teleportation, but I've got the lying down pat."

"Huh?" Ken said.

"Skills, Mr. Manford," I said. "Now you run along and take your grandpa home and I'll hold down the fort."

"Are you sure you can handle it?"

"What's to handle? I haven't seen Jackson in over two hours. Besides, if I get really tired, Caitlyn is at the ready."

"Poor thing. Has she actually got to hold him yet?"

"I don't know. I told you I haven't seen him. Your family has totally monopolized him."

"Don't worry, you will get your chance. I think he's starting to get used to this. He is going to expect us to hold him all the time when we get home."

"I can live with that," I said.

"Me too."

"You get going. I think it's time the twins got their chance to hold the baby." I turned and shouted down the stairs where all the kids were playing, "Caitlyn! Ethan! It's your turn to hold Baby Jackson!" Ken and I heard an excited squeal from below.

"Wow, that was really loud," Ken said.

"Thank you," I said. Now I just had to figure out how to teleport and I would be well on my way to parent of the year.

CHAPTER SEVENTEEN

En Route to Home, May, 2002

"Nothing else is going in there," James said somberly. "We could try strapping it on the top."

"The top of what? The car? For a twelve-hour drive? Are you crazy? Why don't we put a mattress up there too? Just for good measure."

"I just don't know where we can put the rest of the stuff. Seriously, nothing else is going in there." James had been saying this for the last twenty minutes and I had still managed to cram even more stuff into the car. I had tucked a pair of shoes in the tire well, a book under the seat. But I was running out of cubby holes and was beginning to think he was right. I wasn't sure how we were going to get the rest of it in there.

"What do people not understand about small gifts?" I asked him. "I really do not want to unpack all of this again."

"That makes two of us."

James and I had packed, unpacked, and repacked the car for the last hour. No matter what configuration we chose, it didn't seem to matter. There was just no fitting everything in. I really thought we had it figured out the last time we had unpacked and repacked, but there were still gifts sitting in the driveway.

"We need my sister's friend, Ronnie," I told James.

Ronnie was a legend in our family. She could pack anything into the absolute smallest space imaginable. When the three of us went to Florida as kids to stay with my dad for a few weeks, we were all allowed one bag by Cricket. Yes, that was her name. Don't ask. Cricket was Dad's sometimes girlfriend, and she had agreed to drive us down for a visit. Provided she could stay too, of course.

My sister and I were amazed as Ronnie produced a never-ending supply of clothes out of her single suitcase. From that moment forward, Ronnie was called into service whenever anything needed to be packed and space was at a premium.

"Well, unless you can get her up here in the next couple of minutes," James said, "it's going to have to get strapped on top."

"I don't do strap-ons, James," I said.

"Wow, that's a little too much information," James said. We burst into giggles, which took us forever to get rid of. Clearly we were both on the verge of madness from all of the packing.

"At this point I just don't care. Just get it all in or *on* there any way you can. I'm too tired to even attempt repacking it all."

"Alright, I'll get some rope," James said. "And just a word of advice. You might want to think about something other than a Jaguar. Babies have a lot of stuff." James disappeared into the garage.

"I can see that," I muttered to myself. Of course I had traded the Jeep in for the Jaguar because I didn't think Jeeps were well suited to our new family. That and I had always wanted a Jaguar and finally had a good excuse to buy one. I hoped that James would have the decency not to repeat that comment in front of Ken or I would never hear the end of it.

A few minutes later, James returned with some bungee cords and ten minutes after that everything was either in or on the car. A half hour later we were saying our goodbyes.

As expected, Ken's family was very emotional. It wasn't quite *Terms of Endearment* but it was borderline *Beaches*. Lots of hugs and hastily swiped tears. When we finally got on the road it felt like we were leaving a funeral instead of a very successful first visit home for Jackson.

A few hours into the trip my phone rang. "It's your sister," Ken said.

"Answer it."

"Hey Fara. Hang on, let me put you on speaker. Jeffrey's driving." Ken fumbled with my phone until he finally managed to activate the speakerphone feature.

"Are you there?" I asked.

"I'm here, although I was convinced Ken was going to hang up on me."

"Me too."

"You two have no faith in my technology skills at all," Ken grumbled. It was true, but it seemed safer to try to ignore his statement rather than confirm it. He was still in a bit of a funk from the sad goodbyes at his family's house.

"So how's Jackson?" Fara must have thought ignoring Ken was the best course of action as well.

"He's out like a light."

"Did you get out from Joyce's okay?"

"Lots of waterworks, but otherwise everything was fine. Except get this, we have stuff strapped on the roof of my car."

"What! Why? That's very WT of you."

"WT?" Ken mouthed to me.

"White trash," I mouthed back.

"No matter what we did we could not get everything in the car. James and I packed and repacked but it was no use."

"Why didn't you just call Ronnie?" Fara asked.

"I know, we should have," I agreed.

"Pay attention to the road," Ken said to me. "And slow down!"

"Listen, we should go. Ken is wigging out."

"That's because he's driving like a maniac," Ken said.

"Okay, but call me as soon as you get home—"

"Cop!" Ken suddenly squealed.

"Oh shit. Fara, I have to go."

Ken closed the phone and I eased off the gas. *How fast had I been going?*

"I told you to slow down," Ken said. He had twisted around in his seat to see if the cop was going to pull us over.

"How fast was I going?"

"Fast. It felt like you were about to break the sound barrier."

I rolled my eyes. "I was probably only doing eighty."

"Only eighty, huh? Do you remember the bitter dads from New Jersey?" Ken asked.

Of course I remembered them. We had met them at Family Week in August the previous year. Ken and I thought it would be a good idea to attend the annual gathering in Provincetown, in preparation for becoming parents. Each year, hundreds of families descend upon the tiny, little gay outpost for a week. Most of the party boys who are there don't seem to mind, as the babies' naps coincide nicely with their disco naps.

We had met the bitter ones at a seminar called "Being a Dad in a Mom's World." They had told a horrible story of getting pulled over by the police with their infant daughter in the back, and very nearly being arrested because the cop thought they had kidnapped her.

"Well, he hasn't turned on his lights," I said. And then I did something truly insane. By coincidence, we happened to be coming up quickly on an exit, and, without thinking, I pulled over into the right-hand lane and took the exit.

"What are you doing?" Ken asked.

"I'm going to try to lose him. Maybe he will just go on by," I explained.

"Oh my God. This is crazy."

I followed the exit up to the highway. There was a gas station just to the right so I quickly pulled in next to the pump.

"This is perfect," I said. "We needed gas anyway."

Ken was still twisted around in his seat, trying to see if the police car had followed us. "Guess who's awake?" he asked. "Jackson, your dad is a crazy man."

"More like a genius. Did you see that move? I totally gave him the slip." I hopped out of the car. "I'll just fill up the tank and then we can be on our way—no, no, no!"

"What?" Ken asked.

"It's the cop," I said. "He's coming up the exit ramp.

"I'm going to shoot you when this is over," Ken promised.

"You aren't going to get a chance because I'm going to shoot myself." Why had I made that hasty exit off the interstate? Nothing screamed guilt like a quick exit stage right.

The police car eased across traffic and pulled in right behind us. He stepped out of his cruiser and tilted his head at me, the way cops do. "Sir, can I see your license?"

"Of course, officer. Did I do something wrong?" I scrambled around for my license in my wallet and handed it to him. He leaned down in the car and solemnly nodded at Ken, then glanced at Jackson, who was sitting in his car seat with a big grin on his face, like he didn't have a care in the world.

"Cute kid," he said, straightening up. "I clocked you going eighty-five a few miles back. You didn't take this exit to avoid me, did you?"

"No," I lied. "We just wanted to gas up. We are on our way home to Dallas. It was Jackson's first trip home to meet his new family."

"I see. I'll be right back," he said. He started to walk back to his car, but stopped and turned back around. "Don't try to make a break for it."

"Oh my God," Ken said from inside the car. "He's on to you."

"Shut it!"

I finished pumping the gas and got back in the car. I had read somewhere that cops find it threatening when people get out of their car.

After what seemed like an eternity, he finally returned and tapped on my window. I eased it down and did my best to try to look contrite. It's a look I don't feature very often so I wasn't sure whether I was pulling it off or not.

"Mr. Roach, the speed limit on this stretch of highway is sixty-five, not eighty-five. Slow down and get your family home safely. Okay?" He passed my license back to me through the window.

"Okay," I whispered.

"Okay. You two have a good day," he said with another nod. Then he straightened up, walked back to his car, got in, backed out and headed back in the direction from which we had come.

"Eighty-five! Just because you didn't get a ticket, don't think you're off the hook," Ken said to me. "And what was that pervy look you were giving him?"

"That wasn't my pervy look." Damn. I knew I was a little rusty with how to properly show remorse. "I was trying to look *contrite*."

"Well, you failed. I couldn't tell if you were constipated or horny."

"Thank you. It's nice to know that the two are so similar in your eyes. Besides, maybe that's why he didn't give me a ticket." I wiggled my eyebrows up and down a couple of times.

"Please stop," Ken said, trying to hide a grin. "And no more speeding."

"No more speeding," I agreed. "Baby Jackson, you must be our good luck charm."

"At least one of you is behaving himself," Ken said. "You could take a lesson from him. We haven't heard a peep from him since we left Louisville."

"Would you hush! Good Lord, you will jinx us." Although I had to admit that Ken was right. Jackson basically just sat in his car seat and looked around or slept. In the few short weeks since he had come home I was still trying to get used to the fact that most of the time he really didn't do that much.

After carefully checking my surroundings in the most exaggerated way possible, I finally started the car, very slowly eased out of the gas station, and headed toward the ramp to the interstate.

"You're such an ass," Ken said.

"What? What have I done?"

"Going super slow? Being overly cautious? Ring a bell?"

I giggled as I pressed down on the gas pedal and the Jag rocketed down the entry ramp to the interstate. "Just trying to honor my commitment to the po po babe."

"You know, I was really afraid back there," Ken said after we had been back on the road for an hour. "All I could think about was those two guys and the story they told."

"Me too. The first thing that went through my head was *Do we have his adoption papers with us?*"

"Which, of course, we do."

"Of course," I said with a grin. "I wouldn't expect anything less from you. But when I thought that, I didn't know if I should be mad or thankful. I mean why should we be under more scrutiny just because we are two guys instead of a man and a woman? But at the same time, is it so terrible if they err on the side of caution?"

"I know. There are no easy answers and we've only been at this a few weeks. Just think of all the good times we have ahead of us."

"Woohoo! And yet things didn't take that turn. He didn't ask us for our papers, like some border guard from a movie. If anything, he seemed to soften up a little when he poked his head in the car and saw you and Jackson."

"Yes. Who knows, baby, maybe things are changing?" Ken said.

"Maybe. Or maybe the couple from New Jersey were expecting the worst and came across as confrontational."

"Maybe."

"I would like to think that we can find a way not to expect people to treat us unfairly. If there's one thing I've learned on this trip it's that, if you give people the benefit of the doubt, if you expect better things from them, sometimes that's exactly what you get. You know?"

"Maybe," Ken said again. I could tell he was grappling with our new reality as much as I was. It wasn't like we were not prepared to be parents, but neither of us had given much thought to how we would *present* as a family. Although both of us had been out to our friends, families and co-workers for years, suddenly we were both out and on display to the whole world. All day everyday.

"Or maybe," I said, trying to lighten the mood, "maybe he just wanted a little taste of all this." I fanned my hand up and down my body like one of the models on *The Price is Right*.

"Oh my God that's foul!" Ken said.

"Hey! I know I've put on some baby weight, but foul seems a bit harsh."

"Not you, goofy. Can't you smell that? Ugh, that's completely toxic."

"What? Is it a skunk? I don't smell—holy shit." The smell had suddenly hit me in the face and I was pretty sure my eyes had watered up. "Actually, I think unholy shit is more accurate. That can't be natural."

"I have to roll down the window," Ken said, choking. He turned around in his seat to look at Jackson. "What have you got going on in there, buddy?" Jackson just gurgled and choked out a couple of pa pa pas.

"Oh don't overreact, it's just a little gas. And it sounds like he brewed it up for his precious papa."

I was trying to play it cool and act like it wasn't a big deal, but the truth was I was on the verge of losing consciousness because the smell was so incredibly bad.

"Honey, I don't think that's gas," Ken said. "The smell isn't going away. I think Jackson has done his business. We have to pull over."

"Pull over? There's no pulling over. We are halfway between nowhere and *Deliverance* out here."

"Aren't we somewhere close to Little Rock?"

"Look around you! Do you see anything? Anything remotely resembling a place to stop? You know that Arkansas stretches on forever!"

Ken and I had made this drive enough times to know that there is a stretch of highway right around Little Rock where you begin to think you will never get out of the state of Arkansas. It's at that point where you begin to gnash your teeth and swear that you will never make this drive again. Usually, by the time the next trip rolls around you've completely forgotten that promise. And the vicious cycle just repeats itself endlessly.

Ken leaned over into the backseat and gave Jackson's bottom a little sniff. "Honestly, I don't think this can wait," he said grimly.

"Did you just sniff his butt? That is wrong. So very wrong," I said, slowing down and guiding the big Jag over to the side of the road.

"So, who gets the honor?" Ken asked timidly.

This would have been the perfect moment to remind Ken that Jackson had been asking for his papa just a few minutes ago. I was still eager to get back at him for that whole name thing, but Ken was looking a little green and I did not want a repeat of the plane incident. "I'll do it." I threw open my door and stepped out of the car. "Although I'm not sure exactly where, since every inch of space is taken up with stuff. What happened to small gifts?"

I opened the back door and Jackson looked up at me with a big grin. "Don't try to butter me up, stinky," I said to him.

I maneuvered him out of his baby seat and tentatively sniffed his diaper. Yes, we were now the kind of parents who sniffed their kids' bottoms to see if they had left a little present in there for us. The shame, the burning shame of it. Fortunately, no one was around to witness this shame; we hadn't seen another living soul for miles.

"Oh yes, there's something lethal in there," I said to Ken.

"The diaper bag is in the floorboard."

I rummaged around in the bag and pulled out a disposable changing pad, which had been a gift from one of our more clever family members.

I spread the plastic pad out on the tiny little square of backseat that was available, eased Jackson onto it and began to unbutton his onesie.

"Oh, there's major leakage," I said to Ken.

"Yeah, I can see some in his car seat."

"Again I say that this is wrong, so very wrong. Where are the wipes?"

"They're in the diaper bag."

"These?" I asked, holding up a nearly empty package. "Where are the rest of them?"

"That's all we have," Ken said sheepishly. "I thought they would be enough to get us home. Just use them sparingly."

"Sparingly? Ken, Jackson is coated in green, wet shit. His car seat is coated in green, wet shit. And soon, I too will no doubt be coated in green, wet shit. How am I supposed to use them sparingly?"

"Calm down. I'm just telling you that there are no more and I can't magically make more appear."

"I truly hate you right now. Do we at least have some kind of plastic bag?"

"Is there one in the diaper bag?"

I rummaged around in the diaper bag, even going so far as to feel for a false bottom where an emergency wipe or plastic bag might be stowed. "None that's immediately obvious," I said through clenched teeth.

It was at this moment that I heard the distant rumble of an approaching car, and burst into hysterical laughter. I couldn't help myself. The visual of a grown man, kneeling beside an open car door, attempting to rescue a baby from an ocean of green poop was just too much.

I continued laughing hysterically as the semi trailer zoomed by us, tooting his horn in a show of solidarity. The laughter turned out to be good medicine and I made a concerted effort to relax. After all, it was only poop. I carefully peeled away the onesie and used what few wipes I had to get as much of the poop off Jackson as I could. I rummaged around in the diaper bag and located some travel bibs that Jennifer had picked up for us that were not quite cloth and not quite plastic. She claimed that they would change our lives.

After a moment's hesitation I used those to soak up as much of the poop as I could from his car seat. I bet Jennifer had no idea how life-changing those bibs would turn out to be.

After working with whatever I could find to clean up and soak up as much of the damage as I could, I remembered that Ken had started the trip with a bottle of water. "Did you drink all of your water from earlier?" I asked.

"No, but it's probably warm by now. We can stop at the next gas station and get you a new one."

I took a deep breath and tried to remain calm. "I don't want to drink it, honey, I want to use it to hose down your filthy child."

"Oh," Ken said with a laugh. "Great idea. Let me help."

Ken felt around under his seat until he found the discarded water bottle, then opened his car door and popped out with the water bottle in hand. "So, how do we do this?"

"I'm not sure. How about I hold him up and you do your best to try to hose off the worst of it?" And so there we stood along the highway with me holding my naked son up in the air while his papa poured water down his stinky little body. It was all very *Moses and the Ten Commandments*. I was just thankful some moron with a video camera didn't happen by and capture the whole thing for *America's Funniest Home Videos*.

When Jackson was reasonably clean, I used his *My Aunt Loves Me* t-shirt that Fara had given us to dry him off. I was afraid I had gotten poop on his portable changing pad so I balanced him on my legs while I strapped him into a new, clean diaper.

Meanwhile, Ken had braved the trunk to try to find something comfortable to put on him. It had taken nearly twenty minutes, but by the time we had finished I was happy with the results. We had somehow managed to survive our first parenting emergency—the classic *my child has pooped and I am ill equipped to deal with it*. I'd like to say that it was the first and last time we experienced that particular emergency, but sadly that would prove not to be the case. You never realize how many restaurants do not have changing stations in the men's room until you have a child of your own to change. Of course, it only took one trip to a restaurant to figure it out. Sometimes choosing a place to eat came down to whether they had a changing station in the men's room.

"Okay, what do I do with all of this?" I said, indicating the assortment of wipes, bibs, plastic changing pad and one misused *My Aunt Loves Me* shirt.

"Do with it? What do you mean?"

"Yes, where can I put it? Are you sure there's not a plastic bag up there somewhere? You didn't see one in the trunk?"

"There's not one up here and I am not getting back in the trunk. I'm pretty sure that the next time we open it is going to be the last time we open it, because I had to do some creative shoving to get it closed."

Creative shoving? I really didn't want to know. There's a reason why James and I didn't ask for Ken's help with packing everything. Ken was a strong believer in the brute force way of making things fit. "Well, I guess I'll tie everything up in a bundle using the last of my bibs and just leave it here on the floorboard."

"What!" Ken squealed. "Honey, we have several hours left in this car. The smell is just awful. Can't you put it in the trunk? Oh, never mind."

"Even if we could open the trunk there's no room back

there. Literally there is not enough room in the trunk for a—" I paused, searching for something appropriately small "—I don't know, a false eyelash."

"What? A false eyelash? Where did that come from?"

"I don't know. I'm frazzled. I smell like poop. I couldn't think of one of my signature quips. But the point is, no, the trunk is out, so we just have to put up with it on the floorboard until we get to the next exit."

"That could be a while."

"We'll be fine."

"You know there is one other option."

"What?" I had racked my brain to come up with another option, so I was genuinely curious to hear Ken's solution.

"We could just leave it here. By the side of the road."

"What! You mean be a litter bug?" As a child who was blitzed by the *Keep America Beautiful* campaign in the mid-seventies, I was practically programmed not to litter. It was ingrained in my brain that littering was something that nice people didn't do. Ever.

Between *Keep America Beautiful* and *Only You Can Prevent Forest Fires*, it's no wonder that my generation felt like the weight of the world was upon their shoulders. Meanwhile, kids today are told to *Just Do It*; never mind the consequences.

"I don't think we have another choice," Ken said glumly. He seemed genuinely contrite. In spite of our dire situation, I took a moment to note the proper way to appear contrite. I figured I would need it again. Perhaps before we could get home.

"Once more let me say that this is wrong." I gathered up my bundle and gently laid it on the side of the road. I was hoping to somehow lessen the impact by not just carelessly tossing it out the window like the world was my personal garbage can. I got back in the car and looked over at Ken. "So very wrong."

A few minutes later, we were back on the highway, our little package neatly tied up discreetly beside the road, like a gift for the God of Poop. Neither of us had spoken a word since I had climbed back in the car.

"I hope you're happy," I finally said, breaking the silence. "Somewhere Iron Eyes Cody is weeping again."

"Huh?"

"From the commercial. The crying Indian."

"You're an idiot," Ken said with a laugh. "Besides, he wasn't even a real Indian. I remember reading somewhere that he was Italian or Spanish or something."

"No! Yet another childhood delusion falls away."

"Sorry to take that away from you."

I let out a sigh as the Manford-Roach caravan continued on its steady and sure path south, toward home. Toward a future filled with magic and discovery, and a house filled with laughter and joy that only a child can provide.

CHAPTER EIGHTEEN

Dallas, June, 2002

"Ken! The baby!" I threw both of my hands up in front of my face in a defensive manner, as if I were about to be mauled by a bear. "I could go blind!"

"I'm thinking of gouging your eyes out right now." Ken held Jackson out toward me again. "Now, please take your son so that I can take this call." Ken was officially working from home and I had taken a sick day. "What kind of idiot has Lasik surgery with a newborn baby in the house?"

"He is not a newborn! He's practically a year old."

"He's not even eight months old."

"Whatever. Besides, it wasn't like I planned this. It was a spur of the moment kind of thing."

"How can Lasik surgery be spur—you know what, never mind. Just keep him occupied long enough for me to get through this call and then you will be off the hook for the rest of the day."

"Fine, just give me a second to get my glasses." I had been camped out in the media room all day recovering from my impromptu Lasik surgery. The doctor had put the fear of God in me when he casually mentioned that for the next twenty-four hours I should be careful as I was at risk of tearing my cornea. I think he said it was the cornea, but it might have been some other important eye part. I snatched up my oversized dark glasses and put them on my face. "Okay, pass him over."

Ken placed Jackson in my outstretched arms, turned, and stomped out of the room. I heard him praying for strength as he made his way to the office he had set up in the front room of our house.

He had been working from there since we brought Jackson home, which had been a huge advantage for us. So far we hadn't had to deal with day care, which we knew from Marti's experience could be both treacherous and costly. Of course, one day our bubble was going to burst and Ken would have to go back to the office, but right now we were just avoiding thinking about it.

I settled Jackson in on my belly and hoped he might take the opportunity to grab a little nap. He had other ideas. As soon as I let my guard down, he reached for my glasses. "Not a chance, big boy," I told him. "Do you want Ray Charles for a dad? Huh? It's mitts off for the next twenty-four hours."

Jackson grinned and let out a stream of nonsense that sounded something like, "Your eyes will be mine!" Well, maybe not that exactly, but at least he was past his endless stream of papa-ing. And none too soon. I was on the verge of demanding that I be called papa when he suddenly started saying other gibberish. I swear I even heard a da da in there somewhere.

For the next hour or so we lay there, belly to belly, and made a game out of him trying to grab my glasses and me trying to ensure that I would be able to see the next day. I had already decided that when I was fully recovered I was giving him those glasses as a toy.

I really was an idiot for getting Lasik done, but I was never one to delay gratification if there was a no-wait option. I always jumped in feet first and hoped that there was water in the pool. Thinking about jumping in feet first reminded me that I still needed to talk to Ken about the pool I wanted to put in the back yard. I had a feeling he wasn't going to take the news well, especially hot on the heels of my Lasik surprise.

"All done," Ken said from downstairs. "Are you okay with him or do you want me to come get him?"

"I'm fine. I've always felt being able to see was overrated."

"You know what else is overrated?" Ken said, coming up the stairs. He stepped into the media room and took Jackson out of my hands. "What?"

"Being a single parent!"

"It's twenty-four hours. I'll be fully recovered by Wednesday."

"That's good, because the *Dallas Morning News* will be here Saturday morning to interview us." After dropping that little bomb, Ken waltzed out of the room and headed back downstairs.

"Wait! What?" I jumped off the couch and nearly broke my neck on the stupid ottoman, which I didn't even want in the first place. Between the dark room and the dark glasses, I couldn't see a damn thing. I slung the glasses off my face and ran down the stairs after Ken.

"The *Dallas Morning News*?" Ken was settling Jackson into his baby cage. I'm pretty sure that wasn't the official name for it, but that's essentially what it was. He already had a *Baby Einstein* video going on the computer and Jackson's eyes were glued to it.

"Yes, it's a newspaper here in town."

"Ha ha. You are hilarious. But seriously why are they coming here to interview us?"

"They are doing a story about gay adoption—"

"And let me guess," I said, cutting him off. "Family Pride gave them your name?" Ken had gotten very involved with Family Pride, an organization that advocated for the rights of gay and lesbian parents.

"They did, and I have been talking to the reporter, she's great by the way, and she will be here Saturday morning with a photographer to interview us."

"Is that who you were talking to right now? I thought you were on a work call?"

"That was her."

"So you risked my vision to talk to a reporter?"

"Yes. And you made it through just fine."

"I don't know about this." I wasn't sure why, but I didn't love the idea of talking to a reporter about our adoption. "I just had Lasik!"

"Which you will be fully recovered from long before she gets here."

"I don't know how I feel about sharing our private life with the world."

Having finally gotten Jackson situated just so, Ken crossed the room, sat down at his desk, and looked over at me. "We're doing it." With that he fired up his computer and got back to work.

I stood there like a mute for a bit, before eventually climbing back up the stairs and collapsing on the couch in the media room. Since Ken obviously wasn't in the mood to discuss this, I decided to call my mom. I should have known better.

***

"I don't like it." I knew Mom wasn't going to be thrilled with the idea of us being interviewed for the paper. I mean, that's the reason I called her in the first place. I was looking for someone to agree with me.

"Me neither, but apparently it's a done deal."

"Hmm." I could feel her stress level, as if it were somehow being transmitted through the telephone wires. Of course that left me with no option but to switch sides to see if I could reassure her.

"It shouldn't be too bad. I don't think Family Pride would put them in touch with us if they were going to write something negative."

"It's not the reporter I'm worried about."

"Then what are you worried about?"

"I don't like the idea of the three of you being so exposed. The world is full of crazy people."

"No kidding, and I'm related to half of them." I was trying to lighten the mood, but she wasn't going for it.

"Jeffrey, I'm serious. People are crazy. And they are mean. I just—I just don't like it. What does Joyce have to say about this?"

"She doesn't know. We just found out about it a little bit ago."

"I bet she won't like it. You should call her." I promised my mom that we would let Joyce know and that I would let her know what Joyce thought. I was starting to regret reaching out to her in the first place.

After hanging up the phone I went back downstairs to talk to Ken. He didn't look up as I came down the stairs so I perched on the bottom step and waited for him to finish what he was doing. After a few minutes he looked my way.

"Yes?"

"Mom doesn't think we should do the interview."

"You told your mom? Are you nuts? She will worry herself to death about this."

"She's already started. She thinks it's dangerous for us to put our family on display to the world at large. In fact, she thinks we should call your mom and get her opinion."

Ken sat back in his chair and seemed to take a moment to collect his thoughts. "I'm happy to call my mom, but, whether she wants us to do this or not, I think we should do it."

"Okay, but why is this so important to you?"

"Because we have to show the world, or at least Dallas, that two gay men are perfectly capable of raising a baby together. Don't you see?" Ken looked at me for confirmation, but after a minute continued on.

"We are very fortunate that we had the means and the wherewithal to adopt Jackson. Not to mention the unwavering support of our friends and families. Not everyone is as lucky as we are."

"So—"

"So allowing the world—"

"Or at least Dallas," I interrupted.

"Yes, allowing Dallas into our home and our lives is our way of giving something back, of trying to help those who don't have the support we had." Damn that Family Pride. Ken had become downright selfless as a result of working with them. I sat there a minute, taking in what he said, before I slowly stood up and started back up the stairs.

"Where are you going?" he asked. I thought I detected a tiny note of panic in his voice.

"I'm going to pick out something to wear. You did say

she was bringing a photographer with her. Right?"

"Right."

"Then I will need to do what I can to try and camouflage the baby weight I've picked up. Doesn't the camera add ten pounds?"

"I'm pretty sure that's video, sweetie."

"I'm not taking any chances. I'll be upstairs in our closet for the foreseeable future. Please bring me a snack if you don't hear from me by dinnertime.

"Okay. But I'm surprised you're able to function properly, what with your Lasik and all." I stopped at the top of the stairs and turned around. "I'm going to pretend like I didn't hear that hateful, hateful comment."

"Love you!"

"Love you too." I turned and headed toward our bedroom, but stopped and returned to the media room for my discarded glasses. One could never be too safe when it came to one's vision.

***

The reporter from the *Dallas Morning News* showed up promptly at ten on Saturday morning with her photographer in tow. Ken was holding Jackson, so I offered to get the door. "Sara?" I asked.

"Yes and you must be—"

"I'm Jeffrey."

"Nice to meet you. You know you sound just like Ken."

"We get that a lot."

"This is Darren." She motioned to the tall, young guy who was trailing behind her and absolutely loaded down with equipment.

"Hey Darren, nice to meet you. Do you need some help with that stuff?"

"He's fine. I wouldn't want him to get used to someone schlepping all that stuff for him. And I'm trying to teach him not to bring so much."

"It doesn't seem to be working." I smiled at Darren who gave me a little shrug.

"I've got it under control," he said.

Ken had wandered into the hallway with Jackson in his arms. "You must be Ken." Sara stuck her hand out and Ken shuffled Jackson into his other arm to shake it. "And this guy must be Jackson."

"In the flesh," Ken said. "Nice to meet you in person, Sara."

"And the guy with all the bags there is Darren," I said. "And we have been forbidden to help him carry them. Sara doesn't want him to get spoiled." Everyone laughed and I was starting to feel like maybe this wouldn't be so terrible after all.

"Where do you want to set up?" Ken asked.

"Why don't we start at the table"—Sara pointed to our oversized dining room table—"and see where it goes from there?"

"Sounds good. You guys make yourselves comfortable. Can I get you something to drink?"

"Water would be great," Sara said. "Darren, do you want a water as well?" He nodded as he continued to fiddle around with all of his equipment.

"I'll get it," I offered. "Why don't you get Sara and Darren situated? Oh, and give me Jackson. I will put him in his swing." Jackson was in love with this swing we had that connected to a door jam and allowed him to bounce around like a Jackson-in-the-box.

I took Jackson from Ken and put him in his swing,

grabbed the waters for our guests and joined everyone at the dining room table. After I handed out the drinks I sat down in the chair next to Ken and looked around at everyone. "So now what?" Once again everyone chuckled and whatever nervousness we might have had completely disappeared.

"Why don't you two just tell me your story?"

Ken and I looked at each other and I said, "It all started when our friend Marti told us she was pregnant."

"Actually," Ken said interrupting me, "it started before that."

I was a little taken aback. Ken and I had told this story a hundred times. I was confused about why he was deviating from our script, but I gave him a little nod to encourage him to continue.

"I grew up always assuming I would get married one day and have kids." Ken stopped and smiled at Sara. "I was actually engaged to a girl in college. If you can believe that."

"I can totally believe it," Sara said. I bet she could. She had stars in her eyes and Ken hadn't even gotten started yet. "What about you Jeffrey? Did you grow up wanting to get married and have a family?"

"No," I said. "I always knew that I was gay, so I never thought those were options for me." Ken reached over and squeezed my hand. "I'm glad I was wrong."

"Trust me, he doesn't admit that very often," Ken said with a laugh.

Sara smiled and I rolled my eyes. "So Ken, you grew up wanting kids and Jeffrey, you grew up thinking it wasn't something you would ever do. How did you end up with a baby?"

"That's where Marti comes in," Ken said. "Jeffrey and

I had always been in motion. We moved from Chicago, to New York, to Louisville—back to New York and then finally here to Dallas.

Once we were here, we bought our house and started making new friends. For the first time our lives felt settled. So when Marti told us she was pregnant, it reminded me of my old dream of getting married and starting a family. I felt like we were in a place to maybe do something about that dream."

"Jeffrey, how did you react to this?" Sara asked.

"I was shocked when Ken told me that he wanted what Marti had. Not in a bad way," I quickly added.

"He was great," Ken said. "Jeffrey shifted his vision of what our lives were going to look like to support my desire to adopt a baby."

"It wasn't a big shift. It's true that I wasn't thinking about a baby, but the minute Ken told me he wanted to adopt it felt right."

"That's amazing," Sara said.

"He's amazing," Ken said and gave my hand another little squeeze.

"You two are going to make me cry," Sara said. "Okay, back to the story. Marti told you she was pregnant—"

"And that changed everything," Ken said.

We spent the next hour taking Sara through our adoption process. Ken took the lead and once he got going he never really stopped and all that was required of me was the occasional nod or gentle nudge to tickle his memory. All the while Darren roamed around the room taking pictures of us from what I was pretty sure were going to be very unflattering angles.

Sara interrupted with the occasional question, or to ask

me how I felt about a particular event. All the while she just kept scribbling notes, even though she had turned on a portable recorder to tape the whole interview. I guessed that the writing helped to anchor our story in her head in a way that a recording would never do.

Eventually Ken had taken her from our early idea of adopting all the way up to bringing Jackson home and introducing him to our families. I couldn't get over how fabulous our story sounded as he told it. Of course, I might have been just a bit predisposed to think this way.

When the interview was over, Darren suddenly came alive. He had more or less been background noise since they arrived, so we were surprised when he clapped his hands together and announced, "It's picture time!" like a kid on Christmas morning.

"Picture time?" I asked. "Haven't you been taking pictures the whole time?

"Those? That was just me stretching, just warming up the old instrument."

Sara rolled her eyes. "Ignore him. He has a very unhealthy relationship with his instrument."

"Don't we all," I muttered. Darren's face turned a bright shade of red as Sara, Ken and I giggled at his discomfort.

"Moving on," he said. "Why don't you get Jackson and let's set up in the front room. There's some great light in there and I have been eyeing that sofa since we got here. I think it's going to look amazing in photographs. The sofa he was eyeing (although it was really more of a loveseat) put the whimsy in whimsical and was easily the gayest thing in our house. Not counting me of course.

I grabbed Jackson, and Darren put us through our paces

as he snapped hundreds of pictures, many of them featuring the bright yellow and blue striped sofa. There were several moments when I was sure he was going to fall and kill himself as he dangled from the stairs, stood on chairs, and contorted himself into a series of incredibly uncomfortable looking poses, all in the name of his art.

When he was finally finished with us and packing up all of his equipment, I leaned down to talk to him. "Let me guess, you're not a photojournalism major?"

"Actually I am, but I'm much more interested in portraits. The photojournalism is just so my parents don't think I'm going to end up jobless."

I thanked him for all the effort he put into capturing the spirit of our family. He blushed and said that was his job, although I knew he had gone well beyond what the job required.

Sara and Ken returned from the impromptu tour Ken had decided to give her of our house.

"I love your house," she said. "Especially the media room. It must be awesome to just veg out in there and play video games."

"I think I love this girl," I said to Ken.

After making sure she had our contact information, Sara opened the front door. "Are you ready to roll, Darren?"

"I'm ready. Oh, hey Ken, if you give me your email address I will send you some pictures. The paper is not going to use more than one. It'd be a shame to let the others go to waste."

"Really? That would be awesome." Ken crossed the room to his desk and plucked out a couple of his personal cards. He handed one to Darren and one to Sara. "Just in case," he said.

"Thanks again," she said. "Come on, Darren, let's get out of here so they can enjoy the rest of their day."

"I'm waiting on you."

She rolled her eyes and gave him a little push. "Men," she grumbled. "Okay, we are off. Ken, I will let you know when the article is going to run."

"Great. And call me if you need anything."

"Will do. I have your card right here," she said with a grin. "Very fancy."

"Oh, we gays are nothing if not fancy," I said with a smirk. Ken's eyes got wide as he looked over at me. "What? Did you think you would get through this whole thing without me being inappropriate?"

"I was hoping." Ken walked Sara and Darren to their car, but didn't let them drive away until Sara promised that my fancy gays comment was strictly off the record.

When he came back in the house and closed the door I hopped up off the couch and walked over to give him a hug and a kiss. "You did great."

"Thank you. And you behaved. For the most part."

"You're welcome. By the way, where is Jackson?"

"What do you mean?" he asked. "I thought you had him."

"No! You took him with you and Sara on the tour." I started to dash up the stairs when Ken broke into giggles.

"Kidding! He's in his swing." I turned and came back down the stairs. "How many times have I told you that it's not *kidding* if it isn't funny?"

"It was kind of funny."

"You know what would have been hysterical? If I tripped and fell in my panic and broke something.

Wouldn't that have been a riot?" I breezed past Ken, went into the kitchen and grabbed Jackson from his swing.

"Just for that Jackson and I are going upstairs to take a nap. Wake us when lunch is served."

"That's too bad. I was thinking we could head to Mi Cocina for lunch. Maybe meet up with Marti, Greg, and Mason to celebrate." Damn him. He was well aware of my weakness for Mexican food and frozen drinks. "But if you want to nap, I suppose I can make us a sandwich later."

"Call the Phillipses while I go put Jackson and me in something more comfortable. These pants are so tight that I lost feeling in my legs about fifteen minutes ago."

"Based on how tight they are, I'm surprised you lasted as long as you did. Do you need some help getting out of them?" Ken wiggled his eyebrows at me.

"Don't push it, Mr. Manford. You are already on thin ice for that *kidding* business. Just call the Phillipses and I'll be ready to go in ten minutes."

"Make it five," Ken said, picking up his phone. I wanted to say something sassy back to him but there was a very real possibility that I would actually need his help getting out of my pants and I couldn't afford to push him too far.

***

"Honey, I'm having a hard time with this." I looked over at Marti who was balancing Mason in one arm and clutching a ginormous frozen margarita in the other.

"Would you like me to take Mason or the margarita?"

"Not this," she said, cutting her eyes between her son and her drink. "I'm talking about your reaction to the interview."

"What part?"

"All of it! It doesn't make sense. You love being the

center of attention."

"I do not love being the center of attention!"

"You do," Marti, Ken and Greg all quickly assured me.

"I wasn't finished. Yes, I'm perfectly comfortable standing on a stage in front of three hundred people and giving a speech, but this just feels different somehow."

"Greg, you are going to have to take the baby. I'm going to need both of my hands free so I can take some big drinks and talk him through this."

"Put him back in his high chair. I told you not to get him out in the first place." Greg was a lawyer and I swear they must teach a class on how to say perfectly reasonable things and still come across sounding slightly superior. As someone who mastered in sarcasm in college I couldn't help but be impressed.

"Um, that was you, shitter. You started to panic when he threw his pacifier and it landed in the bowl of chips on the table next to us."

"Well, it was a little mortifying. Not to mention unsanitary." Greg reached across Marti and took Mason from her and resettled him back in his high chair. "I can't believe Jackson just sits there and never complains. And he doesn't even have a pacifier."

"Don't jinx us," Ken said. He leaned over and gave Jackson a little peck on his forehead. He looked up and grinned at Ken and then went right back to shoving cheerios in his mouth. "Besides, nothing comes between this kid and his next meal."

"Back to me," I said.

"There's that hating to be the center of attention thing again," Marti said. All three of them giggled and even the boys must have thought it was pretty funny because they both cooed right along with them.

"Yeah, yeah. I guess I'm not exactly known for avoiding the spotlight."

"So what is really going on?" Marti asked.

"I'm not even sure I know," I admitted. "I just feel like we are already under so much scrutiny and this is only going to add more."

"I can see that," she said. "I'm sure it gets old being asked questions every time you try to do something simple like run to Target for diapers. I know that would piss me off eventually."

"Don't get me wrong. People have been pretty great for the most part. But even the nice ones are just so damn *curious*."

"Let me ask you a question."

"Like I could stop you."

"True. Knowing that when the three of you go out to do something together you are going to get the looks and the questions, have you let that stop you?"

"Not at all," Ken and I both said.

"Exactly, so, whether you like it or not, for some people you are going to be the first two guys they ever see with a baby." Marti paused for a moment before continuing, "You can meet that curiosity with openness and kindness and show them how fabulous you truly are, or you can let it drive you crazy and be a total asshole about it." She paused again, but this time to take a drink of her cocktail, letting her words sink in. "Like it or not, you three have become participants in the next wave of equal rights for gay people."

"And what is that exactly?" I asked.

"The right to be as ordinary and boring as the rest of

us."

"Welcome to the club," Greg said with a laugh. He raised his glass and we followed suit.

"You're ambassadors whether you like it or not. Every time you sit in a restaurant, go shopping for groceries together, or show up at the mall in December to get Jackson's picture taken with Santa, people are going to look. Some of them are going to be curious and some of them are going to be angry about what they see."

I hadn't really thought about it that way, but Marti was right. I hadn't worried about what others thought of me since high school and I wasn't about to start now.

"You're right, we haven't changed the way we live our lives since we brought Jackson home," I said. "We do what we do as a trio and that's not going to change, but I still don't see how this fits in with my reluctance to be interviewed."

"I'm just saying that if you are going to be the poster family for gay adoption whether you want to or not then turn it into something positive. Who knows, maybe this article is going to end up changing someone's mind. You three are pretty cute." Ken leaned across the table and gave Marti's hand a little squeeze. "Thank you. I haven't been able to figure out how to say why this is so important to me, but what you've just said—it's like you've given me the words."

"You're welcome. Now, do we dare get another round? Not you, Greg, you're driving."

"Or me," I said. "I'm driving as well."

"I guess it's just you and me, Marti," Ken said. He motioned for the waiter and ordered him and Marti another frozen margarita.

We had been fixtures at Mi Cocina since we moved to Lake Highlands. It was a family owned restaurant with very little turnover, which meant we knew just about everyone who worked there. That's why we were a little surprised when our drinks were delivered to the table by the owner instead of our waiter. She was usually working at the front desk, not delivering drink orders.

"Hello!" she said. "I just wanted to come over and say congratulations. I missed you when you came in. First it was the four of you, then it was five, and now there are six." She leaned in and tried to smooth Jackson's unruly hair into place. She turned to Ken and me with a shy smile. "He's from Mexico? Yes?"

"No," Ken said, returning her smile. "He is from Guatemala."

"Ah," she said. "Well, he is very handsome. Just like his papas." She picked up her empty drink tray from the table. "Enjoy your drinks. This round is on the house," she said with a wink.

After she had walked away Marti gave Ken and me a significant look. "I just have one thing to say."

"What's that?" we asked.

"Ambassadors." We all laughed and raised our glasses in another toast to good friends, good food, and good advice.

CHAPTER NINETEEN

Austin, August, 2002

"So I hear Ken is trotting you guys out on stage again today."

"Yes. He's giving a speech and everything, so we will *literally* be on stage. We are on our way to Austin right now for the rally."

"Technically it's a march," Ken said. "Is that Fara?"

"It is."

"It is what?" Fara asked. You would think at this point I would be expert at juggling multiple conversations. God knows I'd had enough practice. "Sorry, that was for Ken. Oh, and he says it's not a rally, it's a march."

"What's the difference?"

This time I thought to put my hand over the microphone. "She wants to know what the difference is between a rally and a march."

"What?" Ken looked at me like I was crazy.

"Fara asked what the difference is between a rally and a march." I took my hand away from the microphone. "Hang on, Fara, he's trying to think of the difference." We both giggled.

"You two are idiots," Ken said. "I meant that it's called the *March* for Equality. Not the Rally for Equality."

"Well *march* definitely sounds better," Fara said.

"She likes *march* better, she says."

"Great, I will be sure to let the organizers know that she approves."

"Meow! Someone is a little catty today. Jackson, tell Papa to be nice." As usual, Jackson just grinned at me. "It's a good thing you are adorable."

"What?" Fara asked.

"Sorry, that was for Jackson. Listen I should go—"

"That's a great idea," Ken muttered.

"Tell him I heard that."

"She says—"

"I heard her. Your sister definitely has selective hearing."

"Tell him I heard that too!"

"Tell her goodbye," Ken said, grabbing my flip phone out of my hand.

"Goodbye!" Ken closed the phone and tossed it back to me. "I'm not sure I managed to get that goodbye in before you cut us off."

"Don't worry, you can tell her one of the other two hundred times you talk today." This would have been a perfect opportunity to come up with some snarky comeback, but in a move that was uncharacteristically reserved, I decided to hold back. Ken had been a nervous wreck since he agreed to speak at the march.

The feedback from the article in the *Dallas Morning News* was overwhelmingly positive. Ken came across as passionate and articulate and the picture of the three of us on that crazy sofa was just about the sweetest thing I had ever seen. Darren was a very talented photographer. Just as he promised, he had sent digital copies of the entire photo shoot and we had then sent them to everyone we knew. They all seemed to agree: We were definitely camera-ready as a family.

As a result, we had become the go-to family for any press opportunities that came to Family Pride. Most of them had been phone interviews, but a couple of weeks ago they had called and asked Ken if he would be one of the speakers at the March for Equality in Austin.

"Why are you so nervous? You are a pro at these by now."

"This one is different," Ken said.

"How?"

"Well, this one is just me. Out there on a stage in front of all of those people."

"Jackson and I will be there."

"You will?"

"Of course! The wife and kids are always in the background. I'm sure they'll have some place they want us to stand and look supportive."

"And you don't mind?"

"Mind? Why do you think I worked so hard on my hair and Jackson's outfit?"

Ken giggled. "I did wonder what that was all about."

"Seriously, we will be very proud to stand up there with you." I gave Ken's shoulder a little squeeze. "You've got this."

Ken let out a breath and most of the tension seemed to melt away from him. "Thanks. That makes me feel a lot better."

I smiled at him. "You are going to be amazing."

***

After a moment of confusion trying to find parking and

a moment of panic when we thought we had forgotten Jackson's diaper bag, we were finally ready for Ken's big close up.

"Where's the stage?" I asked, looking around.

"It's at the Capitol."

"Okay, where's the Capitol?"

Ken stopped and pointed. "It's up there somewhere." I looked in the general direction he pointed, but all I could see were trees and traffic. "Why have we parked so far away?"

"Because," Ken said just as we rounded a corner and emerged into a sea of people, "we are going to *march*."

"Oh shit. A rally sounds pretty awesome right now."

By the time we had marched up to the Capitol, Jackson was a Sweaty Betty and starting to get fussy. Still, he was holding up better than me. All the work I had put into my hair had been negated by the Austin humidity.

Someone met us at the edge of the stage and motioned for us to follow them. Just as I had predicted, there was a semi-circle of chairs for the friends and families of the three speakers.

Jackson, Ken, and I were directed to two of the chairs closest to the microphone. I was so happy to be off my feet that I almost didn't care what a mess I must have looked. Almost.

"What's the damage?" I whispered to Ken.

"You look great," he said. He put his arm around the back of my chair and pulled me in close to him.

"Sweetheart, I love you, but it's a thousand degrees out here."

Ken laughed and let me go. "Here, give me Jackson until it's my turn to talk. That will give you a chance to cool off a bit. He's like a little oven."

"No kidding." With Jackson off my lap it was definitely cooler, but I was still wilting.

"Here, baby." I looked up to see this giant of a man holding out a fan to me. "You look like you are about to melt."

"You are a life saver," I said, taking the fan.

He laughed and collapsed into the chair next to mine. "Is this your first time speaking at an outdoor event in Texas?"

"Can you tell?"

He threw his head back and laughed again. "A little. Don't worry, you never get used to it. The good news is that if this thing gets boring you can always hide a yawn behind these as well." He motioned to his fan and gave it a little flutter. "Watch and I'll demonstrate." In the midst of fanning he moved his hand forward, as if he was scratching his nose with it.

"Did you see that?" he asked.

"I didn't see anything!"

"Exactly." He stuck his hand out. "I'm Bill."

I shook his hand. "I'm Jeffrey."

"Yes I know," he said. "You know you three are making a difference." I cocked my eyebrow at him. "You are. You are giving people a different look at what it means to be gay."

"Really?"

"Really. Sometimes the only time they see us is when we are dancing naked in the streets during Pride. Not that there's anything wrong with that. I love the sheer joy of that, but it's not the only thing we are." He smiled at me. "Sometimes we are super hot daddies with a baby." We both giggled behind our fans.

"Behave," Ken whispered to me. "I think we are about to get started."

Bill elbowed me and leaned over to whisper in my ear. "I've always had a soft spot for a bossy man." I rolled my eyes and took Jackson from Ken's arms just as he was being introduced to the crowd.

Ken walked up to the microphone and I held my breath and crossed my fingers.

"My name is Ken Manford. I am a gay parent and a proud member of Family Pride. My partner Jeffrey and I have been together for over ten years. A couple of years ago we decided that it was time to grow our family, so we began the process of adoption and within a year brought our beautiful son Jackson home from Guatemala.

We are your typical family. We have careers, we love our son, participate in community events and enjoy spending time with our friends and neighbors.

It is devastating that our country and our state and local officials continue to try and deny our family the rights that our friends, family, and neighbors enjoy. When I talk with people about the many risks our family faces because we do not have equal rights under the law of marriage, they tell me that they had no idea.

That's why it is important that each and every one of us speak up, stand up and demand that we are entitled to the same rights as our neighbors. We pay the same taxes and contribute equally to a country that does not afford us the rights of other citizens.

Jeffrey, Jackson and I were recently featured in an article for the *Dallas Morning News*. While most of the feedback was positive there were people who commented on the legitimacy of gay parenting. It's disheartening to see people try to turn gay adoption and marriage into a political issue. To try and own the word family.

Let me be clear. Love makes a family. My partner of ten years and our son make a family. And our parents and our siblings have welcomed us with open arms.

We will no longer be treated as second-class citizens, forced to file separate income taxes even though we share a home, bank accounts, and the responsibility of raising a child. Stand up with me and tell our legislators that our children are the future of this country and discriminatory laws jeopardize their futures.

I believe it is in the best interest of this country to protect all families and ensure that our nation's civil rights laws provide an environment that will discourage fear and bigotry." The crowd cheered and Ken glanced over at me. I gave him a thumbs up and tried to get Jackson to do the same, but his ended up being more like a fist up.

"Thank you for being here with my family today."

Ken finished his speech and came back to sit with me and Jackson, I leaned over and gave him a kiss.

"What was that for?" he whispered.

"For doing such a good job. And for pushing me to do this and the interviews."

During Ken's speech I had sat there on the stage with Jackson trying to stay focused and be supportive, but my mind was racing.

I had always felt like I wasn't particularly good at being gay. I didn't like going to bars. I always skipped gay pride if I could get away with it, and I never felt comfortable in my skin if we were in a big gaggle of gay boys. It brought out all of my worst insecurities.

Sitting there next to Bill, I realized that I was as guilty as some straight people when it came to stereotyping what it meant to be gay. If I was guilty of believing these kinds of stereotypes as a gay man, why wouldn't people who never interacted with gay people believe them to be true as well?

"You really thought it was okay?" Ken whispered.

"Really. And you were right. Sometimes you have to lead by example. I think I finally get it, so whatever you need us to do. I'm ready."

"Yeah?

"Yes."

"Great, because I'm thinking of joining the Board of Directors for Family Pride." I sat there for a minute, letting his news sink in.

"I waltzed right into that one didn't I?"

"You totally did," Ken said with a smile.

"I think it's a great idea," I said and gave him another kiss. Surprisingly enough, I meant it. In the next few years, Ken would go on to become a very active board member for the organization and eventually serve as the Chair.

During his tenure I would stand by him for countless fundraisers, parties and interviews. I was happy to do it, because I hoped in some way to demonstrate that gay people come in all kinds of shapes and sizes and that some of us are hot daddies with a baby.

CHAPTER TWENTY

San Antonio, September, 2002

Although we had taken measures to ensure that Jackson was as legally bound to me and my family as he was to Ken and his, Ken had not given up on getting me recognized as Jackson's second parent. It seemed insane that we had to go to such lengths to make sure that another adult was legally responsible for the well-being of a child. You'd think the courts would see the wisdom of numbers when it came to having as many people as possible invested in a child's well-being. You would be wrong.

For months Ken had been working with an attorney in San Antonio named Sharon, who had been referred to us by a lesbian couple who had successfully gotten the second mom recognized as a co-parent. Just like the lawyer we had worked with on securing my legal rights, Sharon had a reputation for working tirelessly to help gay and lesbian couples get a second parent adoption in Texas.

I was seriously starting to wonder what we would do if it wasn't for all of these amazing women who were advocating for our rights—with virtually no recognition or compensation. It was yet another reminder that, if Ken and I could do anything to help people become more comfortable with gay parenting, we owed it to future parents to do it.

When the opportunity for our second parent adoption presented itself in September it was like something from the underground railroad. A last minute phone call; a mad dash to San Antonio; an endless wait in the office of our lawyer and then a secret and rushed moment in front of a sympathetic judge. Now that it was all over and we were headed back to Dallas, the long hours and my high-strung nerves had caught up to me. I felt like I had been run over by a truck. After running a marathon. In heels.

We had gotten the call from Sharon at six that morning, telling us we needed to be in her office in San Antonio by noon. We had made the trip a few years ago with my family on vacation, so we knew the drive was right around four and a half hours. That meant we had to be on the road by seven.

"Can you do it or not?" Sharon had asked.

"We can do it," Ken said. We had both jumped out of bed and started trying to get ourselves and Jackson ready, dressed, and out the door in forty-five minutes. Just as we were about to leave we remembered Patsy. For once in her life she had stayed out of our way, but we found her sitting patiently by the garage door when we came downstairs to load the car.

I grabbed her leash and gave her the world's fastest walk, packed up Jackson's diaper bag, found a couple of breakfast bars for Ken and me, and we hit the road.

We had been driving for about an hour when we realized we had forgotten to bring a camera so we wouldn't be capturing this moment for our families. I knew they were going to be unhappy with us, but I felt like we were lucky to even have remembered Jackson.

By 11:30 we were sitting in the waiting room of Sharon's small office in San Antonio, a little worse for wear, but well under the deadline.

"Ken?" Sharon said, coming into the room.

Ken stood up and walked over to shake her hand. "This is Jeffrey and Jackson." We all said hello.

She tapped her watch and looked at the three of us. "Impressive. I guess all those stereotypes about gay men taking forever to get ready are overstated." She winked at us. "Right this way."

We followed her down a short hallway to her office and took a seat opposite her in a little sitting area. There was a stack of papers on the coffee table. I hoped I wasn't going to have to read those on an empty stomach.

"Don't worry. You don't need to read these," she said, resting her hand on the papers. "This is kind of like when you buy a house. You know all those closing papers?" Ken and I both nodded. "Nobody reads those. You just keep signing and initialing until you are done." Sharon looked at the two of us for a second before smiling. "I'm kidding. I'm going to walk you through everything."

She spent the next thirty minutes taking us through all of the paperwork and explaining what everything meant. We were both excited that Jackson would be getting my last name that day. Ken and Greg had attempted to change his name when we first brought him home, but a Dallas judge had refused to do it.

Once everything was signed, initialed, and notarized, Sharon gathered up the papers to go make a copy.

"What do we do now?" I asked.

"Now we wait for a break in the judge's calendar. As soon as that happens her clerk will call me and I will hustle the three of you over to the courthouse."

"Is that far?"

"It's right across the street. You didn't think I picked this office for its décor did you?" Ken and I both laughed. "Once we get to the courthouse the judge's clerk will meet us outside of her chambers and take us in."

"And then what?" I asked. "Anything in particular we should say?"

"Or not say," Ken added, giving me a pointed look.

"Don't say anything until she asks you for information. Believe me, it won't be hard and it won't take long. We've worked with this judge before and it's all very easy. You will be in and out in ten minutes."

"Wow, ten minutes for something that could potentially change our lives. And to think so many judges wouldn't be willing to give us those ten minutes." The look on Ken's face when he said this was so sad that I had to look away.

"You're right. Most of them wouldn't."

"So why does she?" I asked. "Is she a lesbian?"

"No. She's not a lesbian, or an activist or even a liberal. But she is a Texan. And that means she doesn't like being told what she can and cannot do."

"God bless Texas," I said under my breath.

Sharon looked at me and smiled. "Just make yourselves comfortable while I go make copies. We could be waiting here for a while."

After she was out of sight, Ken dropped his head onto my shoulder. "Maybe I should have adopted you instead."

"Are you talking to me?" I asked.

"Yes."

"That's really creepy. I'd be living in delicious sin with my father, raising my brother. Uh, yuck. I need to go shower just hearing you say that."

"I don't know how to break it to you, baby, but you needed a shower before I said that."

"What!" I leaned down to take a discreet sniff of my armpits. "I don't smell anything. Am I stinky?"

"I'm kidding. Sit still, you're jostling me.

"I'm going to jostle you if you don't stop with the kidding. How many times have I told you that it's not kidding if no one thinks it funny?"

"I seem to recall hearing you say that a couple of times."

"More like a couple of hundred. First you try to land us on Springer with your *I married my gay son* routine and then you tell me I need a shower. You are a comic genius."

"I know. Besides, I look way too young to be your father. If anything, you'd have to adopt me."

I shifted around on the sofa and this time Ken's head fell off my shoulder and hit the back of the cushion. "Hey, watch Papa's head, *Son*."

"Shut. Up."

A couple hours later, Sharon rushed into the room and announced that it was time to go. Although we had been waiting for this moment, it suddenly felt like we were being rushed. We started pulling all of our stuff together and trying to shove Jackson's toys into his diaper bag.

"Just leave all that. We will come back here after it's over and you can pack it up then." Sharon turned and walked out of her office and Ken and I had no choice but to follow her or get left behind.

She ushered us across the road and into the courthouse where we were met by the judge's clerk.

"Hey Tammy," Sharon said. "Is she ready for us?"

"She is," Tammy said. "We only have a few minutes so

let's get in there and get these boys on their way back home." She started moving in the direction of the courtroom. "Cute baby," she said over her shoulder as she pulled open the doors.

Sharon led us through the courtroom and right up to the judge's bench. She stepped up and put the paperwork in front of the judge, who picked it up and started reading it.

"Ken Manford?" she asked.

"Yes, ma'am," Ken said.

"Jeffrey Roach?"

"That's me," I said and raised my hand.

"Jeffrey, you are petitioning for a second parent adoption of Jackson Manford. Is that correct?"

"It is," I said.

"And Ken, is this your wish as well?"

"Very much so."

She smiled. "You look like you will make a wonderful family." She scribbled her name on the paperwork and handed it to the clerk who worked with Sharon to quickly get everything finalized. "Congratulations, Mr. Roach. It's a baby boy."

"Thank you," Ken and I both said.

Sharon took us by the arm and led us out of the courtroom. When we got to the door she turned to Tammy. "Thank you."

"Anytime," Tammy said with a smile. Sharon pushed open the doors and we walked out of the courtroom as Jackson's parents of record.

When we stepped out of the courthouse I pulled on Sharon's arm before she could trot us back across the road. "Anything you want to share with us?"

"What?" She could barely keep the grin off of her face. "I never said her clerk wasn't a lesbian."

"This whole lesbian cartel frightens me."

"We are a scary bunch," she said. "Now stand over there on the steps of the courthouse and I'll take your picture. I'm guessing you forgot to pack your camera."

"You are guessing correctly," Ken said. He took Jackson from my arms and the three of us settled ourselves on the steps of the courthouse.

Sharon snapped a couple of pictures with a disposable camera and then handed it over to Ken. "You know if I were a doctor I'd charge you $1000 for that camera."

"And we would happily pay it," Ken said.

"Don't worry, it's on the house. Now let's get back to my office so you guys can hit the road. If you are lucky you can get back to Dallas in time for dinner."

"Sounds good to us," Ken said. Twenty minutes later we were packed up and on the road.

We pulled into the garage at seven, twelve hours after we had left. It was hard for me to believe how much our lives had been changed by the last twelve hours. Ken must have been feeling the same way, because neither of us said more than a couple of words as we got our stuff out of the car and into the house.

Jackson had fallen asleep in his car seat. Luckily you could detach the seat from the frame, so we decided to leave him in it. There was even a handle that made it easy to carry. We sat him next to us on the floor and crashed on to the sofa. Patsy finally heard us and slowly made her way down the stairs. Her tail was wagging like crazy. "I need to walk her," I said. "Poor thing has been cooped up in here all day." I started to get up.

Ken pulled me back down next to him. "Marti came by and walked her for us. Twice. She went out about an hour ago."

"I guess that explains her leisurely stroll down the stairs. I was afraid she had left us a little present upstairs and was ashamed to face us."

Ken laughed. "Let's not talk about dog poop right now."

"Kind of spoiling the moment for you?"

"Kind of," he said. "I'm really happy right now."

"Me too," I said. "I can't believe I'm actually his dad."

Ken took me by the chin and turned my face toward his. "You were always his dad. A piece of paper doesn't make that any more or less true."

"I know, but I'm still happy to have it."

"I am too, but I didn't do this because it would validate you as his dad. I did it because it is the right thing to do. There's no reason we shouldn't be afforded the same rights as any other couple."

"Thank you for sticking with it. I didn't think it would be a big deal, but I was so emotional when she signed the papers I thought I was going to cry."

"You?"

"I know, right? I only cry when I get a paper cut or stub my toe."

"That's you," Ken said. "Hardhearted Hannah."

"Yep." We both burst out laughing. "You are so full of it," Ken said.

"I really am," I agreed.

"But I love you anyway."

"I love you too, and seriously, thank you for doing this."

"You're welcome. Now we just need to get his birth

certificate reissued with both of us listed as his parents."

I sighed and settled back on the couch. *There's no rest for the weary*, I thought. Or for gay parents who have to fight for the same rights that straight couples take for granted. Thank goodness I had my very own activist who was ready to take on the world to make sure that Jackson and I were treated fairly.

CHAPTER TWENTY-ONE

Dallas, October, 2002

On Friday October 11th, 2002, the senate approved the Iraq war resolution by a vote of 77-23. It was a move that would later prove immensely unpopular and lead to Barrack Obama becoming the first African American President of the United States. But the Manford-Roach family's thoughts were much closer to home, as our son Jackson continued his slow march toward adulthood. Or slow crawl I should say, as Jackson had yet to take his first step.

"Who's idea was this anyway?" I asked.

"Yours," Ken said. "You suggested it to my mom at Jackson's baby shower, probably to cover for some smartass comment that she had overheard."

"That's right. She just appeared out of nowhere. A trick I've yet to master, by the way. I was joking that I wanted Joyce to plan my next birthday party, but somehow it turned into everyone coming down here for Jackson's first birthday party."

"And now his first birthday has arrived and they're all on their way," Ken said. "Did you hear that, little guy? The whole crew is coming down to celebrate with you."

Jackson seemed to be taking everything in stride as he

gnawed happily on one of his wooden blocks. He had followed us from room to room that morning as we went about cleaning, organizing, and preparing our house for visitors.

We had strategically set up a number of diversion stations throughout our house so we could clean without worrying what he was up to. He had bounced along happily in his bouncy seat while I picked up his toys, swung from the doorframe of our master bedroom closet while I scrubbed toilets and tubs, rattled the cage of his pop-up play center while Ken cleaned the kitchen, and sat with Ken and watched *Baby Einstein* while I vacuumed and swept the various carpets and hardwood floors.

And now he played happily on the big, colorful mat that dominated the entryway of our house. Our front door opened to a sweeping spiral staircase with rooms on both the left and right. We had devoted the space on the left to Jackson's play area. There was a floor-to-ceiling window that Ken and I sat staring out, expectantly, even though our families were all several hours away.

"I'm excited they're all coming, but I still don't know where on earth we are going to put everyone." Now, just a few hours before their arrival was probably not the time to start thinking about space, but parenting a nearly-one-year-old is exhausting. You can't afford to waste time and effort on things that are too far into the future to matter. But waiting to figure everything out until the day before the big celebration was probably not the smartest thing to do. What was once far off into the future was about to go down in just a few hours.

I had also put off thinking about the details, like sleeping arrangements, because I never believed that everyone would be able (or willing) to take off from work, pile into their cars, and make the twelve-hour trek to Dallas to celebrate our son's first birthday. I was wrong.

"Maybe we should pitch a couple of tents in that giant cement hole you have dug in our back yard."

"It's actually gunite, not cement."

"That makes me feel a lot better."

"Hey, it's not my fault that they are behind schedule. Blame the rain."

"True, but it is your fault that we are having a pool put in our tiny little back yard at the same time as we are about to host both of our immediate families and God knows how many friends."

"You agreed to the pool," I reminded him.

"I agreed to *looking* into getting a pool put in next year."

I sighed and nodded my head. "I know, but you should have known better. You know I have no patience. The only answer I would have understood was, 'No!'"

"So the giant cement death trap—"

"Gunite!"

"Sorry, so the giant gunite death trap in our back yard is my fault?"

"Exactly," I said. "I'm glad we've got that settled. Now, let's get back to the sleeping arrangements."

"Well," Ken said, "I was thinking we could put my mom and dad in the guest room."

"Agreed, and maybe my mom could sleep with Jackson in his twin bed. She's still a little nervous that we have taken him out of his crib so early."

"Are you sure she won't mind?" Ken asked.

"Mind? No, she'll be thrilled, but maybe we should take the bumpers off first."

"As long as you're certain she won't roll out of bed and hurt herself," Ken said with a laugh.

"I'm pretty sure she will be okay. But that still leaves us with Jennifer, James, and the twins, Mike, Josh, Fara, and her three. And Dad, if he decides to come." My dad is the type of person who doesn't commit to going on a trip until the day of the trip. It's maddening.

I dropped my head into my hands. "I think I'm about to have a panic attack."

"Tell Daddy to take a breath, Jackson."

Jackson looked up at me and waved his block. Although it took a little longer than I liked for him to catch on, there was no doubt in his mind who Daddy was. "Dada!"

His entire face was covered in slobber. I reached over and tried to dry some of it off with my sleeve. "You're a mess, buddy."

"Dada!"

"How about this? We'll put the Aero bed in the media room for Jennifer and James. And maybe one of the twins can sleep with them, and the other can sleep with my mom and dad."

"Keep going," I said with a laugh. "You've only got seven more bodies to hide."

"Don't stress about this, baby," Ken assured me. "They're not coming for a vacation. They are coming to celebrate Jackson's first birthday. They won't care where they sleep."

He was right. They would gladly sleep in the car if they had to. Or in a tent in the middle of an empty pool. Except I was determined to fill that pool with water before the party the next day. This was something that I had yet to share with Ken.

When we started planning Jackson's first birthday party, our families tried to convince us it would be easier for us to go to Kentucky to celebrate it with them. But Ken was determined that Jackson should celebrate his first birthday in his own house. He had found an unlikely ally in Joyce, who agreed that the first birthday should be at home, and reminded everyone that was the plan from the very beginning. This, despite the fact that the trip would probably be the most brutal on her and her bad knees.

I was agreeable to staying in Dallas because I didn't want to referee between my family and Ken's on where we would celebrate the actual birth date in Kentucky. So after hours of endless phone calls and negotiations, both of our families had ultimately agreed that everyone would make the twelve-hour drive from Kentucky to Dallas.

Kenny, Joyce, Jennifer, James, Mike and the twins would depart from Louisville. My sister, her husband Josh, Mom, Sydney, Alex and Nick would depart from Hartford. Oh, and my dad would turn up at my sister's house if the spirit moved him on the morning of the trip.

Actually, it was more the flesh than the spirit. My dad was in really poor health, and was determined to die in Kentucky. "The old man isn't feeling very well," he would say. "So I better sit this one out. If I'm going to die I want to die looking at Green River." Yes, this was the reason he would often give for bowing out of a trip at the last minute. Whose brain worked like that?

"Well the couch in Jackson's room makes out into a full-size bed," Ken reminded me.

"You mean the one we gave to Marti?" I asked.

"Uh-huh, I told you we would need it."

"You are so bitter," I said. "Let me think." Just then the

phone rang. "Ah, saved by the bell." I ran into the kitchen and snatched up the phone.

"We're all settled in," my sister said, completely bypassing hellos.

"Fara! You guys are just now heading out? What happened? Did Dad decide he would go and delay you getting on the road?" I was stunned. My sister was a notorious whip-cracker when it came to trips. If she said she was leaving at six, everyone knew she meant five. Anyone who wasn't ready ran the very real risk of being left behind.

"No dumbass, we're here in Dallas. We just checked into our hotel."

"What? Your hotel? Okay, slow down. First of all, how did you get here so fast? You must have left at midnight."

"Is that Uncle Jeffrey?" Alex shouted in the background.

"Dude," he shouted "Arkansas sucks!"

"Alex, get out of my face so I can talk, or I will break your arms and legs," Fara threatened.

"Well, it does suck!" Alex insisted. As Fara's middle child he was the least afraid of her.

"You know what's really going to suck?" she asked. "When your brother or sister has to push you around in a wheelchair for the rest of your life."

"Fara!" I shouted. "Back to me!"

"But—"

"Go! Put on your swim trunks and go explore the pool."

"But the sign said there was no lifeguard on duty," I heard Nick say in the background.

"Well, that's just a bonus," Fara snapped. And then she

was back in my ear again.

"Yeah, as you can see my crew needs a little space to spread out, so I decided to just rent us a couple of hotel rooms. Plus the kids wanted to be able to swim. And since you've screwed up your pool situation—"

"It's not my fault it rained. Besides, it wasn't about swimming. It was just for looks. Who swims in October?"

"Kids. They don't care, they'd swim in December if you let them. Which I probably would if it got them out from under my feet."

"Well, thank you. Because I have to say I'm not sure where I was going to put everyone."

"I figured you were overestimating your space, not to mention your patience."

"True. Tell Josh that we'll pay for the room."

"Josh didn't come."

"What? I thought he was looking forward to it."

"He was, but they wanted him to come in and work a half day today."

"Okay, so why didn't you just wait for him?"

"He knew my schedule. He could have said no."

"Harsh," I whispered, more than a little impressed at her resolve.

"Besides, with Dad, I don't think we could have squeezed him in anyway."

"And the hits keep coming," I said. "So you have Dad with you? And Mom?"

"Of course. Do you think I could have snuck away without her? She practically slept in the car last night."

"What's going on?" Ken finally asked.

"I'm on the phone with my sister, they're staying at some lowbrow motel somewhere on the outskirts of

Dallas."

"We're at a Courtyard you big freak," Fara said in my ear. "I had free nights."

"You see, Ken," I said, "my family is willing to make great sacrifices for our happiness. Fara's kids will be having breakfast with men who have more tattoos than teeth. All so that your family can relax in the sprawl of our perfect home."

"Whatever," Ken said. "I thought you might want to know that my family just pulled into the drive."

"What! Has the whole world gone crazy? They're early. Like several hours early."

"They are," Ken said, heading to the door.

"Fara, I have to go, the Manfords are here."

"Okay, we'll call you in a bit and figure out a plan."

"Okay." I hung up the phone and sprinted toward the door. Ken had picked Jackson up out of his bouncy seat and was waving his little arm at his family as they unfolded themselves from the minivan. Based on how enthusiastically Ken was waving it, I feared I'd be reattaching Jackson's arm later that day.

"So are the kids headed to the pool?" he whispered.

"Pretty much," I whispered back.

"Truck stop, huh? Maybe there's room for me there."

I shot him one of my more deadly glances. "You're not going anywhere. Now smile, we are going to have the best birthday ever, even if I have to shoot someone."

"Hey guys, how was the drive?"

"Long!" they shouted in unison.

"Well, let's get your stuff inside before you melt," Ken said. "Can you believe it's this hot in October?"

"Jeffrey—"

"I'm on it," I said. You guys head in and James and I will get the bags.

"What?" James said. "Thanks for volunteering me."

"You're welcome."

"Every time I see you I'm carrying bags," he said. "But at least there are not as many this time."

"Oh shut up and grab a suitcase. There's a beer on the other side of this for you."

"Beer? I heard there was going to be a pool."

"Don't mention the pool," I threatened. "If you want to live through the weekend, don't mention the pool."

It took several trips, but eventually James and I had everything unpacked and piled in the entryway of the house. It would have probably gone a lot quicker if we had a little help, but everyone else was standing in the dining room, looking at the pool.

"This must be really good," James said, motioning across the room.

"Oh it is," I assured him. He put the final bag down and walked over to join everyone at the windows and immediately started laughing. "Hey, did you guys know your pool is getting a little low on water?"

"Shut up James." I walked over to join everyone else.

"I thought it was going to be finished by now," Ken's dad said.

"So did we," Ken said.

"And it is basically finished," I explained. "We are just a couple of days behind schedule. The only thing left to do is plaster it and fill it up with water."

"Well, the plants look nice," Mike said. "I love the palm trees."

"Me too," Joyce said. "But I guess this means the party

will need to be indoors tomorrow. It would make me a nervous wreck to have the kids out there."

"It would make me a nervous wreck to have you out there," Kenny said. She rolled her eyes at him. "I think I could manage. Why don't you do something useful and take our bags upstairs?"

"Come on," Ken said. "Everybody grab a bag and I will show you where you will be sleeping."

"Not me," Jennifer said. "I've got Jackson." Joyce leaned over and scooped Jackson out of Jennifer's arms.

"Mamaw's got Jackson. You go get a bag."

Ken led the crew upstairs and started getting everyone situated. Joyce and I sat on the couch in the front room and chatted while she played with Jackson.

"Have you heard from Fara?"

"I have. She decided to get a couple of hotel rooms nearby."

"Oh?"

"Yes, she promised the kids they could swim on this trip, and with the pool situation she thought it would be easier to just stay in a hotel." I'm not sure I completely believed Fara's pool excuse, but I didn't want Joyce to feel like her group was pushing my family out of the house.

"Well, that will be fun. Are they coming over today?" Just as Joyce was asking me this question the doorbell chimed. "Wow, look at that. I must be psychic."

"Actually," I said, "I don't think that's them. I think that's the workers."

"The workers?"

"For the pool."

"Oh! Well, this ought to be interesting."

I got up and opened the door and said hello to the guy

who was serving as the foreman for our pool construction. He didn't look particularly happy to see me.

"We are here to plaster the pool."

"I really appreciate you squeezing this in today," I said.

"It wasn't like you gave me a lot of options. Especially when you reminded me that if someone fell in and broke their neck during your son's *first* birthday party it would probably scar him for life."

"You have to admit that would be hard to put behind you. But I really do appreciate you agreeing to come today."

"Yeah, we should probably get started. The entire crew is on overtime right now, since this is our *second* pool of the day."

"Absolutely. What do I need to do?"

"Just unlock the side door so they can get in and we will take care of the rest."

"Got it. I will do that now." I closed the front door and turned to yell for Ken to come downstairs, but he was already on his way down.

"Hey, I was just about to yell for you. Can you come lock the back door behind me? I need to open the side door for the pool guys."

"What?"

"They're here to plaster and fill the pool."

"Today! Why is this the first I'm hearing about this?"

I shrugged my shoulders and headed for the back door. "Lock this behind me." I slipped outside and walked around to the side door to let the workers in. We had been required to add locked doors that led to our back yard as a safety precaution for the pool.

I took a deep breath before stepping back through the

front door. I knew I was probably going to be in a lot of trouble. I had deliberately not told Ken about the pool being plastered today. I figured he would have been against it, since it added another layer of chaos to an already hectic weekend. He thought the pool was being plastered the following weekend.

I didn't actually lie. The pool was scheduled to be plastered and filled the next weekend but I had used every dirty trick in the book to convince our foreman to move the job up a week. I was pretty sure I had made an enemy for life, but I was determined to have water in the pool for Jackson's birthday party.

I opened the front door to find Ken standing there waiting for me with his arms crossed.

"Before you start yelling—"

He stepped up to me and gave me a big hug. "You're amazing. I don't know how you pulled this off, and I probably don't want to know, but you are amazing." I was so surprised by his reaction that I didn't know what to say.

"Oh, and look, here comes your family." That snapped me out of it.

"Woohoo!" I said. "Let the fun begin."

It turned out that getting the pool plastered was a stroke of genius on my part. Kenny, Dad, Mike and James were completely fascinated by the whole process and it kept them busy for most of the day.

The kids were all ushered upstairs to play video games and everyone else was more than happy to spend the day giving me a hard time about what would henceforth be known as the pool fiasco. We had survived our first day and managed to get everyone bedded down fairly early, in anticipation of the big birthday the next day.

***

The record high in Dallas for October 11th is 101 degrees, and the record low is only twenty-four. But on the Friday of Jackson's first birthday the weather was a spectacular seventy-five degrees and sunny.

My eyes had snapped open at six o'clock and I drug myself out of bed, heading downstairs to brew the coffee. I wasn't surprised to find that Kenny was already up as well. Ken's dad had been getting up for work at four in the morning for over forty years and his body didn't quite know what to do with retirement.

"Morning," he said cheerfully as I came dragging into the kitchen.

"Morning Kenny. Do you have coffee yet?"

"Nah, I couldn't figure out the machine."

"Yeah, it's complicated. You pour the beans in the top, it grinds them, and then somehow transfers them to the basket."

"That sounds complicated. I can barely work our Mr. Coffee."

I fussed with the temperamental machine, anxious for that first cup of coffee. Kenny watched me carefully as I went through the motions.

"Did you get all of that?" I asked him.

"No," he said. "I lost you a few steps back."

"That's okay. Remind me before I go to bed tonight and I'll program it for you. That way you'll have fresh coffee waiting for you when you get up in the morning."

"Really?" I nodded. "Well, that's pretty neat." I love Kenny because the little mysteries of life can still make him smile. I can't blame him; a fresh cup of coffee waiting for you when you tumble out of bed is pretty neat.

"All done. We should have coffee in just a matter of moments."

"Is the house alarm still on?" he asked.

"Yes, do you need something out of the car?"

"I wanted to sneak outside and smoke a cigarette before *she* gets up."

"I thought you quit."

"I did," he said with a grin. "Mostly."

I crossed over to the back door and punched in the code to turn off the alarm. "It's off," I said to Kenny, "you better get to it."

"Good morning," Joyce called from the stairs.

I exchanged a quick glance with Kenny. "How does she keep doing that?" I asked. "Just showing up at exactly the right moment."

Kenny shook his head. "Why are you up so early?" he asked Joyce.

"I couldn't sleep. I guess I was too excited. Is that coffee I smell?"

"Yes, it's just about ready," I said. "You may need to add some water to it though, because it's pretty strong." Joyce is notorious for brewing coffee weak enough that you can see the bottom of the cup. She claims it's because Kenny is going to drink a whole pot and she wants to control how much caffeine he has in the morning. She also claims that her recent conversion from butter to margarine is for Kenny as well.

I pulled three cups out of the cabinet and set them down next to the coffee pot. Then I grabbed some milk, sugar and a couple of packets of Equal for Joyce. Everyone fell silent, waiting for the coffee to finish brewing. After a few more desperate grunts, the thing finally seemed to be finished.

"There you go guys," I said to Kenny and Joyce. "Get yourselves a cup of coffee."

"Jeffrey, is there a place around here where I can go pick up some donuts?" Kenny asked. "I figure that's easier than trying to cook a big meal for this crew." I was pretty sure this donut ploy coincided with his need for a cigarette.

"Yes," Joyce agreed, "and we are going to have an early lunch."

"Sure," I said. "There's a little bakery at the end of Kingsley."

"Can you write the instructions down for me?"

"It's really easy. Just follow our road to the mailboxes and take a left. The bakery is in a little shopping center just past the light."

"Sounds easy enough. Now, if I can only find where James left the keys."

"There they are," I said, pointing to the counter next to the back door.

Kenny snatched up the keys and headed to the door.

Mike popped his head up from the couch. "Hang on, Dad, and I'll ride with you."

"Mike, I didn't see you sleeping there or we would have kept the noise down," I said.

"Don't worry, I can sleep through anything," Mike said. He slipped his shoes on and followed Kenny out the door.

"Enjoy the drive," I called after them.

When the front door had closed, Joyce turned to me and said, "Does that man honestly think I don't know that he's sneaking cigarettes?"

"No comment."

"Well, at least he can only sneak in so many a day now.

It's got to be better than the whole pack he used to smoke."

"I think he enjoys feeling like he's getting one over on you."

"We will just let him continue to think that," Joyce laughed. "This coffee is good. Strong but good."

"Do you want me to heat up some water in the microwave so you can dilute it?"

"No, I'm good. Although after half a cup of milk, it is still black."

"Morning, Mom," Ken said as he made his way down the stairs.

"Where did you come from?" Joyce asked.

"You Manfords are a sneaky bunch," I said.

"Where's Dad?"

"He went to get donuts."

"I could have done that."

"That would have disappointed him greatly."

Ken gave me a puzzled look, but must have decided it was too early to pursue it. "What time is Fara heading this way?"

"She said they would be here around ten."

"There better be coffee," Jennifer said from the top of the stairway. "I don't think I can even come down these stairs unless I know there's coffee waiting."

"There's coffee waiting, so come on down," I promised her.

"Strong coffee," Joyce added.

I reached into the cabinet and grabbed another cup as Jennifer came into the kitchen. I handed her the cup and she filled it and took a quick sip. "Mmmm, that's good."

"Where's Jackson?" she asked.

"Asleep," I told her. "The twins?"

"Out like a light."

"How sad is it that we are all up obscenely early while our kids are sleeping? Well, except for James."

"Please do not lump James in with the adults," Jennifer said. "He's more trouble than the other two put together."

"Yes, but he's awfully handy."

"He is," she agreed. "Where's Dad?"

"He and Mike went to get donuts." Although Joyce didn't use air quotes, there was just enough sarcasm in her voice to indicate that the trip was not about donuts.

"Donuts huh?" Jennifer asked. "I think I'll slip out back and see if there's anything there I need to pick up."

"I hope you two don't expect me to nurse you when you both have cancer." Apparently, her campaign to get Kenny and Jennifer to quit smoking was not going as well as Joyce had hoped.

"Well, cancer is better than being fat," Jennifer said as she slipped out the back door. We stood around the kitchen and talked about the plan for the day. I got another pot of coffee going so that Kenny could drink a second cup when he got back. If he got back. I was starting to wish I had written the directions down for them.

"Where are they?" Joyce finally said. It was obvious that we'd all been thinking it.

"Maybe I better drive up there and see if I can find them," Ken offered.

"If they are there then they aren't lost," I said, confused by his logic. "They're just slow."

"Never mind," he said. "I see them pulling into the drive now, and it looks like Dad's bought every donut in the place."

"Naturally," Joyce muttered.

I glanced out the window, and indeed Kenny and Mike were struggling to get out of the car with six or seven large boxes of donuts. "Honey, open the door," I told Ken.

He dashed out the door in time to prevent a donut disaster. Joyce pulled out a stack of paper plates and napkins from the pantry. "We can use real plates if you want."

"For donuts?" she asked. "Not worth it." She arranged the plates and napkins on the counter and then poured Kenny another cup of coffee.

"Here," she said as he walked in. "You're probably dehydrated from that long trip." He rolled his eyes but took the coffee.

Eventually, the twins woke up and it wasn't long before they woke Jackson up.

After everyone was pumped full of sugar, the whole crew headed upstairs to get ready for the big day. I picked up Jackson and walked outside with him to greet my family, who had just pulled into our driveway.

"Morning! How is everyone today?"

"We are doing just the best today," Dad said.

"You're always doing the best," Fara said. "The rest of us, on the other hand, are bitter and filled with hate."

"What! Already? That's a record, even for you."

Mom reached over and took Jackson from me. "Don't ask," she whispered as she slipped around me and into the house.

"What happened?"

"Some asshole pulled the fire alarm around two this morning."

"Ouch. Did you have to leave the building and everything?"

"We were supposed to, but Dad and I refused."

"Hell. There wasn't no fire," Dad said. "I opened my window and told the people in the parking lot to holler up at me if they saw smoke."

I was just about to ask for more details when Alex came tearing back outside.

"Mom! I thought you said there wasn't a pool. You big liar!"

"Did you get the pool finished?" Fara said to me.

"Of course I did. Come take a look." I led my family into the house and over to the wall of windows that faced our back yard.

"Wow, that looks nice. Love the waterfall," Fara said.

"Mom wouldn't let us bring our swimsuits," Sydney said.

"I guess you'll just have to skinny dip."

"No way," Nick piped up. "I'll pass."

"Kidding!" I said, pulling a Ken. "We actually can't use it for a couple of days, so there will be no swimming."

The kids all voiced their unhappiness about this development. At exactly the same time. Loudly.

"Okay, okay! Calm down. There are still plenty of video games and junk food on tap for today. Why don't you guys head upstairs and see if you can find something you want to play?"

I leaned down to Sydney. "The twins are upstairs, if you want to go say hello. I believe Caitlyn brought some of her favorite dolls to play with."

"Are they Bratz?"

"What are Bratz?"

"These terrifying dolls with big heads," Fara said.

"They're cute!" Sydney insisted.

"I don't know, Syd, why don't you go check it out and let us know?" Sydney raced up the stairs after the boys in search of big-headed dolls.

"Okay," Fara said. "What do we need to do to get everything set up?"

"First, Dad, there's coffee and donuts in the kitchen."

"Now you're talking, Son." I pointed him to the cups and he poured one and went outside to talk to Kenny.

"Alright, are you ready?" I asked Fara.

"I was born ready," she said.

"Then let's do this."

"Okay, but first I need a cup of coffee."

"Sounds good to me. Maybe I will have another cup as well. But right after that we really have to get started."

"We will," she assured me.

An hour later, Ken, Joyce, Jennifer, and Mom came down the stairs. Oh, Mom! I had barely gotten a chance to say hello to her before she made a beeline for Jackson. Fara and I were giggling over our absolute last cup of coffee and had yet to get anything ready for the party.

That came to an abrupt halt as Ken started barking out orders and before we knew it the house looked like Sesame Street had exploded all over it. Just moments after the last streamer had been taped into place, the doorbell rang and the guests started to arrive.

The party had been going on for a couple of hours when Joyce announced that it was time for the cake. We had actually had two cakes baked. There was the regular cake for all of us and a small, round cake for Jackson with Elmo's face on it.

"You are going to regret that cake choice," Marti said to me.

"Why?"

"Honey, red icing doesn't come out of anything. Kiss that outfit goodbye."

"It's brand new," I said. "Not to mention adorable."

"And it's about to be red." Mom got Jackson into his high chair and then Joyce sat the cake down in front of him. Everyone had stopped what they were doing to watch Jackson's reaction to his cake.

"Do you have the camera ready, Kenny?" Joyce asked.

"Yes, bossy."

"Ken, do you have our camera ready?"

"Yes, bossy."

I looked over my shoulder and rolled my eyes at him. "I'll show you bossy later."

"I hope so," he said with a grin.

"Gag!" Marti said.

"I just threw up in my mouth," Fara added.

"If you all don't hush you are going to miss him eating his cake," Joyce said.

"I don't know," I said. "He seems a little uncertain." In fact, Jackson was sitting there staring at all of us and had yet to notice the cake at all.

"Who can blame him with this freak show?" Jennifer said.

"Sometimes you have to give them a little push," Mom said. She stepped forward and took hold of Jackson's fingers and grazed them across the icing. Naturally, he immediately put them in his mouth.

He made a scrunched up face and squealed. "Maybe he doesn't like it," Ken said. Just about that time Jackson grabbed the cake in both of his chubby little hands and squeezed as hard as he could.

Cake and icing oozed through his fingers. He must have liked the feeling because he pounded his little fist into the cake and then grabbed two more handfuls.

"Here he goes!" Joyce said. The whole scene seemed to play out in slow motion as Jackson brought both of his cake-covered hands up to his mouth. After hesitating for just a second, he shoved them straight in at the same time.

From what I could see, it looked like he got more cake on his face than in his mouth. But whatever he got in he must have enjoyed because he reached down and grabbed another handful and shoved it in. And then another handful and shoved that one in.

"There he goes!" Mom said. Everyone was laughing and clapping as he tore through the cake. Eventually, I had to look away. He had cake from one end of him to the other. It was in his hair, his ears and all over his birthday outfit.

"I'm not sure I understand the point of this ritual," I whispered to Ken.

"Me neither, but apparently everyone does it." He motioned at our families who seemed to be getting a kick out of the whole thing. "Whatever works."

"Whatever works," I agreed.

"What about the rest of us?" Alex asked. "There you go, hoss," Dad said. "Give 'em hell."

"Does anyone else want cake?" Joyce asked. All of the kids started hopping around talking about cake. Joyce motioned for everyone to follow her into the kitchen where the other cake was untouched. Or at least it was supposed to be. There was a small square missing.

"James!" Joyce said. "You are in a lot of trouble."

"Hey! How do you know it was me?"

"Because it's always you," she said. "Jennifer, hand me

that knife and keep James away from me before I kill him."

"Don't hold back on my account. He has a great life insurance policy."

Joyce cut and dished up the cake while Ken and I tried to pick up the worst of Jackson's mess. Mom came over and unbuckled him from his high chair and lifted him out.

"Hold him still, Betty," Marti said. She quickly stripped Jackson down to just his diaper and Mom headed upstairs with Jackson to get him cleaned up.

"And this goes in the garbage," Marti said. She handed Ken Jackson's little outfit.

"Are you sure?" he asked.

"Ken. Red icing."

He took the wadded up mess from her, but instead of opening the pantry door and sticking it in the garbage, he opened the laundry door and put it on top of the washer. He came back in the dining room where Marti and I were still picking up remnants of cake.

"You didn't throw it away, did you?" she asked.

Ken shrugged. "I have to at least try to save it. It's his birthday outfit."

"Good luck with that. That's why we have a white cake policy in our house."

"For Mason?" I asked.

"For everyone."

After the cake had been eaten, presents had been opened, and most of the mess had been cleaned up, the party settled into a relaxed, lazy afternoon.

Jackson and Mason were in Jackson's playpen, the kids were upstairs, the "men" were outside and the rest of us were sitting around the living room drinking coffee. Syd had latched herself onto me, despite Fara's efforts to get her to go play with the kids.

"This is pretty great," Ken said. "We are so glad everyone could make it." He raised his coffee cup. "To family and friends."

"And good neighbors!" I added, looking over at Ellen. "You're very brave to hang out with this bunch."

"I've had a blast," she said. "Jeffrey, how long have you two been together? Ya'll act like you've known each other forever."

"Almost twelve years," I said.

"Wow! And how did you meet?"

"No!" my sister interrupted. "We are not going to drag out that old chestnut."

"Mom," Sydney said. "Let him tell it. Please!"

"Like I could stop him," she said.

"Actually, Ellen, it's a really interesting story."

"Of course it is," Fara muttered under her breath.

CHAPTER TWENTY-TWO

Louisville, November, 1990

The year was 1990, and my friend Melvin had invited a group of us to Louisville for a big party at his house. It was just before Thanksgiving so I'm not sure exactly what he was supposed to be celebrating. But since Melvin had been to visit us a number of times we knew that not going wasn't an option. Five of us packed into our friend Scott's car and made the six-hour drive from Chicago to Louisville.

Just before the party started, Melvin dragged me to his bedroom. "I want to show you something," he said. He went to his dresser and retrieved a manila envelope and handed it to me. "Take a look."

"If these are nudies you are going to be in a lot of trouble." I reached in the envelope and pulled out a few 8x10 glossy photos.

"Wow. What a handsome guy."

"That's Ken. He's been modeling in Atlanta, but he's just moved back home. He's going to be here tonight."

I handed the pictures and the envelope back to Melvin. He carefully put them back inside and then returned them to the top of his dresser. "He's also a really sweet guy."

"Great," I said. "I look forward to meeting him." As we left I wondered exactly why Melvin had shown me Ken's pictures. It seemed that he thought of Ken as more than just a friend. Did he want my approval? If so, he had it.

Ken arrived at the party really late with a bunch of his friends who I didn't know. Melvin introduced us and we were both polite, but honestly I thought that was the end of it.

We continued to bump into each other the rest of the night and as things started to wind down I found myself talking to Ken and this other guy. I had missed the other guy's name and was having a hard time focusing on the conversation as I racked my brain trying to come up with it. It was either John or Darryl or maybe Fernando. Yeah, I really had no clue.

Mystery Man kept talking about how cute my ears were, which was embarrassing me. I hated my car-door style ears and didn't like anyone calling attention to them. He even went so far as to take his finger and gently trace the contour of my ear. I could feel them starting to turn red from all the attention.

Ken also seemed uncomfortable with the conversation, or was he annoyed? I didn't know him well enough to figure out exactly what was up, but I could tell he wasn't happy.

Eventually, I apologized to the two of them and said I really had to say goodnight. I explained that the drive from Chicago was catching up with me. Mystery Man looked at me expectantly, but didn't make any move to leave. Ken had taken a few steps away from us, but he also didn't seem ready to leave.

Since Mystery Man didn't seem to be taking the hint and Ken seemed determined not to leave me alone with him, I decided to be blunt. "The thing is, guys, we are standing in my bedroom." I motioned to the old sofa in the room. "That's all mine for the evening."

Realization swept across their faces, but still neither of them made a move to leave. Just then, Melvin whirled into the room. *Thank God*, I thought. "Are these boys harassing you?" he asked.

"Not at all," I said. "They've been good company, but I'm afraid I'm not able to return the courtesy for much longer. I'm exhausted."

Melvin eyed them both for a few seconds and seemed to come to some decision. "Tim, come with me. There are some people who are asking for you. Ken, say goodnight so Jeffrey can get some sleep. He's a real bitch when he's tired."

Melvin grabbed Tim and drug him out of the room. He managed a little awkward wave over his shoulder as he was leaving. Melvin was not the kind of guy you said no to.

Tim, I thought to myself. That really shouldn't have been that hard to come up with. I turned to say goodnight to Ken but he started talking before I could manage to get the words out.

"I thought he would never leave. And the way he was pawing you? What an asshole."

"I don't think he meant anything by it."

Ken laughed. "I'm pretty sure he did. I'm surprised he didn't stick his tongue in your ear." This time we both laughed and I noticed that Ken had stepped toward me, instead of toward the door.

"Not to mention that in his obsession with your ears he totally overlooked these." Ken gently trailed his finger through the hair just above my wrist.

I'm sure my eyes nearly fell out of my head. I was

starting to feel like there was a hidden camera in the room.

"My wrist?" I asked him.

"Your forearms. I just about lost it when you rolled up your sleeves. Very sexy."

I looked down at my forearms and then back up at Ken to see if there was some inside joke happening that my sleep-deprived brain was missing. Other than being covered in dark hair they looked pretty typical to me.

"Um, thanks, I guess. I hate to push you out, but I really am tired. And, well, you know I need lots and lots of sleep to keep these forearms looking like this." *Oh God. That was so lame.*

Ken walked toward the door, but instead of leaving he closed it. He started back across the room to me, but seemed to think better of it and turned and went back to the door.

I let out a breath that I didn't know I had been holding. I was relieved and disappointed that Ken had come to his senses and was going to leave me to get some rest. I felt a little silly for even thinking that Ken had been interested in me. "Good night," I said to his back.

Ken reached out and flipped the lock on the door and turned back to me and said, "I'm not ready to say goodnight yet." I thought about pinching myself to see if this was a dream, but I realized that my dreams were never this good.

Ken was leaning against the door staring at me. I knew I needed to say something, but my mouth felt like I had swallowed a bunch of cotton balls that had been rolled in peanut butter. After what felt like hours but was probably only a few seconds, I finally croaked out that I could probably manage a few more minutes if he wanted to talk or something.

Whatever I said must have made Ken happy, because he gave me a big smile and sauntered back over to me. "Sure, let's talk," he said with a smirk, "or something."

***

The next morning Ken and I were inseparable. After saying goodbye to me at least a dozen times he finally left, but not before promising to stay in touch.

Once he was gone, Melvin pulled me aside and told me in no uncertain terms that I shouldn't get my hopes up that Ken would contact me. He explained that Ken had recently burst out of the closet and was exploring his options. I put on a brave face and said I was fine, besides I lived in Chicago and he had just resettled back in Louisville.

On the way home, my friends and I dissected the trip. It wasn't long before talk turned to my out-of-character behavior. "Ms. Roach thinks she's found herself a husband," my friend Scott teased. I knew better than to protest. "Please, I'll never hear from him again."

"You love him," someone else said. I knew the only way to get them to stop focusing on me was to play along until I could redirect the conversation.

"Desperately," I confessed. "Speaking of love. I had no love whatsoever for that toilet in the guest bathroom. I'm sorry, but I can't have a proper movement when my feet don't touch the ground."

"Really? I loved it," Jim said. "It made me feel like a queen on a throne." And, just like that, all talk of my future husband was silenced and the rest of the trip passed without another mention of my foolish behavior. How stupid would it be to fall for a guy you met at a party who didn't even live in the same city you did? Pretty stupid. That stuff only happened in movies.

That's why I was shocked when I got home to find five messages from Ken on my answering machine. I called him back and things accelerated from there. Two weeks later, he asked if he could take the Greyhound bus from Louisville to Chicago to see me. He said he couldn't afford to fly and didn't think his car would make the trip. I told him he was welcome, but I didn't expect him to do that. Ten hours on a bus to see a guy you had only met once was a lot to ask of a person. Ken assured me that it wasn't a big deal and we made plans for the following weekend.

When I went to the Greyhound station, I was half convinced he wouldn't show up at all. My eyes kept scanning the crowd. As the minutes and my happiness slipped away, I resolved myself to the fact that he'd had a change of heart.

All at once I saw him across the crowded station. He wasn't dressed for the Chicago weather. He looked cold and lost and impossibly handsome. Too handsome. "He's not for you," I whispered to myself as I crossed the station to meet him and gently touched his shoulder to get his attention. "You look cold."

"I am," he said. "But seeing you again is definitely warming me up." Even after talking to him every day for the last few weeks it was still hard for me to believe he was interested in me. "Come on, let's get you home before you freeze."

Ken and I barely left my apartment for the three days he was in Chicago. He didn't want to do any sightseeing or go to bars, or even hang out with my friends. He just wanted to spend his time with me.

It felt like we were taking a crash course in getting to

know each other. It was amazing, but as our time was running out I started to panic. I couldn't let him leave without figuring out where we stood.

"We need to talk," I said. We were sitting on my couch, with Ken's bags all packed and waiting by the door.

"I know," he said. He took a deep breath. "I haven't been completely honest with you. Melvin has talked about you guys forever. And when he called to invite me to the party, he told me you all were coming down from Chicago." Ken paused and seemed to collect himself. "He also told me that he wanted to fix me up with one of you who was single." He paused again before adding, "And rich."

I could feel myself on the verge of tears as the puzzle pieces finally fell into place, but I tried to keep my tone calm. "I'm afraid you've been misinformed," I said sadly, "I'm not rich at all."

"Not you, Scott. He was talking about Scott." Ken reached between us and picked up my hand. "But from the minute Melvin said you were coming, I knew it was *you* I wanted to meet. After hearing all of his stories, I already had a crush on you." Now Ken looked like he was about to cry. "I don't want you to think I was there looking for a free ride."

I tried to pull my hand away but Ken held on tightly. "What were you looking for? Because I'm not interested in a fling. When it comes to dating, I don't know how to do casual. I'm looking for true love. The kind that comes with the house and a dog."

He smiled. "I love dogs."

"Ken, I'm serious. I don't spend my weekends dancing in clubs with a bunch of shirtless dudes. I'm more of a movie and popcorn kind of guy. I know you are in a different place right now and that's probably where you need to be, but I don't want that."

"Did I ask you to take me to clubs this weekend?"

"No," I mumbled.

"I know I haven't been out for very long. And, yes, I did try to make up for lost time at first. But honestly I was a mess in Atlanta. I completely crashed and burned."

He looked so sad and lost for a minute that I picked up his other hand. "The truth is I don't know what I want," Ken said. "But whatever it is, I want to see if I can find it with you."

We sat there on my sofa in the quiet until he finally said, "Is that okay with you?"

I pulled him into a hug. "It's more than okay," I whispered into his ear. "But we're going to need to find you a proper winter coat if you're going to be living in Chicago."

Ken pulled back from me and met my eyes with a hesitant smile. He looked like he wanted to believe me but was afraid I wasn't serious. I didn't say anything, I just nodded. Then I pulled him close to me and hugged him like I was never going to let him go.

CHAPTER TWENTY-THREE

Dallas, October, 2002

"I love that story," Sydney said.

"I love that she doesn't understand all the *nuances* of that story," Fara whispered to me, although her whisper volume was loud enough that everyone in the room heard her.

Sydney was doing her best to ignore Fara. "So, do you think the two of you will ever get married?"

I wasn't sure what to say. I was so proud that someone as young as my niece was smart enough to see that the logical conclusion of two people falling in love was to get married, and I didn't want to spoil it for her by letting her know that not everyone was as enlightened as she was.

"Maybe one day, Syd," I told her. "If Ken's lucky." I winked at Sydney and she grinned at the two of us.

"Okay!" Fara said, standing up. "That's enough mushy stuff to last me for the next couple of years. Ken, get the guys in here. It's time we taught Jackson how to walk."

I rolled my eyes at my sister. "I don't think it works that way. It's not like teaching a kid to ride a bike. He's not ready yet." She just looked at me like I was clueless. "What? He can barely crawl."

"Trust me, he is ready. He's been pulling up on

everything within reach all day. Just get everyone in here so we can get started."

Ken opened the back door and poked his head out. "Fara wants everyone to come inside. She says she's going to teach Jackson how to walk."

Everyone shuffled inside and situated themselves on the couch, in a chair, or on the floor, where Fara had positioned Ken and me about five feet apart. She had Ken hold Jackson by the waist while she held her hands up. Jackson reached up and grabbed her hands with his and she slowly walked him from Ken to me.

When he got close to me, she let go of his fingers and he immediately collapsed into my arms. "See!" I said to her. "I told you he wasn't ready yet."

"That's because you didn't give him a chance. You can't snatch him the minute I let his fingers go."

"He was going to fall."

"He was fine. Ken, scoot in a little closer." Ken moved closer to me. We were probably less than three feet apart now. Fara leaned over Jackson and held out her index fingers. He immediately reached up and grabbed them and pulled himself to his feet.

"Good job, Jackson!" she said. "Do you want to walk with Aunt Fara?"

Once again, she began to slowly walk him between the two of us. When he got within Ken's reach she gently pulled her fingers free. "Don't grab him yet, Ken," she warned.

It took Jackson a second or two to realize that Fara was no longer holding him up, but he didn't immediately fall down. He was wobbly, but he was standing on his own.

"Reach out to him, Ken!" Fara encouraged. "See if you

can get him to come to you."

Ken motioned with his hands. "Come to Papa, Jackson." Ken had his arms extended just a few inches from Jackson, who instinctively reached for his hands.

Unlike me, Ken didn't immediately scoop him up, but instead moved his hands back just as Jackson reached for them. Sure enough, Jackson took a wobbly step toward Ken and grabbed his papa's outstretched hands. As they say in the movies, the crowd goes wild.

Ken hugged Jackson tight to him and everyone started congratulating him on taking his first step. But Fara wasn't done yet.

"Okay Ken, turn him around toward Jeffrey."

Ken picked up Jackson and turned him midair so that he was facing me again.

"Jeffrey, scoot in close to him and hold out both your hands, but do not grab him too soon. You have to give him a chance to stand on his own."

I closed the distance between me and Ken until my fingers were almost touching Jackson's. "Come to Daddy, Jackson." I wiggled both of my fingers, trying to entice him.

He just looked at them as if to say, "I'm on to your games, people."

"He's not going to do it, Fara," I sighed. I was disappointed that Ken was able to get him to take a step, and I couldn't.

"Be patient," Fara said. "Try it again and really go all out."

Here goes nothing, I thought, but it was not like I had ever been afraid of making a fool of myself. "Where's my sweet boy?" I asked him. "Do you want to come see Daddy?

Huh? Do you?" Jackson smiled and waved his arms up and down while Ken held him gently around the waist.

"Is that a yes? Do you want to see your dad?" I extended both my arms until they were barely touching his hands. "Come on! Come see Daddy."

Jackson lurched forward and Ken gently let him go. I kept my fingers hovering within a couple of inches of his as he took a wobbly step in my direction.

One step became two and then two became three. I quickly scooted backwards and continued to encourage him to come to me. On the fourth step I could see that he was going to go down, but instead of rushing in and grabbing him, I stayed close enough so that he could safely fall without hurting himself.

He managed the fourth step and then crashed into my arms. "Good job Jackson," I told him. "Daddy is so proud of you." I snuggled him in close for a big hug.

We continued to let him toddle between Ken and me for the next few minutes until he began to move with more confidence. By the time we finished he was actually able to walk from my arms to Ken's. It was a wonky walk, but it was a walk.

Eventually, Joyce said Jackson had practiced enough and that it was the grandmothers' turn to play with him. "Come on, Betty," she said to Mom. "Let's help Jackson open his presents."

"Sounds good to me," Mom agreed, getting up to follow Joyce.

As Mom and Joyce oversaw the opening of the presents, I slid in next to Fara. "Thank you," I whispered. "I'm so glad that you guys got to see him take his first steps."

"You're welcome." She turned and looked at me. "You know sometimes you have to let them stumble a bit in order to be able to stand on their own."

"When did you get to be so smart?" I asked her.

"Practice," she said with a smile. "I've had lots of practice." I gave her a quick hug and the two of us meandered into the living room to see Jackson open his presents.

Later that night, after the presents had all been opened and Fara's crew had gone back to the hotel, Ken, Jackson, and I were in our bed. We decided to let him sleep with us, since it was his birthday.

He was asleep on my belly and the two of us were talking quietly, although once he was out it was nearly impossible to wake him up. Ken had gone so far as to vacuum while Jackson was napping and he slept right through it.

"Today was pretty great," Ken said.

"It was. I'm so glad they all came."

"Me too." Ken rubbed his hand along Jackson's back. "Can you believe he took his first steps today?" I shook my head.

"Although we shouldn't be surprised. You know your sister doesn't take no for an answer."

I smiled at Ken. "No kidding, but she was pretty great today too."

"She was," Ken agreed. He yawned and snuggled in closer to the two of us.

"Tired?"

"A little. It feels like we've been going strong for hours."

"That's because we have," I reminded him.

"Yeah, and tomorrow's another early day. Remember, my family is planning on heading out of here early tomorrow, so we should probably get some sleep."

"Remind me again why they are leaving so early."

"James has to get back for work." Ken shifted around in the bed, trying to get comfortable.

"Maybe I can convince Fara to move her bunch out of the hotel and into our house for her last night in town. Although all of that moving around is going to be a little chaotic."

"I wouldn't expect anything less from our family." I noticed that Ken didn't bother to distinguish his family from mine and it made me smile again.

"Hey, what about what Sydney said?" I asked him.

"What about it?"

"What did you think about it?"

He was quiet for a minute. "I thought it was about the sweetest thing I've ever heard. It gives me hope that things really are changing, that people are changing."

"Me too." I was so tired that I could barely keep my eyes open, but I wasn't quite ready to end the evening and go to sleep. "Wouldn't it be great though?"

"What? If we could get married one day?"

"Yes," I said, trying to hide a yawn.

"Yes," Ken said. "It would be pretty great."

EPILOGUE

New York, September, 2011

"You wrote your vows—right?"

Ken is fiddling with his tie in the mirror. It's already perfect, but I guess it provides him with a distraction, which is a good thing, since he is a little nervous about our pending nuptials. I suppose harassing me about our wedding vows is another way of keeping his mind occupied.

"Yes." I sigh. "The answer is still yes. Just like it was the last fifty times you've asked me." He stops messing with his tie and turns to look at me.

"I just don't want you to wing it. Not that you can't wing it. Nobody wings it better than you, but I really, really want everything to be perfect."

"Really, really?" I ask with a grin.

"Really, really, really," he says.

Marti steps into the bedroom where Ken and I are getting dressed. "Are you two nearly ready?"

"We are actually totally ready," I say. "Ken keeps fussing with his tie, but he has had it perfect at least five different times."

Marti steps up to Ken and gives his tie a little jerk and then pats it. "Perfect!" she says. "I think the rest of us are ready to go and the limo should be here any minute."

"You guys didn't have to rent a limo," I say to Marti.

"But we're glad you did," Ken adds with a grin. One thing that hasn't changed in the twenty years that Ken and I have been together is that Ken likes his with a little side order of fancy.

"Mom!" Mason comes charging into the room nearly knocking me down in the process.

"Careful," Marti says. "You will wrinkle his doll clothes." Mason gives me a confused look.

"It's a long story," I tell him.

Marti and I shared a hotel room at a conference a couple of years ago. She was in the middle of unpacking her suitcase when she announced that there was no way she could hang her big girl clothes next to my tiny little doll clothes. The description stuck and now everyone gives me a hard time about my doll clothes.

I don't care. When I turned forty-five I went on a fitness kick and finally got the body I had waited my whole life for. It's too bad I was too old to enjoy it.

"What do you need, Mason?" Marti asks. "I'm helping the grooms get dressed!"

"The limo is here!"

The three of us run over to the window. Sure enough, a giant stretch limo is parked out front.

"Tell your dad to help Betty and Joyce get down to the car."

"Okay. Dad!" he yells.

"Mason! I could have done that. Go find him." Mason dashes out of the room.

"Okay guys, let's get going." Marti starts to lead us out of the room and comes to an abrupt halt.

"You wrote your vows, right?" she says to me.

I drop my head in my hands and sigh. "Why doesn't anyone have any faith in me?"

"Because we know you, honey. Now did you write them or not?"

"Yes! I wrote them. As a matter of fact, I wrote them weeks ago." I give them both my best glare.

Marti and Ken both start laughing. "Weeks ago?" Marti says. "You had me going until you said weeks ago." She's right of course. I didn't actually sit down and write my vows until last night.

"Okay," I concede. "Maybe not weeks ago, but I promise you they are written and ready to go." Marti gives me a long, hard look before nodding her head. "Let's go."

As we sweep through the apartment, Marti is doing a last minute check to make sure we don't forget anything. Greg must have already helped our moms out to the car because they are nowhere to be seen.

Marti flings open the door to the condo we have rented for the week and shouts down the stairs. "Is everyone down there?"

"Everyone but Fara," Greg shouts back up.

"We are missing The Rev," Marti says. "We can't do this without her." My sister has gotten ordained for the occasion and would be performing the ceremony.

"Fara!" I shout. "Are you ready? The limo is here."

She and Sydney come running out of the bedroom they are sharing with Mom. "Sorry! Sydney had a little hair emergency."

"Don't try to blame this on me, old girl," Sydney says. "I've been ready for the last hour."

"Please don't call me old girl," Fara says. "Today

everyone must refer to me as Reverend Fara."

"I knew getting her ordained was a mistake," Ken says. I giggle and start shooing them all toward the door. "It's just for one day," I remind him. "It won't kill us."

"Are you sure?"

"Now that you mention it," Fara says. "I am considering hanging out my shingle and starting up a side business."

"Honey, you aren't getting paid," Marti says.

"Not for this, but there are plenty of gays itching to get married and I'm happy to offer my services."

"Can we just go?" Ken says.

"Wow, here I am trying to do something for the community and all you care about is yourself. Very sad."

We tromp down the stairs and manage to squeeze ourselves into the limo. It's a tight fit with our moms, Sydney, Jackson, Mason, Marti, Greg, Ken, and me.

Marti gives the limo driver the address of the restaurant in Brooklyn and we are off.

Just a few minutes into the trip, Ken starts to complain about the heat. "I'm burning up," he says. It is hot, but I don't want to agree because it will only make him worse.

"It's warm," I say.

"Warm? An oven is warm. I am roasting."

I glance over at Ken and, sure enough, he is starting to get a little glossy looking.

"Hang on," Marti says. She presses the intercom. "Hello?" Nothing. "Hello? Is this working?" Still nothing. She fiddles with the knob, turning it off and on a half dozen times. "HELLO!"

"Yes," the driver finally says.

"It's hot back here. Can you turn up the air

conditioning?"

"It's on," he says.

"We don't feel it. Is it on full blast?"

"Yes."

"Are you sure? And it also smells like smoke. Are you smoking?" I frown at her. Why is she antagonizing the man who controls our access to cool air? "Well it does," she whispers. Again, she's right, but I'm trying hard to ignore that as well.

"I'm not smoking and the air is on high," the driver says. He clicks off the intercom as if that's all he has to say about the subject.

I lean over and give Ken's hand a squeeze. "Try to think positive thoughts. It won't be long before we get there." This is a lie and I know it. We are going all the way down to the end of Brooklyn and I'm guessing we have at least thirty more minutes in this sauna.

"Feel this!" Marti says as she grabs my hand and drags it over to the vent. "That bastard has the heat on!"

"I told you not to antagonize him about the smoking," Greg says.

"No you didn't," Marti says.

"Well, I thought it."

I can tell that everyone is on the verge of losing it just minutes before we exchange our wedding vows so for once I try to be the voice of reason. "Everyone relax. The heat isn't on. The air is just not very cold. Loosen up a button if you need to. We just have to hang in there for a few more minutes and we'll be there."

Ken finally breaks down and removes his tie and completely unbuttons his shirt. I notice that he has two giant sweat stains on the front of his t-shirt that make it look like he is lactating.

He's not the only one who is worse for wear. Joyce is in the midst of a full-blown hot flash and keeps swiping at little drops of water above her lip.

Marti and The Rev threaten to strip down to their panties if we don't get there in the next few minutes. Mom and Sydney have both fallen into a heat-induced coma and Greg is too busy yelling at Mason to *stop touching everything* to be concerned about the heat.

Jackson is the only person who is unaffected and that's because he hasn't looked up from his DS since he got in the car. I'm pretty sure we could drop him off at someone else's wedding and he wouldn't realize it until it was time to go home and we weren't there.

As soon as the car comes to a stop we throw open the doors and step out into the fresh air. It actually feels cool outside, despite the fact that it's September in New York and the temperature is hovering near eighty degrees.

Once we've all shaken ourselves out of the car, I turn to Marti and Fara and say, "Thanks for renting a limo, assholes." They both start giggling. They try to stop when Ken shoots them a dirty look, but they can't control themselves and soon they are in the midst of another laughing fit.

I shrug my shoulders as if to say, "What are you going to do?" Fara tells me to get Ken into the restaurant and see if I can help repair the damage from the drive.

I pull him into the restaurant and tell the hostess that we have rented the private room for a wedding and reception. She smiles and tells us to follow her.

Ken grabs my arm the minute we step into the area they have set up for the wedding. "This isn't going to work," he says.

They've set the room up in such a way that we will be standing in front of the bathrooms as we say our vows. "It's not terrible," I say.

"Actually it is," Fara says from behind me. She turns to the hostess and says, "Hello, I'm Reverend Hardesty and I will be performing the ceremony this evening." For some reason the hostess seems impressed with Fara's title, as if she is dealing with some holy person instead of someone who got ordained on the Internet.

"Nice to meet you," she manages to squeak out.

"We are going to need to make some changes," Fara continues. "Can you go find me three or four strong boys?"

"Um, I don't know."

"It's okay, Fara," I say but I can tell from her look that she's not going to budge on this. "Come on, honey," I say, dragging Ken towards the men's room. "I don't think you want to be here for this."

"We've got it covered," Marti assures him. "Go pull yourself back together."

Ken and I spend the next fifteen minutes and several dozen paper towels trying to soak up the sweat from the limo ride and reassemble our clothes.

Thank goodness Ken decided we would go with an informal look of dark jeans, crisp, white dress shirts and woven ties. I'm not sure how we would have survived in tuxedos.

When we step out of the bathroom the entire dining room has been completely transformed. The tables have been arranged into three or four clusters and the space in front of the bay window has been cleared out.

Little twinkling lights surround the windows and we can

see shadows of people passing by on the sidewalk through the slightly opaque windows.

There's even a smaller wedding table up front that's separate from the rest of the tables.

"Wow," Ken says. "This looks—"

"Romantic," I finish for him.

"I was going to say amazing, but romantic works. I can't believe they got this done in the time we've been in the bathroom. It's a total transformation."

"Speaking of transformations," I say. "You seem to have worked a little miracle yourself. You look just as handsome as you did when we left the condo."

Ken takes my hand. "Are you ready to get married?" he asks.

"I am."

"Then let's go find The Rev."

Our wedding turns out to be the perfect reflection of who Ken and I are as a couple. It's one part mushy romance and one part slapstick.

Sydney reads us a poem, both our moms end up crying, as does Marti. Our other friends take turns telling stories about our adventures together. Some of them are sentimental and sweet, but most of them are more like the limo ride—funny in the retelling but cringe-worthy at the time they happened.

On the outside ours may look like a storybook romance, but we've definitely had our share of mishaps. But just like the limo ride, most of the time we have ended up laughing about our predicament and being thankful that we are going through it together.

More than one friend ends up serenading us with a song, which isn't surprising considering the creative crew we've collected through the years. There are also a couple of stories that require us to put our hands over Mason and Jackson's ears. They try to pull our hands away, but end up missing the best parts, or the worst, depending on your perspective.

The highlights are without a doubt my sister and Jackson. My sister is a natural at emceeing a wedding. She's funny and sentimental and goes wildly off script, taking the time to explain that, as far as she is concerned, this wedding is just a formality and that the two of us have been *husband and husband* for many years.

We had decided not to follow a traditional plan for the wedding. There are no best men, or flower girls. We have our moms standing up in the alcove next to us and Fara asks Jackson if there is anything he'd like to say before we exchange our vows.

He stands up and unfolds a paper napkin that he used to write down what he wanted to say. He talks about how happy he is for his papa and his daddy and how proud he is that we are going to be legally recognized as a couple. It is short and sweet and I am so proud of him because I know how shy he is and how hard it is for him to stand up there and do that.

Finally, Ken and I are asked to say our vows to one another. Ken goes first, because he says he doesn't want to have to follow me. Everyone giggles.

"I am a little bit of a ham," I confess.

"A little?" Fara says. Now everyone really laughs, which helps Ken to relax and he gets through his vows without breaking down.

When it is my turn I take both of Ken's hands and smile at him. Ken gives me an anxious look when I don't get out a piece of paper. I'm sure he thinks I am going to wing it, but I memorized my vows earlier in the day. I take a deep breath and begin.

"According to Wikipedia, marriage vows are promises each partner in a couple makes to the other during a wedding ceremony.

But our promises were made a long time ago, and those promises have carried us on an incredible journey together from Chicago to New York, to Louisville, back to New York, to Dallas, to Guatemala, to Roswell and home at last to our perfect life in Decatur.

Today we get a chance to renew and share those promises with our family, our friends and our son, who is living proof of their durability.

I promise to love and care for you the rest of our lives.

I promise to listen to you, to talk with you, and to share my life with you.

I promise to wake you up when you fall asleep on the couch, to walk the dogs so you don't have to and to sit next to you, even when you are watching *America's Next Top Model* or *Project Runway*.

I gladly promise these things, because I adore you. And I adore the life that we've created together.

There is no me without you. Just as there is no us without Jackson.

In short, I promise that I am yours for as long as you will have me and I can't wait to change my status on Facebook to married."

Yeah, I kind of kill it. By the time I'm finished Ken is weeping, our moms are weeping and even The Rev looks like she might squeeze out a tear. This is a big deal because my sister and I don't cry unless someone punches us. And sometimes not even then.

Marti decides that it's time for karaoke. It doesn't surprise us that our friends don't need to be asked twice to pick up a microphone. Before you know it the stage is filled with soloists, duos and trios, all belting it out.

Somehow, Jackson and Mason are conned into singing *Eye of the Tiger*. It's mostly Mason singing while Jackson sits there and looks embarrassed.

One of our friends announces that it's time for the happy couple to sing. I look over at Ken and he looks petrified. For the second time tonight I give him the *what can you do* shrug.

I grab his hand and drag him up to the stage. We walk over to the accompanist to see what song our friends have picked out for us.

It's *Endless Love*. Ken's eyes just about pop out of his head. I don't see any way that the two of us can get through *Endless Love*. Plus it doesn't really fit us as a couple. We definitely have an endless love, but ours has come with a certain amount of calamity.

I lean down and whisper something into the karaoke master's ear. He looks up at me surprised and asks me if I'm sure that's the song I want. I assure him that it is.

I grab Ken's hand and lead him to the front of the stage. Everyone has gone quiet, waiting to see what we are going to do with *Endless Love*.

You can imagine their surprise when they hear me say:
I remember when I was a very little girl, our house caught on fire.

I have switched out *Endless Love* for Peggy Lee's *Is That All There Is?* I know Ken won't know the words, but I figure he will enjoy the sentiment. I sing at the top of my lungs while Ken stands there next to me and looks dashing.

By the end, everyone in the restaurant is singing along and Ken and I finish with a flourish, bow, and make our way off the stage.

"Thank you," Ken whispers to me. "That was actually a lot of fun." I smile at him. "I thought you might get a kick out of that."

As the party begins to wind down, Corby and Brian, two friends who have flown in from San Francisco, announce that they have something for the two of us.

They hand us a magnetic sign that says, *Just Married!* "We couldn't manage to get the cans to string together, but we figured you should at least get the sign."

"It's awesome," Ken says. "Should we wear it around our necks?"

"Both of you hold it up and I'll get a picture," Marti says.

Ken and I both grab a corner of the sign and mug for the camera.

"I love it!" Marti says.

"Maybe you can stick it on the back of your limo," Corby says. We all stop dead in our tracks and stare at him. "What?"

"No more limos," Ken says with a laugh.

"Okay," Corby says. "Maybe you can stick it on the back of your taxi?"

"That sounds good," Ken says.

"Absolutely," I agree. "We are definitely more taxi types than limo types anyway."

"Speak for yourself."

"Not a chance," I say. "Now that we're married I get to speak for both of us." Ken just shakes his head.

"You are going to live to regret this," Marti says to Ken.

He leans over to me and gives me a quick peck on the cheek. "Maybe," he says. "But I don't think so."

"Either way," I say to Ken. "You're stuck with me forever now."

"You promise," he says.

"I promise."

A few minutes later, everyone has said their goodbyes and our little group has been distributed across multiple cabs. Ken and I make sure that the cab drivers have the address for the condo, before hailing a cab for the two of us.

When our cab arrives we slip into the back seat and collapse into each other. It's been a long day and I expect that Ken will fall asleep as soon as we are on our way.

I don't mind. After all the noise of the wedding it's nice to have some quiet time to appreciate how much I've enjoyed the evening and how lucky I am.

"I'm going to hold you to that promise," Ken whispers in my ear. I look up to see that he's wide awake.

I pull him down to me and give him a kiss. As a rule I'm not a big fan of public displays of affection, but this seems like a good time to break that rule.

"I'm counting on it," I say. He smiles, and we cling to each other as we make our way back to our son, our friends, and our family. Newlyweds at last.

ABOUT THE AUTHOR

Jeffrey Roach was born and raised in Kentucky and lives with his husband Ken and their son Jackson in Decatur, Georgia.

Jeffrey takes his inspiration from everyday life. His writing revolves around universal themes like love, family, and friendship, with a healthy side order of calamity to keep things interesting. His first novel, PopDaddy, is a memoir that tells the story of how Jeffrey and his husband adopted their son from Guatemala.

Find out more about Jeffrey by visiting his Amazon page (www.amazon.com/author/jeffreyroach) or becoming a fan on Facebook (www.facebook.com/popdaddypress).

36581039R00173

Made in the USA
San Bernardino, CA
27 July 2016